KNOW YOUR PLACE

KNOW YOUR PLACE

Helping White, Southern Evangelicals Cope
with the End of The(ir) World

Justin R. Phillips

Foreword by
David P. Gushee

CASCADE *Books* • Eugene, Oregon

KNOW YOUR PLACE
Helping White, Southern Evangelicals Cope with the End of The(ir) World

Copyright © 2021 Justin R. Phillips. All rights reserved. Except for brief quotations in critical publications or reviews, no part of this book may be reproduced in any manner without prior written permission from the publisher. Write: Permissions, Wipf and Stock Publishers, 199 W. 8th Ave., Suite 3, Eugene, OR 97401.

Cascade Books
An Imprint of Wipf and Stock Publishers
199 W. 8th Ave., Suite 3
Eugene, OR 97401

www.wipfandstock.com

PAPERBACK ISBN: 978-1-7252-6890-6
HARDCOVER ISBN: 978-1-7252-6891-3
EBOOK ISBN: 978-1-7252-6892-0

Cataloguing-in-Publication data:

Names: Last, First. | other names in same manner

Title: Book title : book subtitle / Author Name.

Description: Eugene, OR: Cascade Books, 2021 | Series: if applicable | Includes bibliographical references and index.

Identifiers: ISBN 978-1-7252-6890-6 (paperback) | ISBN 978-1-7252-6891-3 (hardcover) | ISBN 978-1-7252-6892-0 (ebook)

Subjects: LCSH: Christian conservatism—United States. | Christianity—Southern States. Christianity and politics—Southern States. | Evangelicalism—Southern States.

Classification: BL2527.S67 P45 2021 (paperback) | BL2527.S67 (ebook)

04/13/21

Scripture quotations, unless otherwise noted, are from the New Revised Standard Version Bible, copyright © 1989 National Council of the Churches of Christ in the United States of America. Used by permission. All rights reserved worldwide.

For Buck and Gloria.

CONTENTS

Foreword by David P. Gushee | ix
Acknowledgments | xi
Introduction | xiii

PART I: A PROBLEM PEOPLE
—My Introduction to Being White | 1

1. A DISEASED IMAGINATION | 10
2. THEORIES ABOUT OURSELVES: Or, All I Ever Needed to Know about Whiteness I Learned in High School | 19
3. HOW TO BE AN AMERICAN: Joltin' Joe and Kneelin' Kap | 29
4. HOW CANCER MADE ME LESS OF A BASTARD (AND MORE HUMAN) | 38

   WHITE OUTRO: Are We Waking Up? | 47

PART II: KNOW YOUR PLACE
—My Introduction to the South | 53

5. THEORIES ABOUT OTHERS: Or, All I Ever Needed to Know about Blackness I Learned in High School | 60
6. ON BOTH SIDES: The Art of Never Saying What We Mean | 69
7. GONE COUNTRY: How to survive when they try to take it all | 79
8. THE MORAL ARC OF THE UNIVERSE IS LONG, AND IT BENDS TOWARDS US | 90

   SOUTHERN OUTRO: Will We Rise Again? | 101

PART III: **AIN'T NO BODY**
   —My Introduction to Evangelical Christianity | 107
   9   GIVE ME THE BLOOD: American Messiah
       for the Possessed and Dispossessed | 115
   10 THE GAME IS RIGGED | 128
   11 BROKEN AND PUT BACK TOGETHER, I DON'T KNOW
       HOW MANY TIMES (Or, Who's Afraid of Black Jesus?) | 140
   12 MUY RAPIDO: Getting Saved in Uruguay | 151
       EVANGELICAL OUTRO: A Desert and a Sea | 162

CONCLUSION | 169

Bibliography | 173

FOREWORD

I am David Gushee, whom Justin Phillips describes in this book as a "promising, late-thirties southpaw reliever" as of 1999. I wish to begin by saying that I remain a promising southpaw reliever, still wearing #22 and still looking for work in professional baseball as I have since 1984.

But enough about that. To the work at hand.

We live in an apocalyptic time.

I do not just mean that we live in a time in which fires consume the West Coast, protests wrack our cities, gun-toting paramilitaries go looking for trouble, and the US president threatens (as I write) not to honor the results of the 2020 presidential election.

I mean to retrieve the Greek term transliterated *apokalypsis*, which is where we get the word apocalyptic. That term means "unveiling." This is helpful to know. It means something like this: to say that the book of Revelation is an "apocalyptic" work is to say not just that's there's lots of blood and chaos, but that the book purports to unveil the spiritual realities behind the blood and chaos.

Many of us—that is, the white, southern, (ex-?) evangelicals that Justin Phillips describes and addresses in this book—have experienced recent years as an unveiling of the toxic elements in our little subculture. For decades we sat fairly easily with our whiteness, southernness, and evangelicalism. Usually also with our maleness and straightness, for that matter. But now we are discovering that all is not well; indeed, all is not at all well.

It is *not* the case that we lacked resources to get to this unveiling before, say, 2016. Justin Phillips, David Gushee, and many others of us had access to plenty of church leaders, theologians, historians, and regular folk who long ago were saying that white southern evangelicalism was, in one of Justin's most striking phrases here, "a decaying body housing a legion of demonic spirits." But it seems to have taken the election of Donald Trump and

FOREWORD

the "slobbering deference" (another priceless phrase in this book) of many white southern evangelicals to this man to unveil the sickness in a way that we could not miss and that we now find urgent to understand and repent.

I am so glad that the clever student I first met over two decades ago has now come out with this book, which I can only describe as #fire. Writing from ruby-red east Tennessee, with a background in blood-red west Tennessee, Justin Phillips tells the truth about whiteness, southernness, and evangelicalism as it exists in this region.

Justin is an affectionate observer, not a scold. He is a great storyteller. He can write about music, sports, Christian schools, church, or theology with equal skill. There are times that if you know this region you will laugh out loud, embarrassing yourself before whomever you happen to be around. The book oozes home-folks familiarity and great warmth. Justin loves this region and this people.

But make no mistake, this is a plea for repentance. Justin Phillips has seen enough to know that repentance is needed. He makes clear that if we want to be followers of Jesus, we are going to need to unfollow much of the way of life white Christian folk have built here over many centuries.

I understand that this book began as more of a bridge-building exercise. It was a "hey, white Christian teenagers like many I have taught here, I wonder if you might be able to consider this non-Fox News perspective on some things you think you are sure about." That might have been a helpful book, but I don't think it is this book. Nor do I think it is what is most needed in this time. Instead, Justin Phillips makes his own contribution to the unveiling of hard truth in this apocalyptic time. And I am glad.

David P. Gushee
Atlanta, Georgia
September 26, 2020

ACKNOWLEDGMENTS

This book began as my dissertation, which was shepherded by Glen Stassen. I wish he was here to see this completed project. David Gushee, my mentor and friend, has walked with me since my undergraduate days, supported my efforts to find my voice and to use it for the Kingdom. Following Glen and David's lead, I wrote this book for my students, past and present, whose questions, concerns, fears and hopes shaped every chapter.

I've enjoyed a beautiful community of friends who encouraged me to write: Jay Watson, Kyle Wiltshire, John Carroll, Jack King, and Patrick King have patiently listened to me muse or rant for a couple of decades. I'm indebted to so many who talked me through the publishing process or just how to be courageous, including Reggie Williams, Bethany McKinney-Fox, James Love, Lisa Yebuah, Lanecia Rouse Tinsley, Ciona Rouse, Devin Maddox, Chad Eggleston, and the "Justice League" Keith Bates, Micah Watson, and Scott Huelin. A huge word of thanks to those who read parts of this work at various stages, including Landon Preston, Luke Pruett, Clayton Sanderson, Mark Jenkins, Annie Laurie Walters, Zac Settle, and Andrew Smith. Eric Minton's early editorial eye and timely words of often-hilarious encouragement were invaluable. Thanks, as well, to Chris Spinks and everyone at Cascade for getting this project over the finish line.

My talented sister Sarah read drafts, designed my website, and has supported my work for so many years. I'm so grateful for your friendship. To Mom and Dad, who sparked in me the first love of justice and neighbor, I hope you'll put this one up on your refrigerator, too.

I finished this book during the COVID-19 lockdown with my wife, Erin, working near me every day in our living room. Our apartment repaired the roof that summer, and a chain of trash cans was linked together, running down outside our window, in order to send refuse through the chute into the below dumpsters. If ever there was an apt metaphor for 2020

ACKNOWLEDGMENTS

it is being trapped in a confined space, uncertain about the future, while trash rains down upon you from above. And yet, to spend such time with you, Erin, is my comfort and bliss.

INTRODUCTION

My Grandpa Buck and I didn't share much in common other than DNA and a lot of mutual love. He was a quiet man like many in the greatest generation who experienced multiple wars. A career in the army took Buck from a life of poverty in rural West Tennessee, sent him to foreign shores for three wars, and laid the foundation for a good life. Never one consumed by adventure or ambition, he returned home from each war to his wife and seven children. After retirement, he had little businesses here and there, and for the most part I think he just wanted to keep intact what he had pieced together during and following the conflicts. He wanted his children to have it better than he did. Nothing extravagant or anything flashy, just a peaceful, prosperous life, and because of him and my grandmother, my parents ensured that I would grow up a child of the middle class, neither knowing the taste of silver spoons nor of nightly hunger.

Buck and I shared a love of silence. Long, uninterrupted silence, which might explain the reason I pursued the academic life. You could never keep Buck talking for too long. While I'm never certain that my grandfather understood the appeal of my work, I know that he was proud of me because he constantly told me so. I'm reminded of John Adams's words to his wife Abigail that sum up my grandfather's life: "I must study Politicks and War that my sons may have liberty to study Mathematicks and Philosophy."[1] So it came to pass for the Phillips clan.

I often wondered what his reaction would have been had I explained that my passions revolve around the somewhat nebulous idea of whiteness and its effects upon the world. I imagine he would have stared a hole through my head until I concluded, at which time he would have likely said,

---

1. Letter from John Adams to Abigail Adams, May 12, 1780.

INTRODUCTION

"Well, I'm real proud of you. I know you've worked hard." And that was the measure for my grandpa, best as I could tell: Did you work hard?

I learned over the years that, above all, Buck was a helper and a fixer. In his later years, he volunteered with Meals on Wheels and other charitable and civic organizations as he was able, because the "old people" needed help. He listened to Gospel music, a surprising revelation to me, because my grandparents' home was generally a place devoid of music or organized religion. No matter my grandparents' largely indiscernible religious convictions, they were deeply moral people abiding by a "Golden Rule" ethic. My grandfather's helping nature manifested itself through one quirk, which I share with him: Whenever a family gathering created a sensory overload for him from too much noise ringing through his hearing aids, created by his children who never quite shared his love of the noiseless state, he would rise from his chair and begin straightening the house. He would migrate from the kitchen to the garage, and eventually outside with his faithful dog, Missy, picking up anything that was out of place. Every dish. Every coffee cup. Every abandoned, lonely stick. Everything had its proper place and needed to be returned for the sake of order. I find myself doing the same thing.

I believe his generation carried the same sense of place and order into societal issues. Women, people of color, and the LGBTQ community had their proper place: out of sight and mind. Those from the World-War II era felt responsible for building and protecting the nation, and over the years, they saw it transforming into something quite unfamiliar to them. I'm sure the steady diet of books by noted political hacks (an apparent choice of my grandmother) and Fox News, which Buck mercifully turned off when guests arrived, fueled their angst. When they were not conversing on all the children and grandchildren happenings, I imagine politics became a topic of conversation, not particularly hopeful ones either.

Perhaps this is just the nature of each generation giving way to the next that such passing is mingled with sadness and the hope that they adequately prepared their own replacements. I can at least relate to this latter sentiment as I enter middle-agedom, understanding now why the old develop suspicions about the young. Nowhere was this more apparent for me than stepping into a high school classroom for the first time as a Bible teacher at a largely white, evangelical, private school.

To teach high schoolers, you must daily steel your nerves to face down adolescents who possess an instinctual, near-primal ability to smell fear and

INTRODUCTION

pounce on it like a pack of caffeinated, hormonal wolves, Instagramming your carcass to mark their territory. This already-charged environment was unusually heightened in the runup to the 2016 presidential election, which was for many students the first time they had paid attention to national politics or had the opportunity to vote. Attempting to teach Christian ethics amid chants of "build the wall" ringing throughout the nation made for a challenging classroom dynamic. The difficulty teaching in this context crystallized for me when, in the wake of the infamous *Access Hollywood* video (October 2016), I heard a young woman parrot the soon-to-be president's words that this was mere "locker room talk" and not reflective of his character. He was "saved" now. Everything from his past was washed by the blood of Jesus. We know that many white evangelicals shared this opinion.

White evangelicals voted for President Trump in record numbers in the 2016 election, surpassing even their support for professed evangelical George W. Bush, and this voting bloc has remained supportive of Trump throughout the chaos of his presidency.[2] During the election and the Trump presidency, I engaged students on conversations about race and ethnicity. Clear examples of Black genius at the time—films like *Get Out!* and *Black Panther*, and music videos like Beyoncé's "Lemonade" and Childish Gambino's "This is America"—made for poignant conversations with Yeezy-wearing white teens who sensed, but could not fully articulate, the inadequacy of the racial status quo. Every time I excitedly discussed a new Kendrick Lamar or Chance the Rapper album, or geeked out with the theater kids about *Hamilton*, I pondered if their experiences with people of color would move them beyond that of consumers. After all, they lived in—like me, like a lot of us—the homogenous world of white, southern evangelicalism.

Know Your Place is for those waking students, who remind me of my near-lifelong immersion in these spaces. This book is for the teachers that challenged my loyalties by fostering transformational spaces. This book is also for my peers, young Gen X-ers and Millennials. We witnessed significant racial change during our formative years. The icons of my youth were equally white and black. Michael Jordan, Michael Jackson, Bill Cosby, Bo Jackson, and Oprah Winfrey were some of the biggest figures in our imaginations. Hip-hop would explode among suburban, white kids in the early

---

2. Trump secured a greater percentage of the white evangelical vote in 2016 (81 percent) than the Republican presidential candidates in the previous three elections: Romney in 2012 (78 percent), McCain in 2008 (74 percent), Bush in 2004 (78 percent); Cox, "White Christians Side with Trump."

INTRODUCTION

nineties, prompting us to consider perspectives different from our own. Racial flashpoints like the Rodney King/LAPD and O. J. Simpson verdicts were captured on video from beginning to end. Now, at this stage of our lives, as parents and non-stop working professionals already focused on shrinking retirement prospects, we don't have much bandwidth left to educate ourselves on complex matters. With that in mind, I've tried to translate for you, which Willie Jennings describes as "the unrelenting submission to another people's voices for the sake of speaking with them."[3] I hope you hear a shared language through this book that can be a starting point for you.

These pages are also my coping mechanism in the face of deep existential questions: I heard the expression "know your place" within my community (never in my home), as a way of reminding supposed inferiors of their spot in the social hierarchy. "Know your place" was a warning to anyone trying to escape their station by acting "uppity." Thankfully, some things have changed for the better. Some things.

What I've realized is that white, southern evangelicalism has left me ill-equipped to deal with my impending social predicament in the mid-century (2045), when I am projected to become a minority during the twilight of my life.[4] By not really knowing ourselves—the stories that have shaped us—we have turned to figuring out everyone else in relationship to ourselves. Our self-told myth is that we are the sun, and everyone else outside of our communities are but mere satellites in our universe. The first step of coping with this false reality is to truly learn the people, the stories, and places that have shaped us.

Know Your Place is a reflection upon the formative communities of my life—white, southern, evangelical—each one still capturing my affections to one degree or another. I want to be what philosopher Michael Walzer calls a "connected critic," one who is neither "intellectually detached" nor "emotionally detached" from the examined community.[5] Each group considered individually is a confounding community, each having nebulous boundaries and rather elastic definitions. Wendell Berry's words in *The Hidden Wound* resonate with me: "A man, I thought, must be judged by how willingly and meaningfully he can be present where he is, by how fully

---

3. Jennings, *Christian Imagination*, 148.
4. See Frey, "US Will Become 'Minority White' in 2045."
5. Walzer, *Interpretation and Social Criticism*, 39.

he can make himself at home in his part of the world. I began to want desperately to learn to belong to my place."[6]

Belonging addresses our deepest desires, as we are creatures designed for community. That being said, white, southern evangelicals constantly strain my desire to remain connected to them. Whether or not each community sees me as a part of them—and I think that they do—is immaterial. They have left their mark on me in both life-giving and soul-sucking ways, and I have resolved this tension with my people by making two promises: First, for better or worse, I'll keep dancing "with the one that brung me," so long as they keep welcoming me into their spaces. Second, I will tell the truth to those who believe their world is ending with every lost battle in the culture war. Telling the truth without devolving into hagiographies or crouching into a nostalgic, defensive posture means interrogating the good, the bad, and the ugly of my communities. And let me tell you: we have quite a bit of bad news to sort through before we can get to the good news.

This simple formula encapsulates coming to terms with being formed by white, southern evangelicals:

Disembodiment + Division = Disorientation

I have been forged in *disembodiment*, a fact I did not know previously but do now. I have been shaped by *division*, some of which I knew but simply accepted as fact. Learning about my disembodiment and division has led to my *disorientation* in what seems to be a rapidly changing world.

Disembodiment names the idea that I am *not* a body or that I do not have to pay attention to physical matters. I was raised in whiteness, which promoted disembodiment. We were supposed to be "colorblind," to literally not notice race. In other words, we were taught to not notice one of the most noticeable aspects of another person. Evangelicalism taught me to reject being "conformed to this world" (Rom 12:2) or living "according to the flesh" (8:5), awaiting the day that "I'll fly away." My geography contributed to this lack of place, because the South, whatever and wherever it is, imposed customs and gestures that owed more to "the way things have always been" than to their utility for the twenty-first century. Furthermore, we Southerners still cannot agree on the boundaries of this platonic ideal of supposed regional superiority. In short, denying corporeality affects the

---

6. Berry, *Hidden Wound*, 87.

INTRODUCTION

way I understand and enjoy corporate existence, which makes disembodiment a curse that separates me from others.

Historically speaking, white, southern evangelicals are who they are precisely by who they are *not*. *Division* has always been part and parcel of my life: I inherited enemies before I ever even knew they existed. I inherited not just stories of how I came to have these enemies, but an entire world already defined by the presence of these opposing forces: White against non-white; Southerners against Yankees; evangelicals against secularists, mainliners, Catholics, or potentially anything and anyone. I feel as though I've been pitted against someone my entire life.

If you cannot fathom the meaning of your body, to say nothing of others' bodies, and if you inherit division, or at minimum the lingering effects of that division, what happens when you realize that neither of these realities have to be so? For me, the result has been *disorientation*. If all three communal identities are challenged at once, then there are two options: Either interrogate and relinquish old notions, or double-down on them and claim that the world is ending. When I realized my community loyalties—each creating blind spots—I had to revisit my world almost like a first-time traveler.

I am a teacher at heart. Teaching does not mean knowing or saying *everything* there is to say on a topic. This area of study is massive, so I'm offering you a crash-course, trusting that you'll seek out the things that interest you. Thinkers, issues, and events will be left out. Trust me, I'm fully aware of these omissions. We're going broad rather than deep. If you're completely ignorant of the issues, there's no shame in that, but you do have to catch up. The world isn't slowing down for you. Where appropriate, I will define terms. When I use "prejudice," I'm referring to:"Beliefs, opinions and attitudes that are characterized by inflexibility, dogmatism and narrowmindedness. These may be learned, copied or acquired beliefs about another group or other groups (or individuals seen as belonging to that group)."[7] Everyone displays prejudices. "Racism," though, concerns more than just beliefs or attitudes. Racism is "any program or practice of discrimination, segregation, persecution, or mistreatment based on membership in a race or ethnic group."[8]

For the sake of readability, I've written everything in essay form that can largely be read, discussed, or assigned on its own. This is a massive

---

7. Bolaffi et al., *Dictionary of Race, Ethnicity and Culture*, 227.
8 Delgado and Stefanic, *Critical Race Theory*, 171.

INTRODUCTION

topic to cover, so I've found digestible chunks to be a preferable format for myself. Also, trafficking in totalizing labels is a tired mode in our times, as if to say this label or that one is all that someone is or could be (e.g., white, southern, evangelical). David Dark puts it so well:

> Aren't we all made up of a wide variety of influences (like the proffered affiliations themselves)? Too easy identification with one affiliation to the exclusion of the other can get to feeling like the same sad, dysfunctional song of too many a century. The labels we claim are conveniences, only ringing partially true—if at all—and never telling the whole story.[9]

Because the labels never tell the entire story about a person, a place, or an institution, I'll typically use "loyalties" or "communities" over the too-broad "identity."[10] I will also use the first-person singular and plural (I, me, we, us, our) to self-identify with my communities, layering them as we progress. For example, in Part I, "I/we" refers to white people; in Part II it refers to white southerners; and finally, in Part III, those designations refer to white, southern evangelicals. What I mean to model by this approach is a form of grace that allows people to be as messy and inconsistent as I typically am.

For example, my college roommate "Jason" cannot articulate the latest social justice cause or give a thorough take on Black Lives Matter. He also avoids absorbing the constant harangue of fear-peddlers, and this avoidance frees him to live out a kind of Mr. Rogers ethic, which is a preferable politic to the available death-cults. Jason and I disagree on several issues, but because we remain friends it's not uncommon for him to shoot me a text or email to get my take, because I'm his "race" guy, like a trusted plumber or mechanic. What I appreciate about Jason is not that he makes me feel useful, but that this humble man doesn't separate people into wheat and chaff, ready to toss them into the unquenchable fires based on their labels or teams. A quarter-century of friendship does not make one disposable chaff.

My classroom has always been one of stories, conversations, and my own confessions. As I share my life, students reciprocate. If I confess prejudices or confusion, then they follow suit. I've tried to do the same here. I limit my scope to race due to its complexity, specifically the Black-white divide, the reasons for which should be obvious through the book. I have highlighted many thinkers of color to expand your reading list because this

9. Dark, *Life's Too Short to Pretend You're Not Religious*, 117–18.
10. Stassen and Gushee, *Kingdom Ethics* (1st ed.) 59, 63–64.

INTRODUCTION

work should not be your sole book on race and Christianity. So many exciting works are being released in these areas that it's difficult to stay read-up on them all. Any omissions were not purposeful; we just have an embarrassment of riches in this field.

Lastly, much of the Christian story, just like my story, centers upon feeling a sense of possession—possession of land and kingdoms, even possession of the Truth, and then losing it all. A case could be made that the story of whiteness and being a Southerner also rests upon these same themes. Losing it all, though, is *not* a thought many white, southern evangelicals have had to consider in the last half-century until perhaps now. The next quarter century is a crucial time for whites, southerners, and evangelicals to reflect upon their place in the here and now, and in the by and by. I know that I will die one day; I carry no misgivings about the everlastingness of myself or the ways that formed me. My grandparents have died, passing within a couple of years of each other. My parents will be next. I will follow them, and so on. This is the beautiful order of things. We get a blink on this rock. And someone takes our place.

Part I

A PROBLEM PEOPLE
My Introduction to Being White

> There ain't a white man in this room that would change places with me—none of you—none of you would change places with me ... *and I'm rich*. That's how good it is to be white.[1]
>
> —Chris Rock

The first awkward conversation I had about race occurred where all weighty matters do: on the pre-school playground. I asked a Black boy his name, and he replied, "Derrick Brown" (not his real first name).

"Is your name 'Brown' because your skin is brown?" I asked.

"No," he said, "I'm not brown; I'm Black."

I corrected him, saying, "You're not Black. You're brown."

Again, showing remarkable patience for a four-year-old, he said, "My name is Brown, but I'm Black."

I didn't get it, but I was content to leave the matter alone, because after all, it was recess. Mastering intercultural competency would have to wait until after finger-painting and naps.

My whiteness has not always been apparent to me, as everyone else's race has been, but I will tell you that *being* white has been outstanding. I've thoroughly enjoyed it, unless I've been in a non-European nation where

---

1. Rock, "Bigger and Blacker."

PART I: A PROBLEM PEOPLE

my race offered no discernible advantage. At those rare moments it has not been as awesome, standing out like a pale ghost in a country I would not haunt for long. I did not spend much time thinking about my racial identity through my youth unless I was forced to do so. There was "white" and "black" and not much else in my small world. For that matter, I can still remember the name of the one Jewish and one Muslim family I knew through high school. Mine was a fairly straightforward existence in a small, West Tennessee town.

Once I left the safe confines of my hometown for college, new settings, experiences, and friends changed me. As these friendships deepened, I was emboldened to ask people of color what life was like for them. They returned my earnestness with patience in order to address my ignorance. One college friend talked with me for nearly three hours one night, for example, detailing just how lonely our predominantly white college campus was for him. We remain friends to this day. It was a life-changing conversation for me that altered the trajectory of my thoughts and vocation. For him, it was just an explanation of everyday existence. I see now how our reliance upon people of color to be on-call to explain racism, or serve as our personal Wikipedia page on prejudice, is an "exhausting" existence that many folks have decided to forego.[2] I cannot say that I blame them either.

**

At the Republican National Convention, Senator Lindsey Graham noted the shifting national demographics and commented, "We're not generating enough angry white guys to stay in business for the long term."[3]

Graham said this at the 2012 convention.

Robert P. Jones, the CEO of the Public Religion Research Institute (PRRI) and a sociologist of religion, published the ominously-titled book *The End of White Christian America* prior to the 2016 election.[4] Jones (and everyone else) was clearly wrong for at least one more election cycle, because in 2016 lots of white people, including white evangelicals, voted for Donald Trump. The initial election post-mortems focused on lower-middle

---

2. Brown, *I'm Still Here*, 11. See also Eddo-Lodge, *Why I'm No Longer Talking to White People About Race*.

3. Helderman and Cohen, "As Republican Convention Emphasizes Diversity, Racial Incidents Intrude."

4. Jones, *End of White Christian America*.

class, middle-aged whites, who paradoxically held that the future of the nation rightfully belonged to them *and* that there was no longer a place for them. Trump and elected leaders of his ilk made them feel good about who they once were, who they could be, and who they were *not* (i.e., immigrants, Muslims, cultural elites, etc.). Even though the dominant post-election narrative focused on struggling whites, Trump did not simply win their support; he won the support of many white sub-demographics by a significant margin over Hillary Clinton: Trump won white men (by a +31 margin); white women (+9); whites with college degrees (+3); whites without college degrees (+37); whites, age 18 to 29 (+4); whites, age 30 to 44 (+17); whites, age 45 to 64 (+28); whites 65 and older (+19). Trump won the white vote in every economic class, too. Trump's overtly race-based campaign—"Make America Great Again" (MAGA)—garnered broad white support and moved Ta-Nehisi Coates to declare Trump America's "First White President."[5]

Motivating factors for the white electorate have come into view since the 2016 election. Political scientists John Sides, Michael Tesler, and Lynn Vavreck dispel the popular myth that white voters were motivated solely by anger or economic anxiety. Instead, they make the compelling case that Trump activated white voters by enflaming racial tensions during his presidential campaign.[6] They explain these motivating tensions of identity politics in this way:

> People can be categorized in many groups based on their place of birth, place of residence, ethnicity, religion, gender, occupation, and so on. But simply being a member *of* a group is not the same thing as identifying or sympathizing *with* that group. The key is whether people feel a psychological attachment to a group. That attachment binds individuals to the group and helps it develop cohesion and shared values...When gains, losses, or threats become salient, group identities develop and strengthen. Groups become

---

5. Coates, *We Were Eight Years in Power*, 346.

6. Sides et al., *Identity Politics*, 31, 92. One vehicle for forwarding the narrative of white electoral anger came through the national media's praise of J. D. Vance's memoir *Hillbilly Elegy* (HarperCollins, 2016) as the prism through which to view white, rural citizens' economic anger. However, Sides et al. say that "the relationship between economic outcomes in counties and voting in 2016 was murky," because that Trump actually "did better in counties where there was a larger *drop* in unemployment and *more* social mobility" (172).

more unified and more likely to develop goals and grievances, which are the components of a politicized group consciousness.[7]

Sides et al. say, Trump "capitalized on an existing reservoir of discontent about a changing American society and culture," overwhelmingly focused on race, immigration, and Islam.[8] For example, they found that those "most likely to oppose immigration, dislike Muslims, and attribute racial inequality to black's lack of effort were 53 points more likely to support Trump than those with the most favorable views" of those same issues.[9] The president's message was received loud and clear, at least in places like my current home in East Tennessee, when an independent 2016 congressional candidate erected a billboard that read "Make America White Again."[10]

The 2017 white nationalist gathering in Charlottesville, Virginia, remains the "Free Bird" of Trump's deep racist hits catalog, which are numerous: Trump's signature promise of the first MAGA campaign and presidential term was to "build the wall" on the U.S.-Mexico border (with Mexico picking up the tab). Trump insulted a Mexican-American judge accusing him of being unable to be objective on immigration matters. The MS-13 gang was referenced often, as if every little burgh across the nation was besieged by their mayhem. His administration's child separation plan at the border left children still unaccounted for by government records. He campaigned for and instituted a Muslim travel ban. Trump also managed to feud with virtually every Black athlete in the nation, revoking White House invitations for world champions like they were travel visas. The president questioned the intelligence of people of color, like *CNN*'s Don Lemon and Congresswoman Maxine Waters. Trump denigrated "shit-hole countries" populated largely by people of color. Before the 2018 midterm elections, a spate of violent acts were committed by Trump supporters due to racial identity (African-Americans targeted, shot, and killed in Louisville); due to their religious identity (Tree of Life Synagogue in Pittsburgh); due to their

---

7. Sides et al., *Identity Politics*, 3.

8. Sides et al., *Identity Politics*, 71.

9. Sides et al., *Identity Politics*, 90. Sides et al. acknowledge the difficulty of establishing cause-effect for candidate rhetoric leading to votes, yet they attempt to discern voter motivation by studying the 2011–2012 voter survey—Views of the Electorate Research (Voter)—that sought to capture voter attitudes on issues, irrespective of future candidate rhetoric. Thus, voters activated by issues connected to expressions of white identity long before an election can be surveyed again during a campaign to determine what opinions marshaled voter support (73).

10. Jaffe and Siemaszko, "Outrage as Trump Inspired Candidate."

political affiliation or perceived bias (pipe bombs sent to Democratic leaders, including to former Presidents Clinton and Obama).

Prior to the 2018 mid-term election, the president threatened to deploy soldiers to the Mexican border to stop a caravan of people seeking political asylum. President Trump declared southern border crossings to be a national emergency, whereby he could circumvent the power of Congress to fund his border wall. Months later in July 2019, Trump singled out four freshmen Congresswomen of color on Twitter and at a re-election rally, using the hackneyed "go back to where you come from" expression, harkening back to his status as the founding father of the Obama birther controversy. White nationalists were bolstered by Trump's reticence to make clear distinctions between his actual beliefs and those of his most violent supporters. In March 2019, an Australian-born white nationalist called Trump a "renewed symbol of white identity" in a manifesto before killing at least 50 worshipers at two mosques in New Zealand.[11] By July 2019, FBI Director Christopher Wray testified before Congress that the majority of domestic terrorism cases were "motivated by some version of what you might call white-supremacist violence."[12] All of this was prior to the 2020 protests following the killing of George Floyd by Minneapolis police.

Thoughts matter. Thoughts put into words always matter. Public words that affect others matter more so. Public words by the world's most powerful office often means life or death. The net effect of loose words is increased division and violence, sparked by the individual who stands upon the largest platform in the world, the president of the United States.

White people could understand society when it worked as it should with everyone slotted into the proper pecking order. But now, all they can see is their figurative epitaphs signaled by the Obama presidency or immigration or their kids wearing LeBron James jerseys or something. As a nation we are suffering from grieving whites, who feel as if they are losing their place, and I am trying to understand—not excuse—the actions of those who mourn the passing of supposedly better days.

Every person suffers from heartbreak in one form or another, and that grief manifests itself in the public square. The difficulty of being a citizen is remaining connected to others with whom you disagree in order to help them deal with their pain. Parker Palmer names two kinds of heartbreak: Hearts "breaking apart" refers to those individuals who deal with

---

11. *Al Jazeera*, "New Zealand Mosque Attacks Suspect Praised Trump in Manifesto."
12. McCardle, "FBI Director."

loss and failure through anger, disengagement, and often, scapegoating. Those whose hearts are "breaking open" refers to those who can hold the complexities of life in a way that creates the possibility of new life. Palmer thickens the distinction between the two types of heartbreak, saying:

> We will never fully understand why people respond so differently to experiences of heartbreak: there is an eternal mystery about how the shattered soul becomes whole again. But people whose hearts break open, not apart, are usually those who have embraced life's "little deaths" over time, those small losses, failures, and betrayals that can serve as practice for the larger deaths yet to come.[13]

To heal heartbreak, it must be acknowledged. When pain remains unaddressed, it festers and will be manipulated politically. A people's resiliency to political manipulation will depend upon their relationships and the practices they value: At our best, we are bound together by conversation, local associations, and we deal with tensions directly and communally.[14]

**

At the turn of the twentieth century, W. E. B. Du Bois asked a question that captured white notions of Blackness in America: "How does it feel to be a problem?"[15] Du Bois was the first African-American to earn a doctorate from Harvard, and his thought continues to shape modern conversations about race. He famously named the struggle of being both Black and an American as "double consciousness." Black folk were, in his words,

> born with a veil, and gifted with second sight in this American world,–a world which yields him no true self-consciousness, but only lets him see himself through the revelation of the other world. It is a peculiar sensation, this double-consciousness, this sense of always looking at one's self through the eyes of others, of measuring one's soul by the tape of a world that looks on in amused contempt and pity. One ever feels his two-ness,–an American, a Negro; two souls, two thoughts two unreconciled strivings; two warring ideals in one dark body, whose dogged strength alone keeps it from being torn asunder.[16]

13. Palmer, *Healing the Heart of Democracy*, 60.
14. Palmer, *Healing the Heart of Democracy*, 57–67.
15. Du Bois, *Souls of Black Folk*, 7.
16. Du Bois, *Souls of Black Folk*, 8.

PART I: A PROBLEM PEOPLE

A "veil" cloaks Black folk in existential darkness, a kind of exile from Eden, creating a world of spiritual anguish for Black folk—a world marked by stigma, terror, brutality, where one fights to maintain humanity and hope for the long journey through a white supremacist world. The social meaning of being Black was defined and tainted, in part, by white power.[17]

For most white people, there is no such equivalency in our lives of a double-consciousness. Oh sure, we have trifling conflicts from time-to-time, bifurcations of our own making: *It's not personal; it's business. What do my religious beliefs have to do with living in the real world? Why can't sports and politics remain separate?* None of these thoughts, though, carry the weight of Du Bois' recognition that he creates a problem for whites simply by existing in Black skin. As Ta-Nehisi Coates puts the matter to his son in searing terms: "You cannot arrange your life around them ... Our moment is too brief. Our bodies are too precious."[18] *That* reality redirects Du Bois's question to a new subject: Me.

How does it feel to be a problem? I am a problem.

This acknowledgment is not about self-hatred or performative white guilt, but rather a reckoning with my history, that I have either benefited from someone else's hardship or gotten benefits of the doubt along the way that others have not. To be white is to be unaware that most things in the world work for me most of the time, because they were ordered, designed, and enforced by my people. My presence is never considered extraordinary by walking into the door of a church, a school, a neighborhood, a shop. I belong; everything around me confirms my belonging; and because I belong so seamlessly in this society it is easy for me to lose perspective on my surroundings. Instead of the second sight Du Bois describes, I am plagued by a kind of thrice-blinding, where my community loyalties constitute three, largely unified, powerful narratives: white, southern, and evangelical. Each narrative historically reinforces one another. Thus, sometimes we feel that challenging one narrative constitutes a rejection of the communities in which many of us have been raised, and becoming homeless in a sense is too-terrifying a prospect to entertain.

Challenging those long-held narratives are just what we need to do right now. Historian Jacquelyn Dowd Hall's comment on identity helps us think through who we are and who we want to become:

---

17. Lewis, *W.E.B. Du Bois*, 180–83.
18. Coates, *Between the World and Me*, 146.

PART I: A PROBLEM PEOPLE

To be sure, we cannot remake ourselves each morning; we cannot opt out of the matrix of privilege or oppression in to which we are born. At the same time, we are always coming into being; we become who we are in dialogue, in interaction with the world. The challenge and the anxiety of this intellectual moment lie precisely in the tension between these two realities.[19]

One such example of choosing who I would dialogue with came from joining a student group devoted to racial reconciliation at Duke Divinity School. That group helped me consider this tension—between my privileges and my interaction with the world—within a trusted community. Each week we gathered to hear one another's stories. At one meeting, a Black woman, "Nell," shared what was in her estimation a rather small slight at a tire store earlier that week. Nell entered the store to find the counter unattended. Moments later, a white woman walked in too and waited for service. When a white employee eventually emerged, he turned to the white woman and asked how he could help her. The white woman replied that Nell had arrived first and should be served. It was a small story, one that many might dismiss as insignificant, but Nell's last words, delivered with exhaustion, not malice, stuck with me: "I do not wake up every morning thinking about being Black, but everyday someone reminds me that I am." An ordinary interaction had become the occasion for suspicion and hurt, because too often Nell had received disrespect. She lived beneath the veil.

It was a sacred moment for Nell to share her story with us, to expose her daily slights so that we might mourn with her. A slight, like suffering a papercut is a small injury, relatively speaking, but several papercuts a day would drive me into madness, particularly realizing that some people sought to do more than nick me. I learned in those moments among my group to sit, listen, and share, rather than trying to do what we white men always try to do: Fix things.

**

We do not need any more trite Disney treatments of serious issues that leave us feeling like racism is a past problem. The feel-good movies do not help us understand the intricacies of the problem. Ditto to those comfortable Martin Luther King Jr. quotes and memes disseminated throughout social media every January and February. It is time to dig deeper rather

---

19. Hall, *Revolt Against Chivalry*, xxxv.

than settling for surface-level platitudes that literally anyone can find from a simple internet search.

I don't say this from a posture of superiority or perfection. I have benefited from timely corrections from kind colleagues and generous friends. For example, when teaching my first course with a significant number of international students, a colleague brought to light a terribly annoying habit of mine: When a student shared a thought in class, I would boomerang their point back to my own anecdote or perspective. I couldn't simply let their words fill in the room. It was not so much that I had to have the last word, but trying to personally connect with my students through constantly adding my thoughts had the effect of marginalizing their voices. These students were showing courage, speaking in their second language, and I had undercut both their stories and their courage. Part of teaching is just learning how to get out of the way, and I was in the way. I was putting myself in the middle of their stories.

I can imagine scenarios where life could have broken my heart into a thousand irreparable pieces, transforming me into a problem for my family, friends, neighbors, and all of society. Instead of that terrible fate, I grew up in places of love, and life granted me friends who filled my life with grace by telling me the truth. Here's the truth: As white people we possess a racial identity; we always have. Whiteness has social power even if imperceptible to you. Our ignorance, willful or otherwise, has made us into a problem. Let that fact break your heart open to the possibility of your soul being healed.

1

A DISEASED IMAGINATION

So we learned the dance that cripples the human spirit, step by step by step, we who were white and we who were colored, day by day, hour by hour, year by year until the movements were reflexes and made for the rest of our life without thinking. Alas, for many white children, they were movements made without feeling.[1]

—Lillian Smith, *Killers of the Dream*

In the TV series *The West Wing*, White House Press Secretary C. J. Cregg meets with the fictitious Organization of Cartographers for Social Equality who lobby for changing the maps used in public schools. The near-universal Mercator map, they argue, distorts the relative size of European countries compared to non-European nations, and larger European land masses have fostered imperialist attitudes for centuries and created an ethnic bias against the Two-Thirds World.

C. J. asks, "Are you saying the map is wrong?" The cartographers reply that the map is indeed inaccurate and proceed to show her a series of images where Greenland and the African continent appear to be the same size on the Mercator map, even though Africa is the significantly larger territory. Likewise, South America nearly doubles the Mercator-depicted size of Europe, just as Mexico, in actuality, has more land mass than Alaska. As

1. Smith, *Killers of the Dream*, 96.

more distortions are revealed, C. J.'s bewilderment grows: The presentation intensifies as the cartographers reveal the location of land masses on the planet versus where they are shown to be on the map.

C. J. is joined by Deputy Chief of Staff Josh Lyman who had previously teased her about drawing this laborious assignment. When the lead cartographer explains that Germany lies at the northernmost corner of the earth, Josh interrupts and asks, "You're telling me Germany isn't where we think it is?"

"Nothing is where you think it is," the presenter replies.

C. J., now on the edge of her seat, asks where Germany is precisely located, as the cartographer reveals a newly drawn map. C. J. and Josh lean in to get a closer look, now fully engaged. The unveiled image shows newly shaped and positioned nations, vaguely reminiscent of their "normal" appearances, moving C. J. to exclaim, "What the hell is that???!!!"

With a wry grin, knowing he had won a convert, the lead cartographer replied, "It's where you've been living this whole time."[2]

I want white people to ask, Where have we been living this whole time? Answering such a question means pausing from our busy lives to reflect, not exactly a strength of working Americans chasing "the good life." The American Dream is reinforced from the time we learn the importance of standardized test scores; it's like the air we breathe. In other words, all of the education, work, stress, and hustling is done with an end (a *telos*) in mind of the good life. When asked to describe the good life nearly all of my students have given some version of this answer: A progression of graduating from high school and then college, getting a high paying job, getting married and having kids, retiring early to an immaculate beach house.

The good life does not come pre-loaded into our consciousness, however; we learn what the good life is by watching and participating in it. Philosopher James K. A. Smith says this end/telos directs our loves like a compass, and we pursue the good life as its "affective icons" get into "our bones and hearts."[3] Smith says we fancy ourselves to be rational creatures, adhering to Descartes's famous dictum, "I think therefore I am," yet that phrase just doesn't describe a great deal of human experiences.[4] We often act instinctually, led by our hearts more so than our minds. While we *think*

---

2. Yu, *West Wing*, Season 2, episode 16, "Somebody's Going to Emergency, Somebody's Going to Jail."

3. Smith, *You Are What You Love*, 13. Cf. Smith, *Desiring the Kingdom*, 55.

4. Smith, *Desiring the Kingdom*, 42.

PART I: A PROBLEM PEOPLE

that we think our way through the world, we actually *feel* our way through it, intuitively trusting lessons learned, implicitly or explicitly, from our communities.[5]

Our routines and practices become habits, revealing what we love and ultimately who we are becoming. Here's a personal example: I am a creature of habit to the extreme degree. I love my routines. My routines keep me scheduled. My schedule keeps me on task, and the more tasks completed comprise what I believe to be "successful" work days. Waking up, meals, workouts, scheduled blocks of writing, editing, and lesson-planning—I carry these out with metronomic precision. They give me a sense of control. When my routines are disrupted, I feel utterly disoriented. Why? Because normally I exist, as Smith says, on a kind of auto-pilot, reflexively navigating my well-traversed terrain.[6]

Smith utilizes the term "social imaginary," made popular by philosopher Charles Taylor, as a way of understanding one's world that is taken largely for granted. One's social imaginary "incorporates a sense of the normal expectations that we have of each other," Taylor says. "The kind of common understanding which enables us to carry out the collective practices which make up our social life."[7]

Here's the connection to race: Societies have routines, too. We, just by the sheer fact of being white, have been able to enjoy a kind of curated existence, shaped over time by the stories and images that captured our ancestor's imaginations. We inherited a social imaginary that Smith describes as: "frameworks of 'meaning' by which we make sense of our world and our calling in it."[8] At times, these visions are taught to us plainly, but just as often those teachings are *caught* by being a member of the community.

Being white is an inheritance that contributes to what you do and why. When the world feels "normal" and seems to be operating as it should—when everything is in its proper place—our social imaginary just moves us through our day-to-day interactions on auto-pilot. Lillian Smith, writing in the 1940s, described this normal-operating life as "the dance that cripples the human spirit" for whites and people of color alike, one shaped over centuries "until the movements [are] reflexes and made for the rest of our

---

5. Smith, *Desiring the Kingdom*, 57.
6. Smith, *Desiring the Kingdom*, 61; Smith, *You Are What You Love*, 34–38.
7. Taylor, *Secular Age*, 172.
8. Smith, *Desiring the Kingdom*, 68.

life without thinking" and "without feeling."⁹ My question is: Have the steps of the dance changed? None of this is to say your life is easy or that you aren't stressed. It is worth considering, however, the ways in which people of color have more variables to negotiate than you or I.

Where have we been living this whole time?

To answer to my question, I'm claiming that racism must be understood to be a problem of imagination. Yes, people of faith should understand racism to be a sin of individual choices and systemic failures. Those with no faith commitments might call racism simply un-neighborly or un-American. Above all, though, racism is a problem in the way we imagine our world.

Moderates and Other Things

Consider this historical example to illustrate how easily white, southern Christians go with the flow: On April 16, 1963, Martin Luther King Jr. sat in a Birmingham jail cell and began to pen a fixture in American lore. In this letter, King detailed the gradations of white's reactions to the civil rights movement, ranging from the violence of the Ku Klux Klan (KKK) to the systemic brutality perpetrated by groups like the White Citizen's Council, white-collar obstructionists who used courts, schools, and businesses to forward racism. King, however, expressed a greater disappointment with "the white moderate" who was, in his words, "more devoted to 'order' than to justice." Gradualism, the belief that social progress would organically develop as time healed racial wounds, split the ideological difference between the racist segregationists and the activist integrationists. The white moderate was, in King's view, "the arch-supporter of the status quo."[10] In his righteous indignation, King posed several questions to the socially-inert, white, southern Christians who would not pursue justice: "What kind of people worship here? Who is their God? . . .Where were their voices of support when tired, bruised, and weary Negro men and women decided to rise from the dark dungeons of complacency to the bright hills of creative protest?"[11] King's questions served as both a democratic critique of societal injustice and a prophetic reminder to Christians that their worship might just be displeasing to the Lord if divorced from the way they lived their lives

---

9. Smith, *Killers of the Dream*, 96.
10. King, "Letter from Birmingham City Jail," 295, 300.
11. King, "Letter from Birmingham City Jail," 299.

in public. The civil rights movement was a dramatic public confrontation of white, southern Christian complicity with systemic injustice underwritten by, at best, spiritual complacency and at worst intentional bigotry. White Christians' reticence to act for social change preserved the status quo. Racism existed and flourished with Christian support, including the marshaling of the Bible for racist ends. This is not in dispute.[12]

Historian David Chappell, however, offers an interesting nuance to the dominant narrative of a church-endorsed racism and the way many white Christians inhabited the middle ground: "The historically significant thing about white religion in the 1950s–60s is not its failure to join the civil rights movement. The significant thing, given that the church was probably as racist as the rest of the South, is that it failed in any meaningful way to join *the anti-civil rights movement*."[13] White, southern churches, "failed to elevate their whiteness—the institutions and customs that oppressed black folk—above other concerns . . . They loved *other things*—peace, social order—more. They could not make defense of segregation the unifying principle of their culture."[14] What remains clear is that the South worked in predictable fashion for white, southern Christians, and the default, autopilot setting of southern society created problems for people of color.

In other words, the social imagination of white moderates was being exploded by the prospect of losing what they believed they had earned. They had created the world they wanted for themselves. With World War II in the rearview mirror, the U.S. soon enjoyed a booming economy and a booming population. As James Hudnut-Beumler puts it, "Those who came to age as young adults in the 1950s were in no small measure the products

---

12. See Leonard, "Theology for Racism: Southern Fundamentalists and the Civil Rights Movement," 51–52, and Charles Marsh, *God's Long Summer*, 114–15.

13. Chappell, *Stone of Hope*, 107. Emphasis added.

14. Chappell, *Stone of Hope*, 107. Emphasis added. Other historians counter Chappell, claiming white supremacy held in place peace, order, the other things. Glen Feldman states, "There is much in the Southern past to suggest that the rank and file of white Southern believers did not construct an elaborate religious defense of white supremacy *precisely because* it already functioned at a perfectly adequate level" ("Introduction," 9). Mark Noll adds that religious leaders who supported segregation did not have the same cultural authority they would have had a century earlier during the Civil War. Many evangelicals, being reluctant either to spell out a policy of segregation or to perpetrate violence, "moved to the moderate center on most racial issues" (Noll, *God and Race in American Politics*, 132). Noll, too, supports Chappell's thesis. Chappell's thesis remains compelling because, in Luke Harlow's words, "no one has yet published a thoroughgoing critique of Chappell's argument" ("Slavery, Race, and Political Ideology in the White Christian South," 219).

of the fear and expectations of Depression-era parents."[15] The civil rights movement was an interruption to the placid life they had sought to create for themselves. Thus, the white moderate wanted all of the public discord to stop, without their interests being harmed. Preserving these everyday loves begins to explain the white moderates' complicity to racism, all the while feeling *they* were not part of the problem simply because they never lit up a cross or struck someone at a lunch counter.

In Holocaust literature, participation in the atrocities are described by types: perpetrators, victims, and bystanders. David Gushee's assessment of the bystander is instructive, as it mirrors the moral posture of the white moderate in King's letter: "If one is present, one is taking part. The moral issue then simply becomes a matter of moral perception—whether one is able/willing to acknowledge the moral responsibility that is intrinsic to the situation one faces."[16] Very few white moderates would have thought themselves to be racists, oppressors, or even indifferent to African Americans' plight in the mid-twentieth century. In fact, many whites believed Blacks were content living within a segregated society and appreciated white generosity. Jason Sokol summarizes the point, "White assertions of black happiness stemmed more from whites' 'psychological needs' to believe in social harmony than from any evidence that such concord actually existed."[17] White misunderstanding of Black lives showed that *little reflection of any kind*, if and when it ever occurred, could fully undo the years of reflexive habits that seeped down deep into bone and blood. Whites knew one dance, one set of steps, and they danced it, clapping on the one and the three. So, when Dr. King asked "What kind of people worship here? Who is their God?" he is calling out the intention of their Christian worship. Did white Christians actually love their neighbors, or did they actually love other things—safety, security, and personal peace more?

**

What does this have to do with race in America right now?

Just as a map is a background piece, a taken for granted wall decoration, it still communicates valuable information about place, location, and distance, even if we have forgotten its presence. Similarly, social imaginaries

---

15. Hudnut-Beumler, *Looking for God in the Suburbs*, 3.
16. Gushee, *Righteous Gentiles of the Holocaust*, 72.
17. Sokol, *There Goes My Everything*, 59.

create an "implicit 'map' of social space."[18] James K. A. Smith explains it well: "We have an understanding of our environment and surroundings that has been built up from our absorption in it: we've been biking and walking these streets for years. We could get home from the baseball diamond without even thinking about it."[19] Smith's description largely matches my hometown experience with one small adjustment: I rode my bike to most baseball practices, so while I knew the way there and back without thinking, I still had choices to make every trip. Graham Park was the only place I routinely went that forced me to pass through Black spaces, and "trespassing" implied danger. There was no easy way to access the park by bike: One way was the perilous two-lane road with no shoulders. The other possible route took you through government housing, and when you're a young teen everyone is a potential threat, to say nothing of unfamiliar places and people.

Race gets affixed to social spaces, sometimes in coded language as "good" or "bad neighborhoods." Yale University sociologist Elijah Anderson describes "white spaces" as ones where "black people are typically absent, not expected, or marginalized when present." People of color might feel that those spaces are "informally 'off limits'" or that they have to justify their presence in such spaces.[20] The rules do not necessarily apply the other way around, though. For example, every small-town Southerner knows that the best barbeque in town will not be next to Trader Joe's. In Union City, if the craving hit, this meant trespassing into the Eastgate projects, a predominantly-Black housing complex, which was also adjacent to Nina's, a superior restaurant to the other off-brand pork produced by supposedly safer BBQ joints. White people came to Nina's all the time with barely a raised brow. The same free movement, though, was not extended for every person of color. My first lessons in boundaries became etched into my mind—where to go, where not to go, where I should not go alone. While my town, my world, became sectioned off into spaces where I perceived I was welcomed or safe, the reality for people of color was exponentially amplified. Our respective imaginations created new maps for us.

The term "white supremacy" makes white people squeamish, as they think it only applies to historical abominations. However, white supremacy can be much more mundane. White supremacy defined is "a concept that

---

18. Taylor, *Secular Age*, 173.
19. Smith, *Desiring the Kingdom*, 67.
20. Anderson, "White Space," 10.

A DISEASED IMAGINATION

identifies white people and white culture as normal and superior."[21] Nearly everyone will tell you that white supremacy is wrong. But, remember: If racism is a problem of how we imagine our world, then what people claim about racism cannot be the final word. No doubt old school white supremacy still exists, with some voicing it proudly. Most of us fall into white supremacy by virtue of being on auto-pilot where racism permeates the atmosphere.

Even those who just want to be left alone, who think they mind their own business, are captive to some white supremacist ideas just by being white. One people's peace and comfort has been underwritten by controlling the movement and very livelihood of people of color, and when that comfort is threatened—their good life, their kingdom—then those prejudices become activated. Racism is not a problem of reason or rationality. It's a problem of the heart and desires—the stuff that's hidden deep inside of us all.

"Implicit bias" is a contemporary term that begins to describe our hidden prejudices. The Kirwan Institute for the Study of Race and Ethnicity defines implicit bias as:

> the attitudes or stereotypes that affect our understanding, actions, and decisions in an unconscious manner. These biases, which encompass both favorable and unfavorable assessments, are activated involuntarily and without an individual's awareness or intentional control. Residing deep in the subconscious, these biases are different from known biases that individuals may choose to conceal for the purposes of social and/or political correctness. Rather, implicit biases are not accessible through introspection.[22]

Everyone has implicit biases. These deep-seated ideas about others typically favor our particular group, reinforcing the long-held imaginaries of our communities and families, fortifying the boundaries and maps we use to navigate life, often unaware of their existence or their consequences for others. All of our societal norms have a story behind them, whether we know those stories or not. In America, this means those supposedly race-neutral institutions—e.g., science, law, religion, etc.—have creation stories. Tragically, those institutions have colluded to create, in Willie Jennings's

---

21. Tisby, *Color of Comprise*, 16.
22. Kirwan Institute for the Study of Race and Ethnicity, "Understanding Implicit Bias."

PART I: A PROBLEM PEOPLE

words, a western Christianity that "lives and moves within a diseased social imagination."[23]

So, where have we been living this whole time?

Here is the brutal truth about the people and places that I love: The dominant social imagination was, and is, a white-supremacist ideology, employed to enslave, terrorize, dehumanize, or restrict people of color, while at the same time absolving the offenders and their heirs from the guilt of any wrongdoing. These offenses were committed in order to keep people in their place and upon these shared values and stories American life was built, sustained, and defended. My social imaginary has, at its core, white supremacist foundations from which I and many others have benefitted. This is my place in our shared story.

23. Jennings, *Christian Imagination*, 6.

2

THEORIES ABOUT OURSELVES
Or, All I Ever Needed to Know about Whiteness I Learned in High School

Dear Mr. Vernon,

We acccpt the fact that we had to sacrifice a whole Saturday in detention for whatever it was we did wrong. What we did *was* wrong. But we think you're crazy to make us write an essay telling you who we think we are. What do you care? And you see us as you want to see us—in the simplest terms, in the most convenient definitions. You see us as a brain, an athlete, a basket case, a princess, and a criminal. Correct? That's the way we saw each other at 7:00 this morning. We were brainwashed.[1]

Brian Johnson,
Saturday, March 24, 1984
Shermer High School
Shermer, Illinois, 60062

One New Year's Eve, my wife and I gathered with friends. Each of us was enjoying the Christmas break, but for we teachers the all-too-brief respite meant the terminally slow winter session lay ahead, followed

---

1. Hughes, *Breakfast Club*.

PART I: A PROBLEM PEOPLE

by the breakneck spring semester. As they asked me the happenings at my school I shared a couple of my better stories, which prompted one friend to say, "I wouldn't relive high school if you paid me." Most of us nodded and said, "me too," a prayer of benediction to solemnly mark the conclusion of those awkward years. Another friend interjected, though, disagreeing with our consensus, saying, "Oh, I would! I loved high school."

"Yeah?" I replied sarcastically, "because you were cool?"

She smiled, and sheepishly answered, "I was Homecoming Queen."

"Oooh!" we exclaimed with a la-di-freaking-da flourish of exaggerated gestures to show faux humility in the presence of late 1990s royalty from the kingdom of Alcoa, Tennessee. Some periods of life just stick with you even decades after their passing, especially those marked by ruthless labeling and social hierarchies erected upon shaky and arbitrary foundations.

Labels are not just for high school kids, though. The theory of whiteness, centuries in the making and perfecting, concerns, first, what it means to be "white" and second, what it means not to be. Being white, to put it simply, is a made-up thing. There is no white gene. It is a social status like being dubbed a celebrity or VIP, a designation without corresponding accomplishment. You know, like "influencer." The boiled-down history of the theory is that to be white means one possesses a legal, cultural, and psychological meaning within one's body, and in the United States it largely means having control of one's surroundings. Creating whiteness came in response to encounters with others. People have feared or hated one another forever, the reasons for which are seemingly endless, yet no one should be surprised to learn that money and power played a crucial role in making such an arbitrary physical feature like skin color the end-all, be-all.

My academic mentor, ethicist Glen Stassen, once told a story that sums up why people, even moral people, do terrible things. Glen said that he and Dot, his wife, were having a minor disagreement over some mundane thing. Glen stated his desired resolution, likely through an exhaustive ethical explanation. Dot, after considering his argument, laid down a devastating claim: "I think the reason you became an ethicist was so that you could find a way to rationalize what you *already* want to do." Glen laughed as he recounted the story and confessed with a grin, "Maybe she's right."

The creation of whiteness begins in the same spirit, as explained by Boston University professor Ibram X. Kendi:

> Time and again, powerful and brilliant men and women have produced racist ideas in order to justify the racist policies of their era,

in order to redirect the blame for their era's racial disparities away from those policies and onto Black people.[2]

Whether the policy has been slavery, segregation, or mass incarceration, the idea of racial superiority still functions now because it was developed in order to safeguard the accumulated wealth and power acquired by European colonists, slavers, and segregationists. Sometimes we determine what we want to do, first, and then we find the reason to justify our actions.

Theories of organizing peoples have existed since the beginning of recorded human history, but the systematic implementation of these theories has wreaked havoc upon the earth in ways that localized squabbles never could. A few examples, by no means comprehensive, include: Aristotle's climate theory justified Greek slaveholding practices, where "extreme hot or cold climates produced intellectually, physically, and morally inferior people who were ugly and lacked the capacity for freedom and self-government," which persisted for centuries.[3] Various implementations of the Great Chain of Being, an ancient theory (third century CE) developed by Plotinus who said, "All things follow in continuous succession from the Supreme God to the last dregs of things, mutually linked together and without a break."[4] Inanimate and animate objects fall into place, including humans in all their variety.[5] Christian interpreters of the Old Testament prooftexted scriptures to fit their racist needs: the Curse of Ham (Gen 9:18–29) to rationalize institutional slavery in America; the Tower of Babel (Gen 11:1–9) and Levitical passages (Lev 19:19) were marshalled to claim God desired peoples to remain separated; Ezra 10:10, which details a prohibition against inter-religious marriages, is extended to interracial marriages.[6] Global conquests in the fifteenth century by the Portuguese justified the slave trade as missionary expeditions, and other nations followed suit with the full power of their respective monarchies and religious leaders behind them. Stories festered from the frontlines of exploration and were recorded in popular published works for the masses that sparked the imaginations of European intellectuals and necessitated in their view justifiable reasons to enslave some and not others.

2. Kendi, *Stamped From the Beginning*, 9.
3. Kendi, *Stamped From the Beginning*, 17–18.
4. Herman, *Cave and the Light*, 140.
5. Jordan, *White Man's Burden*, 100–101.
6. See Tilson, *Segregation and the Bible* as one who refuted segregationist interpretations during the heightened racial tensions of the 1960s.

PART I: A PROBLEM PEOPLE

In the seventeenth century, scientific societies emerged in the Enlightenment, whereby they could theorize and essentially structure the world. While many thinkers could be highlighted, two stand out: Carl Linnaeus categorized humanity (in *Systema Naturae*, 1735) as a species within the primate genus, then described those human types, not ranking them into an order.[7] Drawing on Linnaeus, Johann Friedrich Blumenbach "advanced" human taxonomy (*On the Natural Varieties of Mankind*, 1776) by measuring, comparing, and classifying human anatomy—the height of foreheads, the size and angles of jawbones, teeth, eye sockets, and nasal bones. Skin color was added to the matrix resulting in five "varieties" of people, where the "Caucasians" were determined to be the cream of the global crop over the Mongolians, Ethiopians, Americans, and Malays. Intelligence, beauty, strength, capacity for morality—all of it could be determined and cataloged just by using a tape measure. American anthropologists drew on Blumenbach's work, as did other European thinkers, and coupled with the foundation already laid by scientific societies' influence over American colonists, it's easy to draw the line from pseudo-science to widespread justification of slavery around the globe.[8]

Here's the point: As the Western world was conceiving the philosophical underpinnings for human equality and democracy—all the while, still a bastion of Christendom, which purportedly taught that all humans are made in the image of God—it was simultaneously instituting systems of racial oppression.[9] The theories found purchase in the soil of old worlds and the new. Our national origin was steeped in a persistent white supremacy among those venerated colonists and founders, propped up by the scientific world's fixation on classifying everything, including people.

The Simplest Terms, The Most Convenient Definitions

Perhaps it seems difficult to believe that powerful people classified others, and then ordered their society based upon preserving their ill-gotten gains. Presumably, though, you went to high school. There you likely witnessed

---

7. Frederickson, *Racism*, 56.

8. Painter, *History of White People*, 72–90. Cf. Kendi, *Stamped*, 179–81; 198. See also Keel, *Divine Variations*.

9. For a good introduction see West, "Genealogy of Modern Racism," 90–112, and Goza, *America's Unholy Ghosts*, which examined the thought of Thomas Hobbes, John Locke, and Adam Smith.

human depravity par excellence and know that it's kind of our thing to classify one another.

Prior to beginning high school in 1991, I felt fully prepared for the pivotal rite of passage, because I had viewed director John Hughes's entire canon of teen dramas, including *The Breakfast Club* (1984).[10] This masterpiece is ninety-seven minutes of hard eye-rolls, angst-ridden complaints about parents, liberal drug use, conversations about sexual exploration, and ultimately, personal identity. *The Breakfast Club* focuses on five white high school students of differing social status, who have been sentenced to Saturday detention. Their punishment includes writing an essay describing "Who you think you are?" in order for them to learn the error of their current paths. Throughout the course of the day each student, already wedged neatly into a tight stereotype, at least according to the gaze of adult authority, learns intimate details about their fellow detainees' lives and begins to see something of their own experience in the other.

The film is memorably bookended by the narration of Brian Johnson ("the brain"), played by Anthony Michael Hall, who recites the group's collective essay to the administrator, set to Simple Mind's pulsing soundtrack of "Don't You (Forget about Me)." The final essay is iconic in its own right as it lays out the metamorphosis of the group from "a brain, an athlete, a basket case, a princess, and a criminal" to the realization that each of them is a complex admixture of all those types. The five students have collided against one another in the forced space of the school library and emerged as changed people, no longer held captive by labels affixed to each of them. The final scene of adolescent agency—casting off imposed types—is meant to be inspiring, punctuated by John Bender's fist pump, and it succeeds on that front, at least somewhat. Brian's initial narration during the opening credits levels an accusation against Vice-Principal Vernon: "You see us as you want to see us—in the simplest terms, in the most convenient definitions." But Brian adds a confession, not included in his final reading of the essay at the end of the movie: "That's the way we saw each other at 7:00 this morning. We were brainwashed."[11]

---

10. The John Hughes's collection has not aged particularly well in the twenty-first century with increased attention rightfully given to matters of sexual harassment and assault. For an apt assessment of Hughes's films, see this reflection from actress Molly Ringwald whom Hughes cast in several of his films: Ringwald, "What About 'The Breakfast Club?'"

11. Hughes, *Breakfast Club*.

PART I: A PROBLEM PEOPLE

Even if "brainwashed" overstates it, teenagers only craft the world they inherit from us, and they will shape that inheritance so it safe-guards their awesomeness. High school social hierarchies are not necessarily nefarious. After all, when the final bell rings and students disperse to baseball practice, to the robotics club, or to the choir room, they have self-selected activities based on talent and interests. Activities can become totalizing identities: We find our people and assimilate, for good or ill. As we mature and gain confidence, we are less prone to denigrate others whose interests differ from our own. Adulthood *should* mean that we no longer need a classification system so rigged that we come out on top, whether commensurate with our actual abilities or not.

Case in point, high school students often slot their teachers into a single classification: Old. They are young; we are old, and our wisdom is not always honored. They understand cognitively that we have more education than they do, but some days it does not matter. Students will, at times, reject every word out of our mouths. Why? Maybe it's just a bad day—a fight with the parents or a breakup. There are days when students do not simply ignore the daily lesson or challenge it intellectually; they dismiss *you* as beneath them. On these rare occasions I'm not sure they could have even provided reasons for disregarding my right to exist. Maybe one day I looked a little scruffy and my clothes were a bit shabby. Perhaps they saw my sweet 2015 KIA Forte in the parking lot, and they knew that I had not achieved the clear markers of American success that they valued. Maybe I mistakenly identified a Sia song and accredited it to Rihanna. (True story). *"What could this guy know?"* Rather than overreact to students' behavior, I try to remember that we humans do many things to guard our egos or forward our desires, including rationalizing the inferiority of others. Ironically, this protective measure of our personhood is the very thing that destroys our humanity. My point is that all of this categorizing, past or present, is arbitrary.

So, what could possibly be the consequences of believing yourself to be prettier, smarter, or better than someone else? What some might think to be nothing more than harmless theories about ourselves actually becomes the foundation for ordering societies. Duke University sociologist Eduardo Bonilla-Silva says, "notions of racial difference are human creations rather than eternal, essential categories."[12] The racial ideology that sprung from "science" was adopted by, or imposed upon, nearly everyone. The creation

---

12. Bonilla-Silva, *Racism without Racists*, 8.

of race, with whiteness as its highest form, is not limited to an attitude of one group of people toward another, like the problem is nothing more than lunchroom meanness. Societies take these theories and make them concrete through the formation of laws. After all, if some beings are considered sub-human (backed by science, law, and religion) then we can legally do to them what we please.[13] According to the law rife with racist ideologies, "white" made "right" and "white" gave rights, as well.[14] Ideas that took hold hundreds of years ago still impact us now. We inherited a particular world, but we also had a hand in shaping it today.

We can still reap the benefits of a "racialized society," meaning this made-up designation of race, that we have accepted and utilize, "matters profoundly for differences in life experiences, life opportunities, and social relationships."[15] This racialized society exists due to humanity's compulsion to dominate one another for self-serving purposes. So, while *The Breakfast Club*'s "you can't label us" sentiment is nice and gives us all the feels, it just isn't true. We categorize people who come into our world. Living without labels might be impossible, precisely because the "brainwashing" Brian and his peers denounce is difficult to combat. At 7 a.m. in the high school library, five high school students came into view before others; each presenting themselves a certain way; each shielding their deepest pains and passions; each operating under the label imposed upon them. This data is all they have to go upon as they form their impressions of the others who come into their midst.

Rightly or wrongly, we categorize people who enter our orbit. The majority of people who I have attended school or church with, and established

---

13. A few examples include: A Virginia law, in 1705, stated that "no negroes, mulattos, or Indians, although Christians, or Jews, Moors, Mahometans, or other infidels, shall, at any time, purchase any christian servant, nor any other, except of their own complexion, or such as are declared slaves by this act" (Jordan, *White Man's Burden*, 51). An 1823 Supreme Court case *Johnson v. M'Intosh* paved the way for coerced removal of native peoples (Charles and Rah, *Unsettling Truths*, 104–13). The Indian Appropriation Act (1871) stated no Indian nation would be an independent entity capable of entering into a treaty with the United States. The Chinese Exclusion Act (1882) made it a crime to employ Chinese workers. The Dawes Act (1887) broke up land Native American tribes held in common, resulting in the loss of almost two-thirds of all Indian land (Delgado and Sefanvic, *Critical Race Theory*, 79).

14. Thomas D. Morris traces the legal heritage of American slave law to English common law that treats slaves not as people but as property, or "things" (*Southern Slavery and the Law*, 56–57).

15. Emerson and Smith, *Divided By Faith*, 7.

friendships with, have been white. I only say this as a matter of fact. Being quite literally *surrounded* by white people has comprised the bulk of my life experiences. Robin DiAngelo says, "Whiteness rests upon a foundational premise: the definition of whites as the norm or standard for human, and people of color as a deviation from that norm." Furthermore, she adds, "the white reference point is assumed to be universal and is imposed on everyone."[16] The great privilege of whiteness is that we are almost never confronted by our race, because the world rarely beckons us to do so. My presence is not a novelty, remarkable, or a point of concern. I move about when, where, and how I desire, which shapes how I view those who deviate from me, the supposed norm.

Angie Thomas describes a perfect example of this norm in her award-winning novel *The Hate U Give*, which follows sixteen year-old Starr Carter and her trials following the killing of her friend by a police officer during a routine traffic stop. One night, Starr is riding with her white boyfriend, Chris, who undergoes a playful interrogation by Starr's brother, Seven, and his friend, DeVante. After a series of questions to determine whether or not Chris can be accepted by his girlfriend's un-appointed protectors, he turns the tables, asking if he can "ask a question about black people?" They agree, and Chris asks,

> "Why do some black people give their kids odd names? I mean, look at you guys' names. They're not normal."
>
> "My name normal," DeVante says, all puffed-up sounding. "I don't know what you talking about."
>
> Seven says, "DeVante's got a point. What makes his name or our names any less normal than yours? Who or what defines 'normal' to you? If my pops were here, he'd say you've fallen into the trap of the white standard."
>
> Color creeps into Chris's neck and face. "I didn't mean—okay, maybe 'normal' isn't the right word."
>
> "Nope," I [Starr] say.
>
> "I guess uncommon is the word instead?" he asks. "You guys have uncommon names."
>
> "I know 'bout three other DeVantes in the neighborhood though," says DeVante.

---

16. DiAngelo, *White Fragility*, 25.

"Right. It's about perspective," says Seven. "Plus, most of the names white people think are unusual actually have meanings in various languages."[17]

If we whites experience the world where *white* is actually a synonym for *normal* or *universal*, it means anything that interrupts our daily existence, or makes us uncomfortable, is abnormal and is cause for swift defensive measures. As the majority culture, our whiteness creates a safe bubble where we are rarely confronted to think about uncomfortable things, and when that bubble is burst by, say, someone calling out an insensitive comment, we tend to melt like, as the internet trolls say, delicate snowflakes. We have no desire or the necessary resiliency to deal with the simple historical fact that our ancestors' actions might have provided an advantage for us. Some of these consistent defensive measures are a tendency by whites to attach less importance to racial identities than people of color do. White people are less likely to accept structural or race-based explanations for inequality. Instead, we often adopt "color-blind ideologies" to explain how individual success in America "is fair, meritorious, and race neutral, that hard work and effort are the keys to success, and that any individual can succeed if she or he tries hard enough," which essentially shields white people from having to consider how structural injustice actually functions.[18]

To summarize for the non-sociologists: White people accumulated power and wealth. They imagined themselves to be fit to rule because of their skin color, a rationalization for their conquests, which then dictated the manner in which they ordered their world. They would say that race did not matter for achieving success, and that the structures were not biased or did not even exist. Finally, in head-spinning logic, whites claimed hard work could secure the good life for *anyone*, even though the good life had previously been deemed unattainable due to their God-given race.

The resulting theories of white supremacy infiltrated every sector of life—science, public policy, art and literature, philosophy, and theology—in order to suit the purposes of those in power. Racial theories became concretized by pseudo-science, ideas of American exceptionalism, and violent practices of enforced separation, all the while being blessed by religious authorities. If this story seems to be a little more than confusing

---

17. Thomas, *Hate U Give*, 401–2.
18. Hartmann et al., "Empirical Assessment of Whiteness Theory," 403, 405, 412, 414, 419.

and contradictory, well humans can be malevolent creatures, prone to self-deception in order to justify our sins.

James Baldwin says, "the great force of history comes from the fact that we carry it within us, are unconsciously controlled by it in many ways, and history is literally *present* in all that we do."[19] Being born white means one's story is seamlessly woven into a long, troubling tapestry. Whiteness was and is so embedded societally that you do not have to rationally assent to its practices, habits, and iconography that enslaved, restricted, brutalized, and dehumanized people of color to benefit from it. These offenses were committed in order to keep people in their supposedly born-station, and upon these lies American life was built, sustained, and defended.

John Hughes said at the release of *The Breakfast Club*: "People forget that when you're 16, you're probably more serious than you'll ever be again. You think seriously about the big questions."[20] I learned in high school how to categorize people for ease of fellowship or dismissal. I learned that I had been slotted into a place, too. I also had the first inklings that those labels were utterly bankrupt.

19. Baldwin, "White Man's Guilt," 321.
20. Ebert, "Review of *The Breakfast Club*."

3

HOW TO BE AN AMERICAN
Joltin' Joe and Kneelin' Kap

> I believe in America. America has made my fortune.
> And I raised my daughter in the American fashion.[1]
>
> —Bonasera to Don Corleone, *The Godfather*

Gatlinburg, TN is a fun getaway near the Smoky Mountains especially if you crave kitsch and the unrivaled joy one experiences when unexpectedly happening upon a Bubba Gump Shrimp. Gatlinburg must also be the nation's leading producer of T-shirts, so much so that its GDP would plummet if tacky phrases were excluded from First Amendment protections. I once saw a shirt that managed to trivialize military service and Christianity with one screen-printing. The tagline "I stand for the flag. I kneel for the cross," showed a kneeling soldier at a small cross serving as a headstone for his fallen comrade, an obvious swipe at the National Football League (NFL) national anthem protests.

I thought about Buck, as I typically do when I see military paraphernalia or references. His framed Army uniform hung in his house. The colorful patches, decorations, with the "Phillips" patch over the heart, are lodged in my memory. My grandfather would have hated the blatant cheapening of

---

1. Coppola, *Godfather*.

soldier sacrifice hawked for $9.99 at the same establishment where you can also adorn yourself with an Old Glory bathing suit. He loved the flag, the anthem was his favorite song, and I'm positive he would have hated Colin Kaepernick.

Joltin' Joe

No athlete of the mid-twentieth century captured the American mythos in the way Joe DiMaggio did, both in the manner in which he excelled on the baseball field and the celebrity he achieved off it. Fans and biographers alike speak of the "Yankee Clipper" with such reverence that those of us born after his playing days have trouble comprehending what he meant for the game and the nation during the mid-thirties through the forties. It's nearly inconceivable to think of a singer-songwriter penning a memorable line about Albert Pujols the way in which Simon & Garfunkel did in "Mrs. Robinson." In what universe would an author speak as wistfully of spending time with Justin Verlander as Ernest Hemingway did about DiMaggio in *Old Man and the Sea*? It wouldn't happen now, because unlike the fiercely private DiMaggio, we seem to already know everything there is to know about public figures.

Joe DiMaggio crafted the image he wanted the public to see by maintaining his privacy, preserving the mystique of being above everyone else without ever having to say so. Joe DiMaggio would never burn waffles and post it to Instagram so that we could all sigh in satisfaction, thinking, *"See. He's just like me."* Joe DiMaggio married Marilyn Monroe. We aren't like him at all. He was a god, and plenty of people have upheld his divinity for him long after his dying day.

Truth be told, the evidence fans needed to judge this deity in pinstripes was overwhelming: In thirteen seasons with the Yankees, DiMaggio was a part of ten pennants and nine championships. DiMaggio, an All-Star all of his thirteen seasons and a three-time Most Valuable Player, was a career .325 hitter who lost three years of his prime to military service. Reporters who covered him detail his grace in the outfield as one of the best of all time. In 1941, DiMaggio became an American legend. Lou Gehrig's death that summer meant DiMaggio was now the undeniable face of the Yankees, and his 56-game hitting streak catapulted him to iconic status, as the statistical accomplishment remains the standard for daily diligence.

While the specter of the United States' entry into World War II created deep anxiety in 1941, the nation's eyes were also turned toward the best baseball player on Earth doing what no one had ever done before: "The nation needed a one-man show that felt like [the hitting streak] would go on forever" one DiMaggio biographer said, "as if the streak itself was a kind of talisman that could keep America out of the war."[2] As the song "Joltin Joe" immortalized him for listeners, DiMaggio exemplified everyman in the way that he punched the clock day-in, day-out: Go to the ballpark, have a cup of coffee (or a dozen), notch a hit, get a win, speak to the media in clipped clichés, and do it all over again the next day. This is the American way. We just do our damn job.

But long before DiMaggio became the beloved possession of all Americans, he belonged to the Italians, specifically to the first-generation Bay area immigrants. Before he annihilated Pacific Coast League pitching for the San Francisco Seals, he was just the son of Giuseppe and Rosalie, Sicilian immigrants, who expected their son would end up on the fishing boat with his old man and brothers. If America at large was slow to accept Italians, the Bay area, had everything they needed to flourish: jobs, local businesses, political power, the church, and schools. Imagine it: When the dream of the Golden Gate Bridge began to take shape, it was an Italian financier and an Italian mayor who saw it to fruition.[3]

DiMaggio's ascension to American hero is remarkable considering Italian immigrants were degraded by being equated with African slaves from the time they arrived in the United States until the time the nation entered World War II. Immigrant children of Italians in the American South were sent to black schools. Italians were lynched in Louisiana in three separate incidents (in 1891, 1896, and 1898). As the United States became increasingly industrialized, Italians found solidarity with other ethnicities, often through labor unions. Irish unions in 1930s Boston worked to keep Italians and Blacks out of the labor force.[4] In this way, "race functioned to distribute the right to full citizenship and access to good jobs" according to David Roediger.[5] Italians were left to figure out how to become an American on their own and thus earn their whiteness. In 1905, Italian-American

---

2. Charyn, *Joe DiMaggio*, 32.

3. Cramer, *Joe DiMaggio*, 100, 40.

4. Roediger, *Working Toward Whiteness*, 47, 52, 82. In 1922, W. E. B. DuBois included the Italians in those who had been disenfranchised under the "Anglo-Saxon cult" (94).

5. Roediger, *Working Toward Whiteness*, 14.

lawyer Gino Speranza voiced concerns for the Italian immigrant, wondering how they could trust "American justice when he ... learns of it through the lynchings of his countrymen or the burnings of negroes."[6] Perhaps the slogan of the times could have been "Italian Lives Matter."

Matthew Frye Jacobsen says racism is a theory "of who is who, of who belongs and who does not, of who deserves what and who is capable of what."[7] When the US entered World War II the general populace had scant knowledge of the Italian people, limited to infamous figures like Al Capone and Benito Mussolini as their frames of reference. Many questioned Italians' loyalty to the United States, asking whether they belonged to their new home or the old world? In this context DiMaggio's legend was born as a necessity to the Italian-American community as much for his clear athletic prowess. "Deadpan Joe," as the local writers referred to him, gave reporters little quotable material to work with, so they authored an American dream come to life.[8] Whether or not DiMaggio actually learned to hit a baseball by swinging a broken oar from his father's fishing boat was irrelevant. He became representative of the Italian-American made good. By 1936, DiMaggio's rookie year with the Yankees, he was already famous due to the California press. DiMaggio became *the* guy for Italians and other fans, particularly due to the absence of Black players in the major leagues.[9] Eventually, he won over the entire nation.

The view has been that immigrants "earn" their American identity by an intentional separation from their culture, such as dropping their native tongue in favor of English, or even altering their distinctive appearance (e.g., dress, hairstyle, etc.) to blend in with the so-called "melting pot." In 1939, *Life* magazine profiled the Yankee Clipper, filling its story with Italian stereotypes, including this passage about DiMaggio's assimilation to American customs:

> Although he learned Italian first Joe, now 24, speaks English without an accent and is otherwise well adapted to most U.S. mores. Instead of olive oil or smelly bear grease, he keeps his hair slick with water. He never reeks of garlic and prefers chicken chow mein to spaghetti.[10]

---

6. Roediger, *Working Toward Whiteness*, 96.
7. Jacobson, *Whiteness of a Different Color*, 6.
8. Engelberg and Schneider, *DiMaggio*, 88.
9. Cramer, *Joe DiMaggio*, 151.
10. Chadwin, *Those Damn Yankees*, 143.

American expectations of assimilation meant you left the old country behind for the promise of a new home. Yet when pressured to change his family name, DiMaggio resisted. "People sometimes mentioned that I should go Anglo, but I never would, never could," DiMaggio reflected. "I knew there was a price to pay, but I was willing to do so."[11] DiMaggio endured as a source of pride for Italian-Americans for his play, the manner in which he carried himself, and how he never forgot his roots. As former New York governor Mario Cuomo said, "He was a symbol of what Italian-American kids like me could accomplish."[12]

So, what if Joe DiMaggio, a military veteran, had taken a knee during the national anthem in 1946, his first year back from the war, to protest anti-Italian policies? After the attack on Pearl Harbor, nearly 600,000 Italians (who were not citizens) were dubbed "enemy aliens" and had their movements restricted, including DiMaggio's father. Giuseppe DiMaggio was not allowed to fish due to the alleged security concerns existing off of the port, which could have affected his livelihood had his son not been the most famous baseball player in the world. Likewise, federal agents deemed DiMaggio's restaurant a threat for its proximity to the coast. DiMaggio family friend Dr. Rock Positano reports in his memoir that this angered DiMaggio greatly, and not just because his family was directly impacted but also because of the many Italian-Americans who were currently serving in the war.[13] Good enough to serve and die but not trusted to earn a living in the land of opportunity.

Italian Lives Matter.

What if Joe DiMaggio, the Yankee Clipper, had refused to remove his cap during the playing of "The Star-Spangled Banner" to draw attention to how Italian-Americans lived between two worlds? What if Joltin' Joe had finally had it up to the top of his 6'2" frame with the racial slurs, the decades of attempts by politicians to curtail immigration from his parent's homeland, with insinuations that he lacked the intellectual capacity to do anything other than play ball? Had he lived in a different era, he might have said, "screw it" and planted a knee firmly into the grass of Yankee Stadium.

And how dirty do you think he would have been done following that little display? Would his unsavory moments, now whitewashed in the twenty-first century, be highlighted in the heat of the patriotic moment?

11. Positano and Positano, *Dinner with DiMaggio*, 61.
12. Engelberg and Schneider, *DiMaggio*, 85.
13. Positano and Positano, *Dinner with DiMaggio*, 61–62.

DiMaggio displayed quite a list of unfavorable traits and acts, like "his tie[s] to gangsters and gamblers, his disregard for his only son, his mauling of Marilyn Monroe."[14] How quickly would he have been blackballed from America's pastime?

What if more attention had been paid to his contract dispute prior to the 1943 season, as DiMaggio held out for more money, when so many men and women were sacrificing during wartime? Would that have been considered disrespecting the military? Would Joe D. have remained a hero to virtually every little boy in America?

This is not to diminish the greatness of the Yankee Clipper. His impact on baseball, to say nothing of his ambassadorship for his people, are undeniable. Yet consider how naive sanctified utterances about an imperfect man like DiMaggio sound today, particularly juxtaposed with contemporary athletes who dare challenge their nation to rise up to its alleged morally-exceptional position in the world. To some, sacrificing your livelihood, even your life, is how you become an American.

Kneelin' Kap

In November 2016, I gathered with my high school students and colleagues for a Veteran's Day chapel. It was the typical God-and-country pep-rally that permeates white evangelical life. Dissent from this particular area of "worship" is tantamount to blasphemy. The school choir sang a few rousing patriotic songs before a medley of the armed services songs. The speaker for the day was a retired military officer who charged the students to pursue a life of service to their country and each other. It was a fine exhibition of boilerplate sermonettes we expect our children to receive when held captive by the mandated school day. That is, until the speaker gave an impromptu lesson on free speech, saying, "And for those who will not stand for our National Anthem, I have nothing but contempt," a line that garnered the heaviest applause of the day.

The NFL was in its fourth month of dealing with the protest of San Francisco 49ers quarterback Colin Kaepernick (and others) during the playing of the national anthem. During a 2016 preseason game, Kaepernick initially sat on the bench in protest of police brutality. The decision to later kneel came at the behest of a Green Beret, Nate Boyer, who himself had spent one preseason with the Seattle Seahawks. Kneeling was a

14. Charyn, *Joe DiMaggio*, 1–2.

compromise Kaepernick embraced after meeting with Boyer, who viewed kneeling as "a sign of reverence," a point our chapel speaker had missed or ignored completely.[15] President Trump predictably used the NFL protest as a wedge issue to fire up his base. At a 2017 rally in Huntsville, Alabama, Trump said about the players, "wouldn't you love to see one of these NFL owners, when someone disrespects our flag to say, 'get that son of a bitch off the field right now.' Out. He's fired. He's fired."[16] Trump routinely framed the issue as one of respect for the flag and military personnel, replicating his binary understanding of so many issues. The very heart of the protest was lost, at the time, in the jingoistic theater, with the president placing himself as the lead star. For no one could love America, the military, or their sacrifice as much as he did.

Whiteness connects itself to patriotism and its symbols, because American values are held to be universal. The flag and the anthem represent the life provided for all Americans, but because America is not experienced equally, these values are not expressed in the same way. Whites, however, believing their experiences to be the norm, take on the role of enforcing expressions of American values, which in effect makes them white values. This enforcement of supposed appropriate patriotism was expressed by New Orleans Saints quarterback Drew Brees during the summer 2020 protests: "I will never agree with anybody disrespecting the flag." Brees attributed his reverence for the flag in honor of his two grandfathers, both of whom fought in World War II, "risking their lives to protect our country and to try to make our country and this world a better place." Brees's limited view of history, though, was countered by his Black teammate Malcolm Jenkins, who noted how Americans held different understandings of patriotic symbols. Neither Brees, nor any veteran's ancestor, was the arbiter or protector of patriotic orthopraxy, because in Jenkins's words, "when our grandfathers fought for this country and served and they came back, they didn't come back to a hero's welcome. They came back and got attacked for wearing their uniforms. They came back to people, to racism, to complete violence."[17] Brees quickly apologized and vowed to learn more.

Even though Trump claimed that most of the athletes "show their 'outrage' at something that most of them are unable to define," Kaepernick clearly explained his reasoning from the beginning of his protest: "I am

15. McEvers, "Ex-Green Beret and NFL Player."
16. NBC Bay Area Sports Staff, "Trump to Anthem Protesters."
17. NFL.com, "Drew Brees Facing Intense Criticism."

not going to stand up to show pride in a flag for a country that oppresses black people and people of color." Kaepernick adds, "To me, this is bigger than football and it would be selfish on my part to look the other way."[18] A 2018 study by the *American Journal of Public Health* concluded that Black and Latino men are twice as likely as white men to die during interactions with the police.[19] This fact can be acknowledged without diminishing the dangerous work of law enforcement. Seemingly anyone capable of critical thought can hold two positions in tension without resorting to Manichean reductions that necessarily cast one perspective as good and the other as evil.

Kaepernick has remained unsigned since 2017 through the conclusion of the 2020 season. Despite the fact that football is still an industry predicated upon winning games, NFL franchises have signed over one hundred quarterbacks other than Kaepernick once he became a free agent, few of which could objectively be thought superior to him.[20] In February 2019, Kaepernick reached a settlement with the NFL in his lawsuit claiming the league colluded to keep him from signing with any team. Although Kaepernick held a workout later that year, it did not lead to a contract offer, raising the possibility that the league was colluding yet again.[21] By 2020, with the cultural opinion shifting and the financial risks mounting for perceived intransigence, NFL Commissioner Roger Goodell apologized about the league's response to the protests and said Kaepernick should be signed. It seems clear throughout this entire fiasco that the unwillingness to potentially upset one's business model is the actually the most American thing of all.

The world will never know what could've been had Joe DiMaggio summoned the courage to decry the mistreatment of his people. Instead, DiMaggio showed up, kept quiet, and played ball. Not everyone decided

18. Frost, "Colin Kaepernick vs. Tim Tebow."

19. Crist, "Police-involved Deaths Vary by Race and Place." The study analyzed data from Fatal Encounters (www.fatalencounters.org/), which documents all incidents of fatal police-civilian encounters. Nearly 6,300 (6,296) police-involved homicides involving a male, between the years 2012–2018, were examined where the cause of death was asphyxiation, beating, a chemical agent, medical emergency, taser or gunshot. Of the average 1,028 deaths per year, African-American men were killed by police at a rate of 2.1 per 100,000 people; Latino men were killed at a rate of 1 per 100,000 and white males were killed at 0.6 per 100,000.

20. Johnson, "All the Quarterbacks Who Signed Since Colin Kaepernick Became a Free Agent."

21. Young, "Colin Kaepernick's Botched NFL Workout."

to take this path. Fellow Italian and American icon, Frank Sinatra, for instance, used his considerable platform to combat anti-Semitism and racism in the short film *The House I Live In* (1945). In the film, Sinatra confronts a group of boys in an alley about to beat up a Jewish boy, asking them if they're Nazis. The boys protest, with one even noting that his father nearly died in combat. No one should question his patriotism, the boy argued. Sinatra asks them, "Do you know what this wonderful country is made of? It's made up of a hundred different kinds of people and a hundred different ways of talking and a hundred different ways of going to church. But, they're all American ways."[22] With lessons quickly learned thanks to Ol Blue Eyes' take on tolerance the gang reconciles with the boy, and Sinatra croons a soaring rendition of the "The House I Live In" for the audience.

Protest has rarely been the path of the privileged, as doing so creates a significant threat to one's bottom line. Even deeper to this conflict is the notion that there are "right ways" of being an American, albeit a notion that has been a moving definition over the years. The bottom line is that being (or becoming) an American has been closely associated with assimilating into the majority-white culture, and Colin Kaepernick will not bend the knee for that cause. Football fans will tolerate scandals involving head trauma, domestic violence, as well as no serious addressment of performing enhancement drugs, yet an individual's act of conscience in the face of police brutality is met with outrage.

For those not "American" enough for whites, their patriotism will always be suspect. This notion is a window into the white patriot's soul: Our ancestors fought and died for this; yours did not. After all, whiteness welcomes even the draft-dodgers if you participate in her ceremonies "the right way." The American way.

---

22. LeRoy, *House I Live In*. The film can be viewed through The Library of Congress YouTube channel at https://www.youtube.com/watch?v=ovwHkb1wEfU&list=WL&index=2&t=0s. See also Norrell, *House I Live In*, 141–42.

4

HOW CANCER MADE ME LESS OF A BASTARD (AND MORE HUMAN)[1]

> Our world is suffering from metastatic cancer. Stage 4. Racism has spread to nearly every part of the body politic.[2]
>
> —Ibram X. Kendi

> Race is a story that shapes the idea of what are bodies are for.[3]
>
> —Brian Bantum

The regional oddity that is Will D. Campbell was beloved among the whiskey-drinking Nashville Christians. Campbell was also considered to be a double-traitor of sorts: First, to poor, white Southerners when he joined the civil rights movement. Second, his fellow activists wondered what would possess a man to minister to the racists after leaving the formal movement.

---

1. Phillips, "How Cancer Made Me Less of a Bastard (And More Human)."
2. Kendi, *How to Be an Antiracist*, 234. Kendi likens his and his wife's cancer and treatment to the state of race relations in America.
3. Bantum, *Death of Race*, 5. Bantum's work is particularly moving, because he, too, addresses the issue of race through processing his grief for his father's cancer.

HOW CANCER MADE ME LESS OF A BASTARD (AND MORE HUMAN)

Will D. Campbell has been called the "conscience of the South," the "white MLK," "part prophet and social critic, part gadfly" and the leader of a "fundamentalist guerrilla ministry."[4] Born in 1924 in Amite County, Mississippi, Campbell began preaching at age sixteen and was ordained at seventeen as a Baptist minister. Campbell dropped out of Louisiana College to enlist in the Army during World War II, where he served as a medic. He returned to school on the G.I. Bill and later earned a Master of Divinity from Yale (1952). Campbell became the Director of Religious Life at the University of Mississippi (Ole Miss), eventually resigning over his integrationist impulses.

The National Council of Churches (NCC) hired Campbell in 1956 to lead "the Southern Project," a targeted effort to foster denominational cooperation in the civil rights movement. Journalist David Halberstam said of Campbell's influence, "his fingers were everywhere, but when you looked around – there were no fingerprints. He was the Invisible Man."[5] Campbell was the only white man present at the formation of the Southern Christian Leadership Council (SCLC), but he was nearly turned away before being welcomed in by King advisor Bayard Rustin who said, "Before this thing is over, we're going to need all the help we can get, so you come on in."[6] Campbell escorted the children of the Little Rock Nine through hostile crowds on their way to school in 1957. He aided the Nashville student movement, and generally, worked as a mediator with white power structures throughout the South.[7] Nashville civil rights attorney George Barrett adds, "If there's any unsung hero of the Civil Rights Movement, it's Will Campbell."[8]

Living in between multiple communities tested Campbell's loyalty and theological presumptions. Campbell's good friend, P. D. East, a journalist and professed atheist, routinely pushed Campbell's buttons as only friends can. East once asked Campbell to describe Christianity in ten words or less. Campbell replied, "We're all bastards but God loves us anyway."[9]

In 1965, a sheriff's deputy, Thomas Coleman murdered Jonathan Daniels, a young seminarian who had just participated in a voter rights

---

4. Wright, *Saints and Sinners*, 157; Kennedy, "Will D. Campbell," 70; Frady, *Southerners*, 360.
5. Wright, *Saints and Sinners*, 159.
6. Campbell, "Reverend Will Davis Campbell," 92.
7. Chappell, *Inside Agitators*, 107.
8. Campbell, "Reverend Will Davis Campbell," 102.
9. Campbell, *Brother to a Dragonfly*, 220.

demonstration in Alabama. Daniels was walking along with two Black teenagers, Joyce Bailey and Ruby Sales, and a Catholic priest, when Coleman confronted them at gunpoint. Daniels shoved Sales out of the way, taking the blast and saving her life. Daniels died instantly. A grieving Campbell was pressed by East to clarify his past definition of the faith, asking,

"Was Jonathan a bastard?"

"Yes," Campbell replied.

East pressed him further: "Is Thomas Coleman a bastard?"

Again, Campbell replied, "Yes, Thomas Coleman is a bastard."

East drew closer and asked the question Campbell credits with changing his life: "Which of these two bastards do you think God loves the most?"[10]

The question pierced Campbell, and he concluded that his life's work to that point had been surrendered to political agendas that simply mirrored the prejudices of white racists. Campbell explains:

> I was laughing at myself, at twenty years of a ministry which had become, without my realizing it, a ministry of liberal sophistication. An attempted negation of Jesus, of human engineering, of riding the coattails of Caesar, of playing on his ballpark, by his rules and with his ball, of looking to government to make and verify and authenticate our mortality, of worshipping at the shrine of enlightenment and academia, of making an idol of the Supreme Court, a theology of law and order and of denying not only the Faith I professed to hold but my history and my people – the Thomas Colemans.[11]

Jonathan Daniels's death led Campbell to conclude, "One who understands the nature of tragedy can never takes sides."[12] He felt he had given himself over to the politics of the era neglecting the South's Thomas Coleman's. This is not to say that Campbell ignored injustices. But, much like a battlefield physician, Campbell committed to performing the equivalent of spiritual triage to the wounded that he noticed everywhere, becoming a minister to anyone in need of one, especially the bastards. His people.

---

10. Campbell, *Brother to a Dragonfly*, 221.
11. Campbell, *Brother to a Dragonfly*, 222.
12. Letcher and Davis, *God's Will*.

HOW CANCER MADE ME LESS OF A BASTARD (AND MORE HUMAN)

**

My own turning point on matters of race didn't hinge on a sudden epiphany. Instead, it was programmed into my genetic code just waiting to emerge within my body. I was a fairly typical Christian college student, who wanted to do well in school, be faithful to God, and maybe even meet my future wife. I was still a college-aged man, which meant that I conceived of my body as little more than a vessel for satisfying my appetites. Beyond that, my evangelical, quasi-gnostic upbringing had trained me not to notice bodies, specifically my own body. Cancer abruptly ended that ignorance. My invisible illness became visible to everyone, meaning my body also became visible. I remained in school, since the treatment center was across the street from my campus. My body became a map of the illness and treatment: Radiation therapy marked me with red and pink splotches like scattered sunburns and the surgical scars told a story of brokenness. Hodgkin's disease, cancer of the lymphatic system, increased my dependence upon others in ways that I previously had not been in the past. I needed notes from missed classes; I needed a hand carrying items in the cafeteria when I felt weak or light-headed. Sometimes I needed simple errands run for me. My body, which I had come both to count on and completely ignore, was now exposed and failing me in undeniable ways.

Two years later, enjoying full remission, I reflected on my cancer as a young seminarian, and I just did not feel eternally grateful for the gift of life. Anyone who has endured serious illness inevitably becomes familiar with these feelings of anxiety. Social ostracism, fear, grief, loneliness, and a near-constant feeling of losing everything—these are the companions of the sick and the recovering.[13] Even though I knew people who could relate to my circumstances, I felt alone with my anxiety and loss. I was a sad bastard who thought about death every single day, because in my worry over another diagnosis my identity had been collapsed into that of "cancer survivor."

Cancer revealed to me, through the relatively brief experience of illness, what it felt like for my bodily sovereignty to be out of my control, and it led me to two realizations. First, the dissipation of my illusions of bodily invisibility was directly connected to the sense of isolation I experienced during my illness, and this forever altered my understanding of racial identities. It is a good thing to notice and talk about bodies. Toni Morrison

---

13. Aldredge-Canton, *Counseling People with Cancer*, 82–83.

PART I: A PROBLEM PEOPLE

suggests that the refusal to discuss race, or to actively ignore its existence as a social reality, is thought to be "a graceful, even generous, liberal gesture" by whites on behalf of people of color. This gesture, though, actually enforces silence on all racial topics, merely allowing "the black body a shadowless participation in the dominant cultural body."[14] Morrison illustrates this idea in her novel *The Bluest Eye* through Pecola, a little girl whose trip to the local store, after having scraped together a few pennies for candy or a doll, is spoiled by the gaze of store owner:

> She pulls off her shoe and takes out the three pennies. The gray head of Mr. Yacobowski looms up over the counter. He urges his eyes out of his thoughts to encounter her. Blue eyes. Blear-dropped. Slowly, like Indian summer moving imperceptibly toward fall, he looks toward her. Somewhere between retina and object, between vision and view, his eyes draw back, hesitate, and hover. At some fixed point in time and space he senses that he need not waste the effort of a glance. He does not see her, because for him there is nothing to see. How can a fifty-two-year-old white immigrant store-keeper with the taste of potatoes and beer in his mouth, his mind honed on the doe-eyed Virgin Mary, his sensibilities blunted by a permanent awareness of loss, see a little black girl? Nothing in his life even suggested that the feat was possible, not to say desirable or necessary.
>
> "Yeah?"
>
> She looks up at him and sees the vacuum where curiosity ought to lodge. And something more. The total absence of human recognition—the glazed separateness. She does not know what keeps his glance suspended. Perhaps because he is grown, or a man, and she a little girl. But she has seen interest, disgust, even anger in grown male eyes. Yet this vacuum is not new to her. It has an edge; somewhere in the bottom lid is the distaste. She has seen it lurking in the eyes of all white people. So. The distaste must be for her, her blackness. All things in her are flux and anticipation. But her blackness is static and dread. And it is the blackness that accounts for, that creates, the vacuum edged with distaste in white eyes.[15]

I hated coming to the realization of what people of color potentially faced every day: I was a body; I experienced the world as a body now. In turn, others experienced me, first, as a body—a failing body—not as a soul,

---

14. Morrison, *Playing in the Dark*, 9–10.
15. Morrison, *Bluest Eye*, 48–49.

an intellect, or a conscience. My illness thrust me into a vulnerable space, and in that space I became a little more human. When I finally noticed my own body other bodies came into focus. Even though reflection did not come easily for me during that trauma, I was becoming a student of a new pedagogy, one of bone and blood. As Brian Bantum puts it, "Race is a de-creating word that signifies and separates; it renders some people always visible, always unique persons with names and stories, while other bodies are trapped within a story told about their bodies, making them utterly invisible or violently visible, unable to be anything other than their skin, eyes, and hair."[16] Whites tend to live as if we are unmarked racially; we exist within a sociopolitical norm where personal autonomy is taken for granted. The longstanding invisibility of people of color, coupled with the freedom of whites to navigate society unmolested, creates an empathy-gulf for most whites that is difficult to bridge.

My second realization gleaned from illness was the importance of communal presence, even though this lesson did not become apparent until years into remission. When I was sick and still living on my college campus, I became a curiosity. In the white evangelical world my peers saw it as impolite to *not* mention my illness. I was the subject of endless prayers and petitions, which meant I was the subject of constant attention. I couldn't go unnoticed, and it was driving me crazy. The longer I endured the attention, I came to accept these gestures from well-meaning peers who viewed their own mortality through me as though I were an icon of God's potential healing. The blessing of Christian community is that people drew near to me, even if they did so simply out of curiosity. To come close to me was to experience a primer in conceiving of, perhaps for the first time, one's body and mortality. Threatened, weakened, and vulnerable, I could no longer navigate my day-to-day existence surreptitiously. I was the subject of concern, prayers, and mystery, whether I wanted to be or not.

Jesus Sounds

Will Campbell's life exemplifies how whites can be transformed through drawing near to suffering. Campbell knew well that the poor, white or Black, could not shelter themselves from the harsh realities of disease and death, because he grew up in deep poverty himself. This fact crystallized for him during childhood after witnessing the funeral procession for Noon

---

16. Bantum, *Death of Race*, 104.

Wells, a Black tenant farmer who was employed by a family member. He recalled Wells's mother leading a train of mourners who echoed her loud cries of "Lord Jesus" and her supplication for Christ to "Bring my baby home!" These "Jesus sounds," as Campbell called them, were the pleas of a peasant mother in Mississippi to the son of a poor Jewish mother who surely understood her plight and pain.[17] Campbell said the sounds were "the articulation and recitation of two hundred years of pathos. An emancipation which still had not reached them, or us, if in fact it had reached anywhere at all."[18]

Campbell never shied away from being in the presence of those who suffered. His work in the civil rights movement, though, would cost him dearly with this brother, Joe, a man incapable of finding community or healing due to his addictions. Joe Campbell suffered from bouts of deep sorrow, frequent violent outbursts, and sociopathic behavior, but he also showed occasional moments of lucidity, even if the message was submerged under deep prejudices. In one interaction he lashed out at Will, claiming his brother's activism did little more than separate him from the white trash who needed him. Will recalls Joe's charge:

> You think you're going to save the . . . South with integration, with putting niggers in every schoolhouse and on every five-and-dime store lunch counter stool . . . What you're saying is that you're going to use the niggers to save yourself. What's so Christian about that?[19]

Joe's racist, addiction-fueled invective was meant to get under his brother's skin, and it worked. Will Campbell was learning the cost of presence with his brother: it meant stepping into tragedy, which also meant no longer denying the systemic forces that oppressed poor whites like his own family members. Will would lose his brother not long thereafter; however, his ministry to Klan members, murderers, and prisoners was sparked by his confrontation with Joe. Will spent his remaining years in the presence of those similarly diseased like his brother and the people of his homeland. Pursuing this strange work meant Campbell allowed himself to be misunderstood in order to be a minister to anyone and everyone. He was never quite at home again on any of the acceptable political or denominational teams. He was a bastard for the rest of his days.

17. Campbell, *Brother to a Dragonfly*, 60.
18. Campbell, *Brother to a Dragonfly*, 62.
19. Campbell, *Brother to a Dragonfly*, 201.

Ruby Sales, who Jonathan Daniels saved from Thomas Coleman's shotgun blast, has continued to work for racial and economic justice.[20] Sales says it's important for our times to ask people, "Where does it hurt?"[21] Asking questions—Where does it hurt? What are you scared of? What do you think you'll lose?—has been a better tact for me in teaching, rather than trying to shame people into submission. The apostle Paul's admonition to "put on the whole armor of God" (Eph 6:11) is followed by a reminder that "our struggle is not against enemies of blood and flesh, but against the rulers, against the authorities, against the cosmic powers of this present darkness, against the spiritual forces of evil in the heavenly places" (v. 12). The battle is not against my people, but against the forces that have convinced them that life is better lived in constant fighting.

Will Campbell knew the fight was against such powers. Campbell's close proximity to death helped him understand a new aspect of his ministerial calling. Those moments were conversion experiences for him. I can relate. Cancer was my second baptism. Just as baptism prepares us for death by submerging our old self beneath the waters, cancer revealed to me a world that did not require my presence. Understanding mortality showed me that while I was not essential for the world to keep spinning, I was loved deeply by my community. I also heard, in new ways, the old lessons from my parents that not every child of God feels loved in the world. Not everyone gets a fair shake. Not everyone is given the benefit of the doubt by the powers that be. For this reason, when I hear the death wails of our day, I must be moved from compassion to action. When I hear the Jesus sounds, I am called to rage against death and for those who are its targets.

Trayvon Martin. Jordan Davis. Tamir Rice. Sandra Bland. Laquan McDonald. Philando Castile. Ahmaud Arbery. Breonna Taylor. And on and on.

When I hear Eric Garner and George Floyd gasp, "I can't breathe," it must be an echo of my own baptismal vow, and I must hear it as a man's last affirmation of his humanity and his condemnation of the forces that killed him. Christopher Marshall explains the parable of the Good Samaritan as Jesus calling us to be motivated by "sharing in [the victim's] personal suffering and isolation." Compassion for one's neighbor "is the emotional signal that we all participate in a common stream of humanity and it is this

---

20. For more detail of Ruby Sales's work in the Student Nonviolent Coordinating Committee (SNCC) see Branch, *At Canaan's Edge*, 291, 299–300, 303, 314, 346.

21. Tippett, "Ruby Sales."

shared humanity ... that evokes the obligation to love others as creatures of equal worth and right as oneself."[22] If Jesus truly shows us how we are to be human, then our ears and our hearts must be trained to hear these death wails—these Jesus sounds. Otherwise, we deny something essential in our created intention.

Of course, not everyone hears the Jesus sounds immediately. Whiteness does not tune our hearing all that well. A people with no body feels no pain, or so we tell ourselves. I received a harsh vessel of transformation that mercifully does not come to everyone, and, for that reason, the lesson from remission is that I am called to welcome all. The Jesus sounds changed me forever. Not everyone has heard them though, and until they do, Jesus remains for everyone, especially the bastards.

---

22. Marshall, *Compassionate* Justice, 73, 78.

WHITE OUTRO

Are We Waking Up?

> I would strike Babe Ruth out every time.[1]
>
> —Adam Ottavino, Yankees pitcher, 2019

Prior to the 2019 baseball season, newly-signed reliever Adam Ottavino made waves by claiming "The Great Bambino" would not stand a chance against his devastating slider-sinker combination. Ruth, as Ottavino pointed out, gorged on hot dogs and drank beer before every game, not to mention swung an absurdly oversized bat compared to today's lumber. "It was just a different game," Ottavino noted, clarifying his prior comments, originally taken to be disrespectful of a baseball icon. Regardless of whether or not Ottavino was right (he was), his claim highlights how judging our progress against the past remains a precarious task. Ruth was great in his era, particularly when judged against his peers, but he would absolutely struggle in today's game if transported from the 1920s. Ottavino is not judged by hypothetical dominance against the game's past great, however; he's evaluated by how he fares against Mike Trout.

Walter Rauschenbusch, father of the Social Gospel, uses an apt parable for how each era thinks of its own accomplishments and others' failures. In his story, Rauschenbusch describes the Spirit of the Nineteenth Century giving way to the Twentieth Century and descending into the dwelling place called "the Past," where he begins to extol all of his accomplishments:

---

1. ESPN News Services, "Adam Ottavino Says 'No Disrespect' Intended."

PART I: A PROBLEM PEOPLE

> I am the Spirit of the Wonderful Century. I gave man the mastery over nature . . . . I freed the thoughts of men. They face the facts and know. Their knowledge is common to all . . . . I broke the chains of bigotry and despotism. I made men free and equal. Every man feels the worth of his manhood . . . . I have touched the summit of history. I did for mankind what none of you did before. They are rich. They are wise. They are free.[2]

The Spirit of the First Century spoke after a long silence and noted how each of the prior centuries had also made bold proclamations of successes when they first entered the Past. The First Century then noted how each of them shrunk into shame realizing just how little things had progressed under their care, before asking the question that moved the Nineteenth Century into deep reflection of his era's failings: "Your words sound as if the redemption of man had come at last. Has it come?"[3] The First Century continued, enumerating the societal ills that remained from the unintended consequences of the fruits of the "Wonderful Century"—industrialism, enlightenment, wealth, etc.—moving the Nineteenth to confess the unresolved problems. The Spirit of the Nineteenth Century relented under the evidence and said, "Their freedom and knowledge has only made men keener to suffer. Give me a seat among you, and let me think why it has been so."[4]

Each one of us possesses a limited social imagination for conceiving progress. First-century peoples could no more anticipate twenty-first century problems than they could solve all ills of their own time. Modern folks' superiority to the past should be of little consolation. That said, when prophetic voices rise in our time, calling out the distorted imagination of our day, will we listen? Trotting out the tired, old slogan "things are so much better now" is like saying "I would strike Babe Ruth out every time."

Disembodiment + Division = Disorientation

Disembodiment

We white folks do not think of our physical existence, because we are rarely required to do so. We don't think about whiteness because our world is

---

2. Rauschenbusch, *Christianity and the Social Crisis*, 177.
3. Rauschenbusch, *Christianity and the Social Crisis*, 177.
4. Rauschenbusch, *Christianity and the Social Crisis*, 178.

designed for us to not have to think about it in the same way lungs were designed for breathing. If you live in such a way that you're rarely beckoned to consider your surroundings and physical existence, then you can float through life on auto-pilot unless something interrupts the monotony. For me, cancer interrupted those familiar patterns of *not* noticing.

One of my graduate students had a similar experience: "Kate," a second-career student who had gone back to seminary, made sure other students found their way around her local church, which was hosting our first class of the term. Kate directed people to the kitchen where fresh coffee awaited them and to the restrooms. It was a joy to have such a hospitable student get us settled in our new digs. As the weeks progressed and we read challenging readings on racial injustice, Kate was running into some mental roadblocks, and she worked up the nerve to say what had been troubling her.

"I don't know quite how to say this, but some of this just feels like . . . complaining," Kate said with a grimace, awaiting the backlash.

"I know there are real problems with police officers, but it just seems like *everything* is about race."

All of this was delivered, mind you, through great pain and a clear invitation to help her understand more deeply. Two Black students shared their school, church, and professional experiences in Knoxville and around the South. They named points at which they agreed or disagreed with this particular protest or that one, and they asked Kate probing questions. Kate receptively listened to everyone and promised to keep reflecting.

When our class gathered two weeks later, Kate shared that she was a widow. She had lost her husband within the last couple of years after a long, wonderful marriage. Kate, still grieving, expressed that her support group of family, friends, church members, a dinner group, and hiking buddies all surrounded her in love. As the well-wishers in her life increased, however, so too did unwanted attention and labeling. Her husband's absence, his body no longer present alongside hers, created a new identity for Kate, collapsing everything into a single word: Widow.

Everyone noticed her. Every movement and every gesture.

"Is she okay?" "I wonder what's she's going through right now?"

She was noticeable in a way that was completely out of her control. Just as the totality of Kate's life experiences had been reduced to what Chimamanda Adichie calls "a single story"—the story of being a widow—people of color are often similarly reduced in white spaces. Their being noticed or not noticed largely escaped their complete control; they were at the mercy of how the majority white culture viewed them.[5] This revelation was an awakening for Kate.

Division

Race divides peoples into categories—categories within a hierarchy, best to worst, highest to lowest. The lesson is our bodies have meanings, inherited definitions. Sometimes the hierarchy is explicitly talked about; other times you absorb it and the lessons create a division between us and people of color. For this reason, "white" has a societal meaning in the United States: Normal. Universal. Supreme. But, whiteness also creates policies and protections for its own gain, and because of this, it engenders anger, bitterness, resentment, and suspicion among all races when things do not appear to work as they should. The greatest privilege of whiteness is that I am rarely confronted by my race at all, and that comfort often prevents me from walking the proverbial mile in another's shoes, maintaining our divisions.

Disorientation

The twenty-first century has witnessed a great awakening on matters of discrimination not just in personal interactions but through seemingly trustworthy systems and authorities. This means that if we have not been paying attention to the cultural awakening our knee-jerk reaction might be to dismiss movements for justice; however, when those in our circle—family, coworkers, trusted mentors, or pastors—begin using unfamiliar language or concepts regarding race and affirm current movements, we may feel as if we no longer know the world or our place within it.

Our disorientation in these moments leads to a number of possible responses. Some will *reject* the changing world and refuse to acknowledge grievances by people of color. They reject anything less than a fully-realized, post-racial, colorblind world. To raise racial matters means you're "being political," which ironically, proves the point they reject: Noticing race is a political act *to them*, because the noticing is not behaving in a post-racial way. Certain bodies remain "political," because we have made them so through virtually every societal mechanism. The truth is that there has

---

5. Adichie, "Danger of a Single Story."

always been a race-based, identity politics in the United States forwarded by white men. We do not consider ourselves susceptible to identity politics because we assume our perspective is unburdened by a racial identity. Couple this ignorance with an increasing frustration over the shifting vocabulary, standards of conduct, and public accountability, and we struggle to adapt to a world that does not take our every word as Gospel-truth.

Other whites will assume a posture of *resignation*, overwhelmed by the pace of the world's change. They do not know where to begin in order to educate themselves. Their hearts and minds are usually in the right place; it's just that they've stepped into an arena within which they feel massively underqualified. They need a nudge and patient friends to walk with them, through new terms, concepts—really, a new imagination.

Ibram X. Kendi's term "anti-racist" has offered white people a language for how to address injustice: "The opposite of 'racist' isn't 'not racist.' It is 'anti-racist' . . . One either allows racial inequities to persevere, as a racist, or confronts racial inequities, as an antiracist. There is no in-between safe space of 'not racist.'"[6] Kendi's acknowledgment that "racist and antiracist are not fixed identities" means the pursuit of anti-racism is a lifelong processes of making antiracist choices.[7] White supremacy mutates, infects new hosts, and develops resistance to old remedies. In our reluctance to learn from the past generations' mistakes, and our continuation of those same sins, we retrench into familiar mindsets. Neither can we be content with simple progress judged against past horrors. In other words, we cannot pat ourselves on the back realizing we could strike out Babe Ruth every at-bat. No generation is perfect—imperfect in progress, in love, and justice. Such will be the fate of every generation, but for now, we can consider why our current turmoil exists and be moved to act, whether we remain disoriented or not.

To those who are learning about injustices for the first time, and feel the necessary righteous anger to affect real change, a slight word of caution: During my earliest awakening days, I called out racism in all its variant forms, but I perceive now that I was difficult to be around, despite the rightness of my words or cause. I learned that shame-based approaches could change some people, but shame could also become a religion, one which

---

6. Kendi, *How to Be an Antiracist*, 9.

7. Kendi, *How to Be an Antiracist*, 10. Kendi's broader claim is that, "There is no such thing as a nonracist or race-neutral policy" (18). While I think this creates too stark a binary choice for literally every decision, "antiracist," opposed to simply "not racist," remains a helpful beginning framework for individuals to assess their personal actions.

PART I: A PROBLEM PEOPLE

replicated the very kind of divisions I was trying to repair. David Dark writes,

> Bad faith begins in the disavowal that will own up to little or nothing. And in turn, bad religion is the disavowal of relationship, a denial made plain in any practice we have for dividing ourselves from others, those ways we have of turning away from the fact of kinship.[8]

Buck's brother, Clint, was a family therapist, and he coined a phrase that my father, also a family therapist, preached to me often: "If you hold onto your right to be right, you can be right and alone."[9] I do not have it all figured out, but I know more about myself and my racism than I once did. I've made the decision that I would rather be on the journey with others, problematic as they may be, than be utterly alone yet content in my righteousness.

---

8. Dark, *Life's Too Short*, 131–32.

9. My dad credits two sources for this phrase: H. Stephen Glenn's "Developing Capable People" training programs developed from Glenn and Warner, *Developing Capable Young People*, and Phillips and Corsini, *Give In or Give Up*, xv.

Part II

KNOW YOUR PLACE
My Introduction to the South

> Kentucky was my fate—not an altogether pleasant fate, though it had much that was pleasing in it, but one that I could not leave behind simply by going to another place, and that I therefore felt more and more obligated to meet directly and understand. Perhaps even more important, I still had a deep love for the place I had been born in, and liked the idea of going back to be part of it again. And that, too, I felt obligated to try to understand. Why should I love one place so much more than any other?[1]
>
> —Wendell Berry, *Jayber Crow*

One of my favorite rituals while teaching high school in Knoxville was the year-end chapel celebrating students' college commitments. Graduating seniors stepped to the microphone in front of the assembled school, wearing the T-shirt of their college choice, announcing their decision with confidence and exuberance, intermixed with timidity, as only teens can present. Most of the assembly was thirty minutes of polite applause followed by cake. The niceties ceased, however, when a brave student proclaimed her allegiance to a Southeastern Conference (SEC) rival of their hometown University of Tennessee Volunteers. Auburn or Kentucky loyalists received a healthy jeering, no matter how well-liked the student

---

1. Berry, *Jayber Crow*, 143.

had been up to that fateful moment, and hostilities did not cease until the next student declared they were headed to UT, appeasing the orange-clad throngs. The deepest enmity was reserved for the poor soul who dared venture down to Tuscaloosa to join the reviled Crimson Tide. Lusty boos would fill the cafeteria, all directed toward the future University of Alabama freshman. Some students would just stride away from the microphone as quickly as possible; others would egg it on like they were pro-wrestling villains. It was a perfect picture of our tribalism.

The irony of the South is that while we strictly enforce all sorts of boundaries—physical and cultural, seen and unseen—we cannot agree on our geographic boundaries, a clear sign of our disembodiment. Demarcating "the South" by the Mason-Dixon line means Maryland/DC makes the cut. Neither Missouri nor Texas should be considered the South, in my opinion, even after the SEC expanded to include the Missouri Tigers and the Texas A&M Aggies into its ranks. Virginians are clearly Southerners with Richmond as the capital of the former Confederacy, but honestly, I forget about them. West Virginia never entered my mind as a southern state until I moved to East Tennessee, which shares the landscape and Appalachian culture. Southerners disavow Florida until it is time for a vacation. Beyond this border or that one, Southern snobbery emerges clearly when one state dishonors the reputation of the entire region. Most Southerners can attest to perusing the latest national statistics on education or public health, scanning for their home state's rank on the ignominious list, and whispering a quiet "Thank God for Mississippi." We stratify ourselves this way because we know our homeland is no monolith.

Tennessee bears this regional diversity out in its three Grand Divisions, each of which has been "home" for portions of my life: West Tennessee is largely flat farmland, politically conservative (outside of Memphis), and generally lags behind the rest of the state in accepting cultural norms. Nashville has a gravitational pull on the rest of Middle Tennessee, ever-expanding its reach into soon-to-be suburbs, while not fully exporting its glitz or politics to its rural neighbors just yet. East Tennessee is a natural wonder filled by the Smoky Mountains, hiking trails, rivers, and a robust outdoor life. East Tennessee prides itself on a fierce, political independence, possibly due to its resistance to secession prior to the Civil War, while generally still leaning to the right politically today. In fact, most southern states can claim similar variations in landscape, culture, and politics not so easily known to outsiders.

PART II: KNOW YOUR PLACE

We are not, and never have been, one people. Colin Woodard details in *American Nations* the American South's regional cultures: The traditional rendering of American history begins in April 1607 in Jamestown, Virginia, the first English colony to survive, and the beginning of the South. Woodard names the coastal lands of Virginia, North Carolina, and Maryland the "Tidewater" region, marked by its abiding connection to English customs in governance and social hierarchies. Tidewater maintained the Greco-Roman understanding of "liberty" across the Atlantic, where "most humans were born into bondage." Woodard says, "Liberty was granted and was thus a privilege, not a right."[2] Tidewater attempted to replicate rural English life, where a lord ran his home, ruled over those who worked his land, and passed on his wealth to his eldest son. Maintaining such a society required an underclass, one which largely came from England's struggling class who would trade three years of indentured servitude (white slavery) for a fifty-acre plot of land. These indentured servants made up 80 to 90 percent of the seventeenth century European immigrants to Tidewater.[3]

The "Deep South" encompasses the entirety of South Carolina, Georgia, Alabama, Mississippi, and large swaths of North Carolina, Arkansas, Texas, and Louisiana. South Carolina brought the chattel slavery economy to American shores in 1670 from the English settlement of Barbados. The Deep South makes for beautiful images in southern magazines; yet the backdrop of the staged scene was a culture propped up by its caste society where one could never rise above their born station.[4] Aristocratic expansion of land, financial wealth, and political power would threaten the unity of the young nation, creating two visions of America, the vestiges of which still linger today in the Deep South.

The final regional culture, "Appalachia," extends well beyond what is commonly considered to be the South, including large portions of the Midwest. Appalachia also includes West Virginia, Kentucky, nearly all of Tennessee, and slivers of Virginia, North Carolina, and Arkansas. This "decidedly rural nation" welcomed outcasts from the British Isles from the early eighteenth century.[5] The Scots and Irish brought with them a warrior mentality, forged in bitter clan struggles, that established a lasting defense of individual liberty, personal sovereignty, and suspicion of governing forces.

2. Woodard, *American Nations*, 55.
3. Woodard, *American Nations*, 47.
4. Woodard, *American Nations*, 82–91.
5. Woodard, *American Nations*, 190.

These elements "wove itself into the Southern mind," according to W. J. Cash, particularly a propensity to respond violently to factors he could not control or affronts to his ego.[6] Those "Don't Tread on Me" decals affixed to gigantic trucks throughout the South are more than decoration; they signal back to a regional resistance against British forces during the Revolutionary War that birthed the motto. These fiercely independent people moved westward in such massive numbers that by 1800, one-fifth of the American population had settled into the territory between the Appalachian mountains and the Mississippi River. As Nancy Isenberg puts it, "Both crackers and squatters—two terms that became shorthand for landless migrants . . . lived off the grid, rarely attended a school or joined a church, and remained a potent symbol of poverty."[7] Even today, this people is characterized by their opposition to big government (at least in theory) and fight for what they have secured, evidenced by their vigorous support of every American war.[8]

The same factionalism exhibited by my students in their assembly is not so far detached from the southern virtues of fidelity to place and tradition. There remains an abiding conviction that Southerners are a people called to a promised land, yet exiled there. They live in hope that their prayers will be answered by a faithful God who speaks with a slow drawl. The more pressing point for Bible-believing Southerners is to consider whether or not we are as hospitable as we believe ourselves to be, because exclusion and division is the thick air we breathe. Our cultural mosaic is more than Charleston plantation photo shoots, NASCAR, or Duck Dynasty. The South is also Fannie Lou Hamer's activism, the music of Beale Street, the greatest literature and food on the planet, and the lingua franca of Christendom that allows me to say, "I'll pray for you" and for you to know that I'm not part of a cult.

Wendell Berry, whose writings populate the syllabi of a range of college and graduate courses, has contributed to the increased awareness of not just one's surroundings but to the concept of "place," which is far more than just a plot of land. For Berry, place refers to "a locally understood interdependence of local people, local culture, local economy, and local nature."[9] Berry's life embodies this commitment to place. After leaving a prestigious

---

6. Cash, *Mind of the South*, 42–43.
7. Isenberg, *White Trash*, 105–7.
8. Woodard, *American Nations*, 285–94.
9. Berry, "Sex, Economy, Freedom, and Community," 120.

professorship at New York University, Berry settled back onto his family's farm in Port Royal, Kentucky, where he continues to write poetry, fiction, and essays to this day. Being present in a place creates affections, and those affections can form deep, abiding loyalties that never leave us. For Berry, Kentucky was with him no matter his location; it marked him so much so that he felt it was fate to return.

Every person is inextricably connected to where she spends much of her life either embracing her place, rejecting it, or settling into some mediated relationship between these two poles. This "complex inheritance" from a particular place, as Berry calls it, helps us find and make our life.[10] Places are like organisms, full of vitality and potential, interdependent with their surroundings. But, these places are also vulnerable to "diseases" such as being disconnected from the land; isolation from one another; disregarding our obligation to the common good; and excluding others from communal decision-making processes.[11] Places, like individuals, are just as susceptible to self-deception, and at those times, a community relies upon its memory to bridge the gap between self-perception and reality in order to ward off these diseases. For Berry, reckoning with his family's slaveholding history was one such disease for which he sought a cure.

> I am trying to establish the outlines of an understanding of myself in regard to what was fated to be the continuing crisis of my life, the crisis of racial awareness—the sense of being doomed by my history to be, if not always a racist, then a man always limited by the inheritance of racism, condemned to be always conscious of the necessity not to be a racist, to be always dealing deliberately with the reflexes of racism that are embedded in my mind as deeply as least as the language I speak.[12]

10. Berry, "Native Hill," 4.

11. Berry claims three cultural inheritances—Agrarianism, Democracy, and Christianity—that inform his personal standard for what makes a place "healthy" (Berry, "Is Life a Miracle?" 181). Berry does not overtly connect these three cultural inheritances directly to his notion of "healthy" communities; this is my observation. Berry utilizes the inheritances throughout his work to judge whether a community is living up to his standard. Conversely, the distortion of each inheritance contributes to the "disease" of a place. It is important to note that Berry does not hold each inheritance to be the exclusive standard by which all places must be judged (e.g. a place does not have to be "Christian" to be considered "healthy," but a distorted Christianity will certainly make a place "diseased"). Rather, Berry is acknowledging precisely how he has been influenced by living in a particular place and its attendant qualities, which for Port Royal, Kentucky, would be the three inheritances.

12. Berry, *Hidden Wound*, 48–49.

Berry names for me how southern loyalty is the connective tissue that holds together "white" and "evangelical" loyalties. In trying to understand myself—the question of whether or not I'm doomed by my "reflexes of racism"—Berry knows how it feels for that evil to be present in one's body and mind. If being white fosters certain impulses toward protecting the tribe, the South deems those impulses to be virtuous in service to your kin. As Berry puts it, "To be known is to be protected."[13] Aside from the obvious value of having a people for protection, our collective memory can help protect us from our own worst impulses. When we go astray we must say to one another, "This is not who we are."

My West Tennessee town left its marks on me: I only possess a slight southern accent on the spectrum of regional dialects, but it's one that becomes more pronounced when I'm around my people. In our neck of the woods "barbeque" is pork smoked in a pit, and nothing else, especially not the fraudulent vinegar-based imposter foisted upon us by North Carolinians. A "coke" is *any* variety of soda. I understand that fall weddings are scheduled around the football schedule of one's favored SEC team (except for Vanderbilt). I know what it means to live somewhere long enough that you give and receive directions based on where things "used to be." In the same intimate way, southern identity grounds the "white evangelical" in the contextual soil of a place. The southern social imagination is captured by the phrase "our way of life," which is a complex inheritance of often unsavory moments I'll address in this section. The legacies of slavery and evangelical Protestantism have undergirded southern culture for over two centuries, meaning that race and religion are always in plain view, embedded in our hearts and minds. Tracy Thompson asserts that the South is the "nation's first truly biracial culture"—whites and Blacks together in close proximity, understanding their experiences in light of the other—meaning that Southerners have essentially been the "beta-testers" of American democracy.[14] This testing has been, and continues to be, undeniably messy, evidenced by Southerners' understanding of personal liberty and self-sufficiency; its confounding gender roles; and a notion that this people and its causes are ordained by Almighty God.

Each constitutive part of my communities tells a story about my people and my place, with few nooks and crannies free from influence. As a Southerner and American I'd like to believe that I have total control over

13. Mangine. "Seeing Life Full Size," 46.
14. Thompson, *New Mind of the South*, 8, 10, 14.

my fate. As one steeped in evangelical Protestantism, which shaped me to be suspicious of any fatalism masquerading as a cultural Calvinism, I'm doubly conscientious that my designs of free will simply names me master of all that I achieve or the misfortune that befalls me. Time, however, is a teacher, and I know now that I have picked up habits, even half-baked beliefs, without my full cognitive awareness. I am not nearly as impervious to influence as I like to believe myself to be in the fantasies I tell as part of the American Dream.

I am deeply influenced by the places my feet have trod. My place is about West Tennessee cornfields, baseball diamonds, and First Baptist Church. My place is about humidity so thick that tornado sirens hardly cut through it. My place is about Stonewall—Drive, not Jackson. Well, it *is* also about Stonewall Jackson, the Confederate general, but mainly, it is about the street where I spent my entire adolescence. It's the quarter-mile stretch that includes my childhood home on Stonewall Drive, along with a dozen other homes near mine. Our remarkably stable neighborhood had only three families move during my time on Stonewall. I went to church or attended high school with the people in all but one of these homes. Most were friends, some were not, yet they were all my neighbors. I was never unknown. If you asked anyone from the old neighborhood what they recall about me, their memories would conjure images of my constant running up and down that street, in all weather and seasons, nearly every day. I ran the same route throughout high school in preparation for my track season. Still today, when I see a half-mile remaining on the treadmill, my mind drifts back to the only flagpole on my street, which meant I was about a quarter-mile from the crest of the slight hill, where my home would come into view at the apex with a final quarter-mile to go. That "map" is still embedded in my feet, my lungs, and my heart. I pounded the asphalt which bore Stonewall Jackson's name, traversing my entirely white, nearly entirely evangelical neighborhood, which was my place among my people. And, even though I'm a significantly different man two decades later, there are certain things you simply cannot outrun.

5

THEORIES ABOUT OTHERS
Or, All I Ever Needed to Know about Blackness I Learned in High School

> We have been enslaved for 244 years, but we decide not to create a black version of Al-Qaeda. We've been terrorized for 244 years, but we're not going to create a counter-terroristic organization, going around and terrorizing white slave holders who have been terrorizing us. No![1]
>
> —Cornel West

In the spring of 1992, I was a freshman in high school, struggling through algebra, playing too much Nintendo, and listening to a lot of hip-hop. Arrested Development burst onto the scene as one of several conscientious groups that transformed the genre for me from consumer product to pedagogy. On the contemplative "Tennessee," their first hit, Arrested Development's emcee Speech chanted like a weary psalter about part of his childhood spent beyond Dyersburg and in Ripley. Those places—practically in my backyard—being name-dropped on MTV, was not a happy reminiscing for Speech, because the trees he rapped about, the ones from

---

1. West, "Untitled Address."

which his forefathers hung, still stood in West Tennessee hollers.[2] Like Abel's life soaking into the soil, the blood always calls out.

Rural West Tennessee has farmland for miles, and I know very little of this soil. My disconnection to the land extends to my family, too, knowing virtually nothing about my family beyond my great-grandparents. All I really know is that my ancestors were poor, meaning they were not slave owners, which is enough knowledge to assuage any fears that my family tree's roots were pulsing with villainy. So, it brought only a tiny measure of comfort to learn that even though Black bodies were the conduits for creating generational wealth for landowners, it was not the case for my people. These are the small "victories" we claim when sorting through our problematic history.

W. Fitzhugh Brundage says, "memory provides a genealogy of social identity" for groups and individuals.[3] Memory is a communal endeavor, creating crucial bulwarks against misremembering. After all, to be embedded in a particular place with others prevents, in Charles Pinches's words, "memory from being cheapened into nostalgia."[4] There are always two sides to every story, and too often we never hear the underside, or even teach it well.

I learned in high school just how touchy a subject slavery remains for Southerners. One English teacher clumsily brought up race, presumably trying to manufacture an "Oprah moment." What she got instead was Jerry Springer. Earnest white teachers were still a couple of years away from channeling their inner-Michelle Pfeiffer from *Dangerous Minds* to connect with Black youth, so this young teacher was a true pioneer. And, by "pioneer" I mean that she nearly died in her mid-twenties like an Oregon Trail character. Referencing slavery in rural West Tennessee in the early 1990s was near suicidal. Our rival high school, ten minutes down the road, was nearly all-white, claimed the Rebels as their mascot, and proudly flew the stars and bars at athletic events. As the multiracial school in the area our racial tensions were typically close to the surface. Our school's racial makeup mattered, because at the time the national racial landscape was an exposed nerve with harrowing scenes like Rodney King's assault by the Los Angeles Police Department (1991), the officers' subsequent acquittal, and

---

2. Arrested Development, "Tennessee."
3. Brundage, *Southern Past*, 4
4. Pinches, "Stout, Hauerwas, and the Body of America," 23.

the following riots rested firmly in everyone's mind that a local inferno was just a moment away.

My teacher's actions were fairly pedestrian, posing what I recall to be a bland question like "What do you think about prejudice?" A couple of Black students shared carefully guarded answers, and predictably white kids in the room lost their damn minds as if Malcolm X had burst through the doors and called them "white devils." One especially surly white girl, spun around toward the Black students, and yelled, "Nobody whipped you!" Her explosion hung in the air for about two seconds before the most mild-mannered young man in our class, responded with, "You goddamn right! Nobody's gonna whip me either!" Terror came across our poor teacher's face who realized there would be no feel-good moments this day, but I learned a valuable lesson from my classmate: Although he did not possess the memory of slavery, he shared in the history transferred upon his body.

**

"Why do we still have to talk about slavery?" remains a consistent question inside and outside of classrooms. The assumption behind the question is that everyone agrees slavery was awful, but Lincoln, King, and Obama fixed it, so why belabor the point? What's at stake, first, is just an accurate description of the atrocity: Slavery was the practice of "killing, torturing, raping, and exploiting people, tearing apart families, snatching precious time, and locking captives in socioeconomic desolation."[5] Second, slavery remains relevant, because its effects are currently felt. A 2019 Pew survey revealed a racial divide between Americans on the impact of slavery:

> Black adults are particularly likely to say slavery continues to have an impact: More than eight-in-ten say this is the case, including 59% who say the legacy of slavery affects the situation of black people a great deal. By comparison, 26% of whites, 29% of Hispanics and 33% of Asians say slavery affects the position of black people in American society today a great deal, though majorities of each group say it does so at least a fair amount.[6]

For some strange reason, conversations about slavery so often are received by whites as personal indictments. Southern honor kicks into high gear.

---

5. Kendi, *Stamped from the Beginning*, 98.
6. Horowitz, "Most Americans Say."

Lillian Smith provides one of the clearest descriptions of how community loyalty maintains a hold on its members:

> We who were born in the South call this mesh of feeling and memory "loyalty." We think of it sometimes as "love." We identify with the South's troubles as if we, individually, were responsible for all of it. We defend the sins and sorrows of three hundred years as if each sin had been committed by us alone and each sorrow had cut across our heart. We are hurt at criticism of our region as if our own name were called aloud by the critic. We have known guilt without understanding it, and there is no tie that binds men closer to the past and each other than that.[7]

Three generations after Smith wrote these words, I still encounter students who say they feel no guilt about slavery, and then ratchet up the conversational tension so quickly that their intonation betrays their words. They do this, because they've been initiated into a tradition that simultaneously disregards the lasting impact of slavery and still adheres to the destructive mythologies upon which slavery was built. Even though I never witnessed chattel slavery, myself, every historically-debunked piece of racial pseudo-science was reified through commonplace slurs and theories that I heard by the time I was a teenager. Racial theories never remained theories, though; they became enfleshed into societal practices. Ideas, it would seem, are tougher to eliminate than bad behavior.

One reason we in the South have never grasped slavery's severity is that there is no analogous experience for southern whites that gets placed upon *all* of us. Maybe Hollywood's attempts to mimic our varied accents, which result in caricatures, stings a bit, because if our voices are deemed to be dumb, then our minds probably match. But for the most part, white people can laugh at themselves when the stakes are relatively low and the barbs pretty tame.

White supremacy damages its victims and perpetrators by remaking peoples and worlds. W. J. Cash, a white Southerner writing in the forties, realized the intertwined fates of Blacks and whites, stating, "Negro entered into white man as profoundly as white man entered into Negro—subtly influencing every gesture, every word, every emotion and idea, every attitude."[8] Slavery—from abduction, to "the middle passage" across the Atlantic Ocean, to family separation—created a world shaped by the white

---

7. Smith, *Killers of the Dream*, 16.
8. Cash, *Mind of the South*, 49–50.

imagination with lasting effects upon Blacks in America. In the minds of whites, less intelligent, morally-suspect beings, slotted at the bottom of the divine pecking order, were ready-made laborers to serve their more intelligent, industrious, and righteous betters.[9] African peoples were denigrated as beastlike, childlike, soulless creatures, that neither possessed the capacity for reason nor morality. Blacks were driven by lust and sexual aggressiveness and reportedly possessed enlarged genitalia, rapacious sexual urges, and venereal diseases. After all, if a person isn't *really* a person, then they must be something else: a beast of burden or cargo, the kind that can be tightly packed onto tight shelving under ships docked off the western coast of Africa. An endless supply are ready to replace those that died in the vomit and shit-filled festering stews of the ship's hold. Slavery altered the normal pattern of creation, too, as sharks learned to follow the boats across the Atlantic, because the bodies of the one-eighth who did not survive the trip would be tossed overboard.[10]

The horrendous, nearly two-month trip across the ocean led to weeks-long marches to the auction block en route to a lifetime of enforced labor. Fitbit users know that a 10,000 step-day, roughly five miles, is a great goal to maintain physical fitness. Men and women were unloaded off of slave ships, burdened by iron chains, shackled to one another, and then forced on a journey that would take 40,000 steps a day until the journey to the plantation or auction block was completed, sometimes weeks after docking.[11] Field work lasted through the daylight hours, and workers went to bed soon after supper upon little more than a few blankets on a cold floor. Those who remained awake tended to washing and mending clothes. This life was the status quo even before the possibility of whippings, brandings, or rape.[12]

The meaning of slavery, for master and slave alike, went deeper than just the conditions slaves endured. Edward Baptist painfully details the disembodying aspects of the American slavery economy. For example, the right hand symbolized the power a slaveowner held by their signature: "They produced concrete results at distance, using words that their hands

---

9. Jordan, *White Man's Burden*, 6–7.

10. Jordan, *White Over Black*, 32–5; 158–59; Kolchin, *American Slavery*, 18–19, 21–22; Hartman, *Lose Your Mother*, 47, 53; Quarles, *Negro in the Making of America*, 22–23.

11. Baptist, *Half Has Never Been Told*, 2.

12. Douglass, *Narrative of the Life of Frederick Douglass*, 21, 33.

wrote on pieces of paper."[13] White men changed economies, financial fortunes, and worlds through the near divine-power possessed in the right hand, a kind of *creatio ex nihilo*, to write something into existence. Slaves, or "hands," became extensions of their masters' wishes, putting flesh onto these ideas. Working hands remained connected to the land, while white hands were removed from it.[14] For slaves, picking cotton had to be a two-handed job in order to meet their daily quotas to avoid savage beatings. Utilizing one's left hand to pick meant doing something unnatural for most. Slaves had to train in such a way that they had to "disembody oneself," Baptist says, "to become, for a time, little more than a hand."[15] The southern economy was built upon this continually dehumanizing, disembodying experience that demanded that "one become a different person—or not even a whole person, but a hand, and the wrong hand at that."[16] White folks, even the so-called "white trash," knew they possessed the most valuable currency in this land. To be "white" in the United States came to mean primarily *not* of African descent or "Black," which is also to say the difference between being considered "free" or "slave."[17]

Even a kind of forgetting was enforced upon African peoples. The slave population came from various nations, tribes, and spoke different languages. Such diversity contributed to their fracturing in America. As Albert Raboteau says, "no single African culture or religion, once transplanted in alien soil, could have remained intact."[18] By 1865, the slave population was now 99 percent American-born, a shift from one comprised primarily of African-born slaves. Memories of the homeland faded—safeguarded insofar as oral records could be kept, told and retold.[19] Saidiya Hartman puts the matter in the most searing, heartbreaking terms:

> In every slave society, slave owners attempted to eradicate the slave's memory, that is, to erase all the evidence of an existence before slavery. This was as true in Africa as in the Americas. A slave without a past had no life to avenge. No time was wasted yearning for home, no recollections of a distant country slowed her down as

---

13. Baptist, *Half Has Never Been Told*, 89.
14. Baptist, *Half Has Never Been Told*, 100–101.
15. Baptist, *Half Has Never Been Told*, 136–37.
16. Baptist, *Half Has Never Been Told*, 139.
17. Painter, *History of White People*, 42.
18. Raboteau, *Slave Religion*, 8.
19. Kolchin, *American Slavery*, 38–39.

she tilled the soil, no image of her mother came to mind when she looked into the face of her child.[20]

White Southerners' systematic attempt to dismantle a people, families, cultures, and worlds is an unspeakable evil, making those whites who now plead ignorance on their ancestor's behalf little more than mouthpieces for white supremacy. Frederick Douglass, for one, saw the beatings he received at his master's hands to be an extension of slavery's brutality, an intentional dehumanization: "I was broken in body, soul, and spirit. My natural elasticity was crushed, my intellect languished, the disposition to read departed, the cheerful spark that lingered about my eye died; the dark night of slavery closed in upon me; and behold a man transformed into a brute!"[21] But, Douglass's life offers a counter-testimony: White abuse did not transform him into a brute.

Slavery's Lasting Impact?

How do we explain slavery's impact in our times? In *Deep Roots: How Slavery Still Shapes Southern Politics*, the authors detail how "Black Belt" counties have maintained racially repressive policies into the twenty-first century. The Black Belt—large swaths of Mississippi and Alabama named for their dark soil—were largely economically dependent upon slavery until the end of the Civil War.[22] These researchers say the political culture of a place can be mapped over time: "Significant historical forces, and the attendant political economic and political incentives that they produce, can create patterns that pass down through generations over time—and these patterns can outlast the original institutions and incentives."[23] This means that slavery's impact in areas where it "was a cohesive part of their culture, economy, and political life" lasted beyond the Civil War, Reconstruction, and the civil rights movement. Their research shows how southern whites in these areas remain more conservative on racial matters, more opposed to affirmative action, and show "cooler feelings toward African Americans" compared to whites in areas that were less reliant upon slavery.[24]

---

20. Hartman, *Lose Your Mother*, 155.
21. Douglass, *Narrative of the Life of Frederick Douglass*, 58.
22. Acharya et al., *Deep Roots*, 28.
23. Acharya et al., *Deep Roots*, 12.
24. Acharya et al., *Deep Roots*, 75, 64.

We know that we inherit attitudes and behaviors individually, e.g., political, racial, religious attitudes, but a second way of cultural transmission occurs by what Acharya et al. refer to as "institutional reinforcement," meaning "culture and institutions work in tandem," allowing behaviors—ways of life—to linger.[25] Every place reaches a crossroads where they have to choose a behavioral path, not just for themselves, but in essence for the generations that will follow them. Slavery ended, but the theories behind it did not, in part because our ancestors poured the spoiled wine of defeated ideologies into the new wineskins of legal and extra-legal practices, rather than choosing the post-bellum path of integration. Southern whites inherit a particular imagination—centuries worth of unholy theories catalogued and implemented, both behaviors and blind spots—that communicate who is worth seeing. We might not accept these "reflexes of racism" outright, but they are ours with which we must reckon.[26]

In high school it became impossible to look past my Black peers any longer because of burgeoning Black pride. Distinctly Black clothing brands and styles filled the school hallways—Cross Colours, Fila, FUBU. Black garb accented by gold, green, and red—those unfamiliar "African colors"—were everywhere in the nineties, and Union City High School might as well have been a De La Soul concert the way teens were sporting these fashions. And if FUBU's "For Us By Us" wasn't clearly communicating the message, one t-shirt bootlegged by thousands of hustling entrepreneurs, made it clear that *"It's a Black Thang. You Wouldn't Understand."* It was true. I did not understand, and that fact made me extraordinarily uncomfortable. Now it was being made abundantly clear by my schoolmates that not only did I *not* know something, but even if I were to observe the "it" in question I would not understand it precisely due to my race.

When I noticed these expressions of Blackness in school, I was experiencing what bell hooks describes concerning white perceptions of Black people in their midst. Whiteness conjures the belief that we are invisible to people of color, almost like a spell has been cast upon every path where white feet trod. White people move about society, supposedly unnoticed, by God-given right. In other words, the privilege of whiteness, hooks says, "accorded them the right to control the black gaze," and in turn, Blacks assumed a kind of invisibility, which made them "less threatening servants."[27]

---

25. Acharya et al., *Deep Roots*, 35, 38.
26. Berry, *Hidden Wound*, 49.
27. hooks, *Killing Rage*, 35.

For a time, I could progress through my daily routine undisturbed by anything that did not fit into my construct of what the world was or should be. The young people at my school altered their clothing choice just a tad, by a pattern or a collection of words that made me notice them. They made it impossible to look away or imagine that they were not actually there in front of me.

It's a Black Thang. You Wouldn't Understand.

Back in the day, those revolutionary t-shirts were met with knock-off counter messages, that spoke to whites' most transparent, long-held contempt: "It may be a black thang, but I don't give a shit" adorned with Confederate flags and burning crosses. Give white folks credit: We have always had a thing for cultural appropriation.

I bore witness, though, to the genesis of a generation who would no longer suffer the impositions placed upon them by so-called "science" or custom. They honored their fathers and remembered their mothers with near-biblical faithfulness. "I am a reminder that twelve million crossed the Atlantic Ocean and the past is not yet over," Hartmann says. "I am the progeny of the captives. I am the vestige of the dead. And history is how the secular world attends to the dead."[28]

Some kids wore new shirts to school one day hinting toward two sides of our shared history. And I, in turn, had to alter my inherited theories about myself and others in order to imagine the world anew.

---

28. Hartman, *Lose Your Mother*, 18.

6

ON BOTH SIDES

The Art of Never Saying What We Mean

> Over the years I have come to the judgment that Southern civility is one of the most calculated forms of cruelty.... Texans have many faults, but usually we do not try to control you by being nice. Tell us what you want. We will either give it to you or kill you. That is not the way you negotiate life in the South. Courtesy forbids direct speech.[1]
>
> —Stanley Hauerwas

Days after the 2016 presidential election, Roland Martin's interview with alt-right leader Richard Spencer took an unexpected excursion into Christianity. Spencer had just said that identity rested "at the heart of my ideology," so Martin asked Spencer if he was a Christian. Spencer replied, "I'm a cultural Christian." After incredulously asking, "What the hell is that?" Martin sharpened his question: "Have you professed that Jesus Christ is your Lord and Savior?" Spencer repeated that he was "culturally Christian." When pressed to clarify, Spencer replied, now visibly nervous: "I grew up in a Christian background. I resonate with Christianity and so on."[2]

---

1. Hauerwas, *Hannah's Child*, 180–81.
2. NewsOne Now, "Roland Martin Confronts White Nationalist Richard Spencer."

PART II: KNOW YOUR PLACE

Months later in the spring, Spencer, a University of Virginia (UVA) alum, organized a protest against the Charlottesville city council's planned removal of a Robert E. Lee statue and renaming of Lee Park. Spencer returned to Charlottesville for the "Unite the Right" rally on August 11–12, 2017, first gathering on the UVA campus chanting "blood and soil" and anti-Semitic chants: "You will not replace us. Jews will not replace us." The following day a clash between protesters and counter-protesters escalated into violence, culminating in a white nationalist driving his car into counter-protesters, killing 32-year-old Heather Heyer and injuring dozens. President Trump's tepid response had the notable line, "I think there's blame on both sides. You look at—you look at both sides. I think there's blame on both sides."[3]

"On both sides" is the kind of response you give, when you just don't want to upset anyone, a trait Southerners should recognize. One of the peculiarities of southern life is the manner in which we care for our speech, so much so that it often turns us into liars. Only a people so conflicted by the truth and reticent to fully voice it would go to such lengths to keep from saying things plainly. In an attempt to avoid rudeness or a quarrel, our speech transforms into prattle. Our verbal oddities are most obviously on display when we try to describe an individual or group outside of our sphere. The hemming and hawing exhibited by a Southerner who is backed into verbally describing a delicate intercultural situation beyond their comfort level combines the gymnastic artistry of Cirque de Soleil with the promise of disaster matched by an Evil Knieval stunt. Only a people so steeped in deploying "bless their heart" as a fleet of stealth drones could easily say so much by attempting to say so little. We talk out of both sides of our mouths.

Such is the way we have dealt with the Confederacy for too long.

"Heritage, not hate" is not just a failure of language. It's a deception that begins with the soul. "History has happened to the South," as Edward Queen puts it. We are the only white Americans to have suffered a defeat on our home soil, and the relics adorning our land prove our ancestors wanted to re-narrate the past.[4] The Confederacy was a self-proclaimed Christian nation adopting the national motto *Doe Vindice*, "With God as our defender."[5] The South had critics of slavery, but many of them coalesced

---

3. "Transcript of President Trump's Remarks at Trump Tower on Charlottesville."
4. Quee, *In the South the Baptists are the Center of Gravity*, 50.
5. Stout, *Upon the Altar of the Nation*, 47, 98, 409. For a summary of how historians

to craft the idea of Confederacy once the southern life and economy was threatened. In the infamous "Cornerstone Speech," Vice President of the Confederate States of America, Alexander H. Stephens, said of the new government:

> its corner-stone rests, upon the great truth that the negro is not equal to the white man; that slavery subordination to the superior race is his natural and normal condition. This, our new government, is the first, in the history of the world, based upon this great physical, philosophical, and moral truth.[6]

The ways in which Southerners conceived these physical, philosophical, and moral "truths" determined the routes they took to defend slavery. South Carolina, Charleston in particular, including its clergy, welcomed scientific professional communities and innovations, making it one of the national centers of scientific interest. The polygenesis debate found new life in the South, as one way to justify the lower station of slaves. For example, South Carolinian Dr. Josiah Clark Nott forwarded the polygenesis thesis in 1843 that whites and Blacks emerged from separate creations.[7] This thesis, of course, challenged the Bible's creation narrative, and the South ultimately defended the Bible and used it to forward a slave society, sometimes in creative ways. South Carolina Presbyterian pastor-theologian James Henley Thornwell, an architect of the Confederacy, interpreted the Golden Rule to mean "we should treat our slaves as we should feel that we had a right to be treated if we were slaves ourselves."[8] By the 1850s, southern pastors adopted similar theological rationalizations and led their flocks accordingly.[9] Thornwell understood human history to unfold by God's design—one that came about slowly, so insuring relative stability. Humanity protected God's order against anything that would "threaten the organic structure of society

---

have examined Christianity within the Confederacy see Berends, "Confederate Sacrifice and the 'Redemption' of the South" in Schweiger and Mathews, *Religion in the American South*, 99–124. Harvey, "'Yankee Faith' and Southern Redemption: White Southern Baptist Ministers, 1850–1890" in Miller et al., *Religion and the American Civil War*, 167–86.

6. Stephens, "Cornerstone" Speech.

7. Farmer, *Metaphysical Confederacy*, 82–89.

8. Farmer, *Metaphysical Confederacy*, 225.

9. James Farmer, commenting specifically on southern Presbyterian acceptance of justifications for slavery, says, "when theology clashes with the dominant ideology of a culture, theology is revised" (*Metaphysical Confederacy*, 201). Cf. Genovese, *Consuming Fire*, 14.

and undermine the divine plan for progress."[10] In their view, God had positioned Blacks as slaves for a reason that only God could know, and those who attempted to change society too quickly acted outside of God's will.

During the war, the Union and Confederacy made claims upon God's favor. Both sides called for public fasts and days of thanksgiving and prayer. Both sides saw victories as God's blessing and their losses as prompts to purify themselves. Revivals were held in Confederate camps under the belief that if certain gestures of personal piety were followed, God would bless the nation.[11] Nevertheless, the South's fall necessitated a theological audit of its beliefs and practices, particularly after a quarter of a million Confederate deaths. Surely the Lord had not brought his people to heel for no good reason. Slavery was again midrashed with claims made that it remained a just and right practice, and others believing it to be unjust bringing God's chastening. Regardless, Baptist, Methodist, and Presbyterian churches—95 percent of southern church membership—split over slavery in the antebellum period and remained divided following the war, making slavery one, if not the, defining mark of the southern church.[12]

The nation remained divided, too. The Confederacy's story had to be rendered in a manner to make sense of their great losses to ease their psyche and galvanize those who remained to carry on the holy cause. The result of this careful framing came to be known as "The Lost Cause," a new southern civil religion, coined in 1866 by Richmond editor Edward Pollard in his book of the same title.[13] Lost Causism charted a way of maintaining southern identity, i.e., white supremacy in the face of reconstructionist efforts, and shaping their collective future by re-narrating the past. Southern "Redemption" was underway.[14]

10. Farmer, *Metaphysical Confederacy*, 167.

11. Stout, *Upon the Altar of the Nation*, 289, 409. During the Confederacy nearly three-fourths of all printed sermons called for public fasts, times of thanksgiving, or were political in nature and often related to the war (51). Not all military leaders adhered to such theology, as one Confederate General Edward Porter Alexander was a bit dubious about the efficacy of their prayers, writing after the war: "I think it was a serious incubus upon us that during the whole war our president & many of our generals really and actually believed that there was this mysterious Providence always hovering over the field & ready to interfere on one side or the other" (Genovese, *Consuming Fire*, 45–46).

12. Ahlstrom, *Religious History of the American People*, 715.

13. Wilson, *Baptized in Blood*, 7.

14. Henry Louis Gates, dates "Reconstruction" from 1865 through 1877, and says the "Redemption" period should be understood when the final Confederate state was recaptured by southern Democrats in 1877 through President Woodrow Wilson's screening of

Southern clergy, some of whom had served as Confederate chaplains, assumed the roles of high priests of the Lost Cause religion, calling Southerners to see their time of suffering—with Yankee rule as the new Babylon—as the necessary path to redemption. Southerners were called to remain faithful to the theological and social principles upon which their society had been founded to be victorious. White, southern Christians understood their participation in this religion as "an extension of the cosmic struggle between order and disorder, civilization and barbarism, white and black."[15] God's chosen were merely in exile, a faithful remnant ready to rise again if God restored her to prior glory.

The South set out in proto-Orwellian fashion to alter the memory of its crushing military and cultural defeat, filling public spaces with Confederate monuments and school textbooks with stories of southern valor against Northern aggression. Southern defenses of slavery (and later segregation) were couched in the language of "states' rights" and our "way of life" offered a way to say something other than what our ancestors really meant. As UVA history professor, and descendant of enslaved Virginians, John Mason says, "To memorialize history in public spaces is to make it visible—that is, to make interpretations of history visible."[16] Whiteness was placed front and center in town squares and in schools. By 1875, Confederate veterans gathered in Richmond to dedicate the first statue in honor of Stonewall Jackson. In 1907, an estimated 200,000 people came to Richmond for the dedication of a statue to Confederate President Jefferson Davis.[17] Monument funding and erections peaked between 1890 and 1910, during Jim Crow's dark shadow, as the *Plessy v. Ferguson* (1896) instituted the "separate but equal" doctrine. The Southern Poverty Law Center reported in 2016 that over 700 Confederate monuments rest on public property, 95 percent in former Confederate states, with 167 of these being dedicated after 1950.[18] Southern rehabilitation was an elaborate re-narration of the past: Edenic plantations, a truly "civilized" Civil War without the carnage, happily enslaved blacks, and a general racial harmony that was interrupted by Northerners.

Klan propaganda film *Birth of a Nation* in 1915 (*Stony the Road*, xv).

15. Harvey, *Freedom's Coming*, 40.
16. Mason, "History, Mine and Ours," 24.
17. Wilson, *Baptized in Blood*, 18–19, 29.
18. The Southern Poverty Law Center, "Whose Heritage? Public Symbols of the Confederacy."

PART II: KNOW YOUR PLACE

The Lost Cause became the religion of the public square, finding renewed implementation upon the passage of *Brown v. Board of Education* (1954). The ruling was a call to arms for a "holy war" of civil religions with both sides, once again, claiming God to be on their side.[19] The Lost Cause was renewed and marshaled its affective images to preserve their way of life. Confederate iconography, e.g., flags, songs, and chants, was revived by dispossessed men, riled up by political evangelists who claimed that the promised land was theirs by divine right.[20] For example, following the *Brown* decision, Georgia adopted a new state flag in 1956 that incorporated the Confederate battle flag, joining other states whose state flags had elements of the Confederate flag, all adopted after the Civil War.[21]

**

When Alabama governor and famed segregationist George Wallace ran for President of the United States in 1968, he received over 100,000 telegrams congratulating him on joining the race, half coming from Northerners. "They all hate black people, all of them," Wallace said of his Northern supporters. "They're all afraid, all of them. Great God! That's it! They're all Southern! The whole United States is Southern!"[22] Seemingly proving true Rust Cohle's dictum that "Time is a flat circle," President Trump's affinity for protecting Confederate relics throughout his Presidency—monuments, military bases, the flag—along with the other overtly bigoted aspects of his presidency led Henry Louis Gates Jr. to dub it "the Neo-Redemption Era."[23] The first impeachment trial spurred some Trump supporters to gesture at the possibility of a new Civil War, and several publications ran pieces that portended violence: "Donald Trump's New Lost Cause" (*New Republic*), "How America Ends" (*The Atlantic*), "Nothing Less Than a Civil War" (*The New York Times*).[24]

Not long after the Charlottesville clash, President Trump said of monument removals, "They're trying to take away our culture. They're

---

19. Manis, *Southern Civil Religions in Conflict*, 87.
20. Wilson, *Judgment and Grace in Dixie*, 25–27.
21. NBC News, "These 5 States Still Use Confederate Symbols in Their Flags."
22. Anderson, *White Rage*, 101–2.
23. Fukunaga, *True Detective*; Gates, "'Lost Cause' That Built Jim Crow."
24. Ford, "Donald Trump's New Lost Cause," Applebaum, "How America Ends," Herndon, "'Nothing Less Than a Civil War.'"

trying to take away our history."[25] Richard Spencer said, "We're being demographically dispossessed. We're losing our culture, we're losing our sense of being."[26] What do two non-Southerners mean by "our culture" and "our history"? Factor in that from 2018 to 2019 distribution of white supremacist propaganda doubled for the second year in a row, according to the Anti-Defamation League's Center on Extremism report, and you could understand why people of color questioned what their nation was becoming . . . or returning to.[27] The conflation of "white supremacist" and "southern" seems to be complete with a wink, a nudge, and a tip of the red cap.

Even perfunctory governmental administrative duties continue to tell false stories that shape our imaginations. For example, on July 13, 2019, Tennessee Governor Bill Lee signed the annual proclamation of "Nathan Bedford Forrest Day" honoring the former Confederate general, slaver, war criminal, and founder of the Ku Klux Klan. Lee, like every governor who preceded him since 1921—Democrats and Republicans alike—has been bound by the Tennessee constitution to make odious proclamations like Robert E. Lee Day (January 19), Confederate Decoration Day (June 3), the birthday of Jefferson Davis, and the Forrest proclamation. Early in his tenure Lee was asked whether he would remove a bust of Forrest that sits in the state capitol's rotunda, one installed in 1978, a year after I was born. Lee exhibited a clear reticence to do so, saying it would be "a mistake to whitewash history."[28]

Governor Lee seemed to grasp the significance of the bust's presence only when massive, organized protests began filling the streets across the nation. At Lee's summer 2020 press conferences for COVID-19 updates, the Forrest bust issue would not go away. Governor Lee said he was committed to "racial reconciliation," which he did not define beyond saying that it required him to listen to others: "What's really important is that we not draw lines and choose sides. It's that we understand that these answers are complicated and they require dialogue." That dialogue would include "those who advocate keeping it" and "those who advocate getting rid of it."[29]

25. Greenwood, "Trump on removing Confederate statues."

26. Huppke, "Trump uses textbook white supremacist language."

27. Alund, "Report finds 103 incidents of white supremacist propaganda in Tennessee since 2018."

28. Allison, "Tennessee Gov. signs Nathan Bedford Forrest Day proclamation."

29. TN Office of the Governor, Transcript, June 10, 2020. In the following weeks, Lee stressed that racial reconciliation was a "spiritual issue" because "every human being is created by God in His image" (TN Office of the Governor, Transcript, June 18, 2020).

PART II: KNOW YOUR PLACE

Lee's most curious statements came when it appeared imminent that a vote would be taken on the Forrest bust in July 2020 by the legislature. Lee acknowledged that, "Symbols matter . . . They're a window into what we value, and while the Nathan Bedford Forrest bust creates a clear tension between heritage and symbolism, we'd be wise not to make this a referendum on his place in history." Lee said of Forrest that "in a particular season of his life, significantly contributed to one of the most regretful and painful chapters in our nation's history." Lee petitioned the Capitol Commission "to consider whether the current placement of Nathan Bedford Forrest's bust allows for his full story to be told, and his contribution to our history to be fully understood." Lee's suggestion to move Forrest's bust to the Tennessee State Museum ventured into "both sides" territory, saying that Forrest "died a reconciled man, who recognized the mistakes he had made, and he turned from his ways. And at a minimum, there should be context around Forrest, to acknowledge his complexity to the legacy of Tennessee."[30]

Lee's comments over those weeks were curious for a number of reasons: First, the desire to provide context for most situations is one I would generally welcome; however, such a decision by Lee must also be read within the *current* context, one in which it is now politically expedient to remove a heinous figure like Forrest. Campbell University Christian ethicist Ryan Newson, writing in 2017, articulates a warning that applies not just to leaders like Lee, but all of us: "White memory is short, and taking down these monuments should be done carefully—not because it is 'too quick' but because it is a move that many well-meaning white persons may support because we would prefer to forget and thus relegate to the unconscious and invisible and evil that is with us yet."[31] Second, Lee's care for a metal bust of one of the world's infamous racists, all to insure "context" for Forrest's legacy, while refusing to meet with his own constituents who protested for months in order to dialogue with Lee, remains curious for one committed to racial reconciliation. Furthermore, by mid-August the Tennessee legislature convened a special session, which included passing legislation that would make camping out on state property a felony.[32] Finally, Lee referenced the "historic point in our country" during the summer of 2020, and that he wanted to "take advantage of that historic moment"

---

30. TN Office of the Governor, Transcript, July 8, 2020.
31. Newson, "Epistemological Crises Made Stone," 137.
32. Allison, "Tennessee Legislature Cracks Down on Protesters."

to move the state toward racial reconciliation.[33] On July 9, 2020, the State Capitol Commission voted 9–2 to remove the Forrest bust from the capitol's rotunda. Due to prior legislation to protect historical monuments, a full vote for removal might not occur until the following year.

What changed between 2019 and 2020? Was there not a chance to engage Black leaders the prior year? Were they not concerned in 2019 with a host of issues related to their community the year prior? Why did it take national outrage over police killings to move Lee (minimally) on the Forrest bust, but not yet to the point of acknowledging the rightful presence of peaceful protesters? The best-case scenario I can imagine for Lee is that he, like many in power, remains captive to controlling the narrative. For Southerners, we've been well-practiced in this attempt since the war's end. It also means in the hyper-polished twenty-first century that we get few unvarnished moments of pure honesty, where a leader says "I was wrong. I see differently now." The worst-case scenario is that too many white southern leaders confuse the sacred with the profane, bending their language—even of the faith—to mean something it never did or could. For instance, to say you favor racial reconciliation, yet do not take the necessary steps to reconcile, then you are merely speaking out both sides of your mouth. Too many southern leaders, including current governors (Democrat and Republican), have troubling histories of bowing at the altar of this disturbing civil religion—wearing blackface or Confederate cosplaying—making sacrifices to the gods of white supremacy like the latest priests of the Lost Cause.[34]

Not every Southerner feels the pressure to speak in unnecessarily balanced ways concerning heinous periods of our history. Russell Moore, president of the Southern Baptist's Ethics and Religious Liberty Commission and a descendant of Confederate veterans, for example, in the wake of the 2015 mass murder at Mother Emanuel Church in Charleston, South Carolina, clearly said, "The cross and the Confederate flag cannot co-exist without one setting the other on fire."[35] In these strange days, where lost causes are reconsidered, we need direct declarations—ones so clear, that the daylight between "both sides" shines ever the brighter through a chasm created by plainest of speech.

33. TN Office of the Governor, Transcript, June 18, 2020

34. Allison, "Gov. Bill Lee Pictured in Auburn Yearbook Wearing Confederate Army Uniform"; Kelly, "Virginia Governor Apologizes for 'Racist and Offensive' Costume"; Taylor, "Alabama Gov. Kay Ivey Apologizes For Wearing Blackface During College Skit,"; Pittman, "Lt. Gov. Tate Reeves' Fraternity Wore Black Face."

35. Moore, "Cross and the Confederate Flag."

Of course not everything in the South is fated to devolve into a Charleston or Charlottesville tragedy, but long before the bullets start flying our short memories lead to unthinkable moral equivalences. The absence of every last Confederate monument, bust, memorial, or flag would be a good thing in my view, but no one should be foolish enough to believe that white supremacy will whimper away and be silently celebrated only in dusty museums. Habits of the heart and mind, even those we assent to unbeknownst to us, do not die so easily.

Oh, and one last thing:

Should you ever find yourself blazing up a Tiki torch and walking with a khaki-clad white supremacist mob, shouting "Jews will not replace us," there is something you should remember: One already did on a cross in AD 33. It's a basic tenet of faith for a Christian, cultural or otherwise.

7

GONE COUNTRY

How to Survive When They Try to Take It All

> Southern self-consciousness was created by the need to protect a peculiar institution from threats originating outside the region. Consequently, the southern identity has been linked from the first to a siege mentality. Though southerners have many other identities, they are likely to be most conscious of being southerners when they are defending their region against attack from outside forces: abolitionists, the Union Army, carpetbaggers, Wall Street and Pittsburgh, civil rights agitators, the federal government, feminism, socialism, trade-unionism, Darwinism, Communism, atheism, daylight-saving time, and other by-products of modernity. This has produced an extreme sensitivity to criticism from outsiders and a tendency to excuse local faults as the products of forces beyond human or local control.[1]
>
> —Sheldon Hackney

East Tennessee is filled with the most beautiful landscape I've ever seen. The mountains shine on sunny days providing the breathtaking backdrop to our lives. Yet, for all of the natural splendor, when I'm *in* the mountains, *in* the woods, I see nothing but threats. Every wave of a leaf in my

---

1. Hackney, "Southern Violence," 924–25.

periphery. Each twig that snaps from something other than my foot. I do not control my surroundings. The forest lets me know that I am incapable of surviving it for much longer than a casual hike.

During these moments, my thoughts turn to how disappointed Hank Williams Jr. would be in my inadequacy to carry on the survivalist tradition. Bocephus's 1982 ode to southern ingenuity, "Country Boy Can Survive," opens with an apocalyptic warning that the end is near, and everything that follows sounds like doomsday-prepper braggadocio, because Southerners are resourceful, connected to the land, and most importantly, different from the rest of the world. Hank enumerates through the song the ways in which the country boy survives: by shotguns and 4-wheel drives; by plowing our fields and catching catfish; by making whiskey, smoking tobacco, hunting and fishing.[2] This is how we survive.

But survive what exactly?

I am not alone in my inability to survive. On one hike, my wife pointed to the downed Fraser firs that covered the Andrews Bald trail in the Smoky Mountains. Greyed trunks lacking foliage of any kind line the way of the heavily shaded trail like ancient tombstones, a visual likely distressing for many a hiker, because the park's website explains:

> You'll immediately notice that many of the trees in this area are dead, or in the process of dying. This is mostly the result of the balsam woolly adelgid, a small insect that infests and kills Fraser firs. Since these trees have little natural defense against the adelgids, which were first introduced from Europe in the early 1900s, more than 90% of the Fraser firs in Great Smoky Mountains National Park have already been killed.[3]

The Fraser's history is an apt metaphor for southern fears: Outside elements will fundamentally change us into something other than what we have always been. Or, they'll kill us. The "muh rights" crowd, among whom I live and congregate, will buck the system just because you told them not do something. Anyone who's ventured into a Wal-Mart beyond August 2020 (when their COVID-19 mask policy went into effect) knows what I'm talking about. And not to stereotype, but every little slight brings about the dilemma of whether they'll express their displeasure with the establishment by choosing between their "Don't Tread on Me" or Punisher tee. I love them;

---

2. Williams, "Country Boy Can Survive."
3. "Andrews Bald," http://hikinginthesmokys.com/andrewsbald.htm.

they're my people, but southern system-buckers routinely display the "siege mentality" Hackney names, coming to change slowly and begrudgingly.

The first targets of southern fears were freed slaves and their descendants, who faced a multitude of legal and extra-legal schemes designed to maintain the closest facsimile of slavery. The failure of Reconstruction to remake the South actually *united* Appalachians with Deep South oligarchs, and Jim Crow's reign began.[4] The estimated 2000 Black men who served in government offices during Reconstruction were ousted.[5] By 1899, registered Black voters had plummeted. Louisiana's 130,000 registered voters fell to just 6,000. Likewise, Alabama had only 3,000 registered from 181,000 voters.[6] "Black Codes" were instituted, making it difficult for a Black country boy to survive. Self-sufficiency itself was at stake. In Mississippi, for example, Blacks were banned from employment other than manual labor or domestic service unless given consent by a judge or another official. Likewise, Blacks were banned from hunting or fishing, and carrying a gun was a crime. Even an insulting gesture could be grounds for imprisonment.[7] Sharecropping, debt bondage, convict leasing, medical experimentations, redlining, aggressive policing and mass criminalization, voter suppression—these policies left in their wake reduced possibilities for a person of color in America.[8]

By the late nineteenth century into the early twentieth century, white men felt they were losing societal control, and not just in the South. Staving off that loss required a masculinity that was equal parts "kindhearted manly chivalry" and "aggressive masculine violence."[9] This is why "Country Boy Can Survive" is a familiar parable for Southerners of the long tension between surviving as a civilized man versus a primal man. The settler impulse to tame the wide, open spaces and heroically face the dangers that lay "out there" is a component of southern lore captured by legends like Tennessean Davy Crockett, who my dad's generation feasted on through Disney's TV show, *Davy Crockett, Indian Fighter* (1954). Davy Crockett was born in the woods, knew every square inch of the forest, and knew no fear. But alas, my people's bear-killing days were long-behind them, and with no

4. Woodard, *American Character*, 108.
5. Gates, *Stony the Road*, 8.
6. Gates, *Stony the Road*, 186–87.
7. Anderson, *White Rage*, 19, 28.
8. Gilliard, *Rethinking Incarceration*, 31–42; Acharya et al., *Deep Roots*, 134–55.
9. Bederman, *Manliness and Civilization*, 172.

wild frontiers left to conquer, the mid-fifties became a period of surviving all manufactured threats, beginning with protecting segregation.

Gone Country

My home-state's rich musical heritage is a source of pride for Tennesseans: The blues and soul of Memphis, the folk and bluegrass of Appalachia, and of course, country music of all varieties. My grandparent's house was a haven for old-school country music; the new stuff could not withstand Buck's harshest review of "that ain't country." Willie Nelson—that "dope-smoking Commie"—was too new school for my grandpa. *Being* country, however, differed from one's musical choice. Alan Jackson described this phenomenon in his 1994 song "Gone Country,"[10] which depicted people who adopted southern speech and dress for financial gain. The Garth (Brooks) years were a gateway for even Southerners to step up their country-game a notch, to try out being a redneck. Whatever style they had before was abandoned in favor of boots, Wranglers, and new shiny belt buckles rivaling the championship strap carried by "The Nature Boy" Ric Flair. Some started dipping Skoal depending upon their level of commitment and tolerance. The cosplaying meant you could look the part without the accompanying economic hardships or occasional cultural derision.

Digging deep into our roots and rediscovering our love of a place can be a psychological staving off of extinction, i.e., going country.

Resisting outside pressures is ingrained in us from birth, as we come to understand our division from some place called "the North," which is only partially about geography and much more so about the role of the federal government. As W. J. Cash bluntly puts it, "the conflict with the Yankee . . . really created the concept of the South as something more than a matter of geography, as an object of patriotism."[11] Our obsession with regional identity has not cut both ways, however, as James Cobb says:

> The idea of a "North" as a fundamental source of identity and an object of attachment has been far less important historically to Americans above the Mason-Dixon line than has the idea of a "South" to those who lived below it . . . . northerners have been

---

10. *Who I Am*, Arista, 1994.
11. Cash, *Mind of the South*, 65–66.

more likely to characterize their own identity as simply "American" and define that in contrast with the South.[12]

Journalist Curtis Wilkie, explains how Northerners existed in the southern imagination: "All Northerners were Yankees, and all Yankees were aliens, a threat to the Southern way of life.... This was not something taught in my home but learned by osmosis."[13] Again, we see here how habits of the mind and heart form without our full consent, lessons learned from a variety of teachers. "Yankee" ideas—a pliable concept that can incorporate any intrusion—infiltrating the South means eventually y'all are gonna try to change or kill us. As the saying goes, "Yankees are Northerners who visit the South. Damn Yankees are the ones who stay."

Masculinity and self-sufficiency are southern virtues directly tied to provision and protection. The hard country life contrasts with city life, one too civilized to deal with the realities of a dangerous world. Case in point, Hank Jr. mentions how the life of his friend, a New Yorker (presumably liberal), ended tragically, when he was mugged in the city for forty-three dollars. Hank growls that he would love to exact some retribution on the mugger at gunpoint, implying it never would have happened to him. Those with the necessary survival tools—be they cultural, religious, or otherwise—can survive the federal government's invasion or even Times Square in the 1980s, or so we all learned.

Earthquakes and Intimate Things

Even though East Tennessee is my home, West Tennessee is my birthplace and houses its own unique topography. Reelfoot Lake, a massive swamplike body of water, was formed by a series of massive earthquakes between 1811 and 1812 when the New Madrid Fault shook, causing the Mississippi River to reverse flow and flood 15,000 acres, approximately twenty miles long and seven miles wide.[14] It remains the defining mark upon the Choctaw land, housing a bald eagle preserve and changing the area's way of life by drawing tourists and outdoor enthusiasts.

May 17, 1954, was an earthquake of a different sorts for Southerners, when the Supreme Court unanimously ruled in *Brown v. Board of*

---

12. Cobb, *Away Down South*, 7.
13. Cobb, *Away Down South*, 215.
14. Walker, "Fascinating Story Behind Reelfoot Lake."

Education that Black children attending schools in separate facilities violated the Fourteenth Amendment's guarantee of equal protection under the law.[15] The *Brown* ruling was a crushing indictment of the South's way of life, reinforcing their rejection of northern influence as equated with federal power. One need not understand the legal minutia of the *Brown* decision to see how white Southerners' response to a foundation-shaking federal imposition was little more than a continuation of the regional narrative of victimhood.

Fifty-four weeks after the Supreme Court's initial ruling, after little-to-no action by southern states, a unanimous Supreme Court ruled that integration in schools should occur "with all deliberate speed" (commonly referred to as *Brown II*). The vague deadline to act with all deliberate speed provided segregationists more time to bolster what was already deemed a "massive resistance." Virginia Senator Harry Byrd called desegregation "the most serious crisis that has occurred since the War between the States."[16] Massive resistance included legal challenges to the initial *Brown* ruling, as well as implementing state constitutional reforms and school policies that would appear to comply with the Court's ruling but would actually slow desegregation to a crawl.[17]

The White Citizens' Council formed in July 1954 in Indianola, Mississippi, and organized in the former Confederate states, suppressing Black rights through political levers and economic intimidation. Maintaining the southern way of life attracted many dejected whites, helping the Citizens' Council gain a quarter of a million members within a couple of years.[18]

---

15. *Brown v. Board of Education* refers to the consolidated case of five separate school desegregation cases filed by the NAACP. Chief Justice Earl Warren spoke the word "unanimously" as he read the decision, which did not appear in the written text. The Supreme Court justices came to the decision that even one dissenting vote in the case might lead to great civil unrest and only the Court's unified voice would provide the necessary mandate to make this marginally popular position the accepted law of the land. Justice Felix Frankfurter wrote to Justice Stanley Reed, who was persuaded at the last moment to join the majority, "I am not unaware of the hard struggle this involved in the conscience of your mind. I am not unaware because all I have to do is look within. As a citizen of the Republic, even more than as a colleague, I feel deep gratitude for your share in what I believe to be a great good for our nation" (Kluger, *Simple Justice*, 710–12).

16. Bartley, *Rise of Massive Resistance*, 110.

17. Patterson, *Brown v. Board of* Education, 94.

18. Bartley asserts that there were no verifiable membership numbers. He cites a Southern Regional Council survey report of 300,000 members as being inflated before settling on the cited approximation of a quarter of a million (*Rise of Massive Resistance*, 84).

If southern businessmen and local law enforcement acted as the hands and feet of massive resistance, the US Congress was the mouthpiece of southern angst. On March 12, 1956, Senator Strom Thurmond (SC) entered into the congressional record "The Southern Manifesto" portraying Southerners as the victims of "a clear abuse of judicial power" perpetrated by a court influenced by "outside mediators," "outside meddlers," and "agitators and troublemakers invading our States." Further, Congress chastised the Supreme Court for "creating chaos and confusion" and "destroying the amicable relations between the white and Negro races" where "there has been heretofore friendship and understanding."[19] The signees claimed that segregation was inextricably tied to southern life, as made clear by their defense of the *Plessy v. Ferguson* decision upholding the separate but equal doctrine: "This interpretation, restated time and again, became a part of life of the people of many of the States and confirmed their habits, traditions, and way of life."[20]

Deeper fears resided in the imaginations of southern whites. In 1956, W. A. Criswell, pastor of First Baptist Church in Dallas, addressed the South Carolina Joint Assembly, where he railed against outsiders meddling into southern affairs:

> Don't force me by law, by statute, by Supreme Court decision . . . to cross over in those intimate things where I don't want to go. Let me build my life. Let me have my church. Let me have my school. Let me have my home. Let me have my family. And what you give to me, give to every man in America and keep it like our glorious forefathers made it—a land of the free and the home of the brave.[21]

By "intimate things" Criswell was voicing the long-held notion that integration would lead to interracial marriage, biracial children, and the destruction of the white race. Again, it's important to place Criswell's fears within what was, at this point, an over two-hundred-year tradition of racial science.[22] Henry Holcombe Tucker, Baptist minister and former president

---

19. "Southern Manifesto."
20. "Southern Manifesto."
21. "Address by Dr. W.A. Criswell, Pastor, First Baptist Church, Dallas, Texas, To the Joint Assembly." See also Freeman, "Never Had I Been So Blind," 10–11.
22. See Hall, *Conceiving Parenthood*, which details how Christians supported various eugenics movements, particularly under the auspices of ensuring healthier families. Hall's work focuses on Mainline Protestants, but her attention paid to advertising and the massive public relations campaigns that accompanied these movements in the twentieth century speaks to the ubiquity of the thoughts and images. Hall describes the mentality

of Mercer University and the University of Georgia, posited in an 1883 editorial four key litmus tests for racial orthodoxy: First, human races are and will be forever unequal. Second, Blacks are inferior to whites. Third, intermarriage was detrimental to all races. Fourth, free social intermingling of Blacks and whites "must have its origin in sin."[23] At the turn of the twentieth century, concerns over intermarriage was being expressed in the highest of ivory towers. In 1902, British thinker James Bryce, delivering the prestigious Romanes Lecture at Oxford University, said, "That races of marked physical dissimilarity do not tend to intermarry, and that when and so far as they do, the average offspring is apt to be physically inferior to the average of either parent stock, and probably more beneath the average mental level of the superior than above the average mental level of the inferior."[24] President Theodore Roosevelt (1901–1909) was obsessed with what he termed "race suicide," the breeding out of whites which would be exacerbated by lenient immigration policies and white couples who did not perform their civic duty of having large families.[25] Still today, "the great replacement"[26] conspiracy theory—espoused by mass-shooters in Christ Church New Zealand (March 2019) and El Paso, Texas (August 2019)—remains a fever-dream of white supremacists.[27]

Southern whites believed intermarriage was the primary goal of civil rights advocates.[28] Virginia Governor Thomas Stanley received hundreds

of the times as, "If planned domesticity is the hope of the world, and the United States is the world superpower, then aptly ordered domesticity is arguably the salvation of the planet" (16).

23. Smith, *In His Image, But*, 264–65.

24. Bryce, *Relations of the Advanced and the Backward Races*, 26. See also Painter's chapter "Refuting Racial Science" in *The History of White People*, 327–42.

25. Bederman, *Manliness and Civilization*, 202–5.

26. Charlton, "What is the Great Replacement?"

27. Hayden, "Stephen Miller's Affinity for White Nationalism."

28. Myrdal, *American Dilemma*, 59. Swedish sociologist Myrdal found the primary reason for southern maintenance of their white caste system, or what he termed an "anti-amalgamation" posture, rested chiefly upon the threat of interracial marriage or sexual contact. He said that in Western civilization "sex and social status" are for most people "danger points"—in other words, the areas in which one "fears the sinister onslaughts of his personal security" (59). His survey of American Southerners lent support to this conclusion: Whites were asked to rank those discriminations held to be most important. He found "intermarriage and sexual intercourse involving white women" presented the greatest threat to the racial status quo with economic opportunities as the *least* threatening to whites. In contrast, issues of economics and enfranchisement were of paramount interest to blacks, with intermarriage to whites being a nearly non-existent concern

of constituent letters questioning how he would comply with the *Brown* ruling and voicing concerns about "miscegenation."[29] Mississippi Senator James Eastland believed the *Brown* decision was "a program designed to mongrelize the Anglo-Saxon race."[30] Judge Thomas Brady, founder of the White Citizens' Council, proclaimed Anglo-Saxon superiority, saying, "the loveliest and purest of God's creatures, the nearest thing to an angelic being that treads this terrestrial ball is a well-bred, cultured southern white woman or her blue-eyed, golden-haired little girl."[31]

Rev. Criswell concluded his address to the South Carolina Joint Assembly by admitting that some things should be available for all people, particularly economic opportunity and transportation, but pivoted to those "intimate things" that captivated the attention of Southerners: "But there are some things that get way down on the inside of us . . . Whom are you going to marry? Those things are personal . . . Wherever you cross over those social lines . . . that's going to get in your family."[32] Southern Baptist pastor and president of the Alabama Baptist State Convention Leon Macon put the matter more crudely, saying, "The half-breed child of an integrated marriage" would be the gravest result of desegregation.[33] No matter what claims for equal rights Blacks stated they desired through civil rights advancements, whites perceived a sexual threat.[34]

The *Brown* decision, coupled with the growing global threat of communism, created an environment of paranoia in the South. Even racially-progressive Southerners took the Red Scare seriously. For example, Southern Baptist Christian ethicists, Henlee Barnette and T. B. Maston worked for civil rights but also decried communism to be a "rival faith" to Christianity.[35] Blacks who petitioned the international community for

---

(60–61). From the same time period, see Logan, *What the Negro Wants*. Of the fourteen black contributors, only two—W. E. B. Du Bois (66) and Charles H. Wesley (109)—express any desire for the freedom to marry anyone of their choosing.

29. Dailey, "Sex, Segregation, and the Sacred after Brown," 126–33.
30. Jacoway, *Turn Away Thy Son*, 359.
31. Manis, *Southern Civil Religions in Conflict*, 83.
32. "An Address by Dr. W.A. Criswell," 7.
33. Flynt, *Alabama Baptists*, 471.
34. Lubin, *Romance and Right*, 3–38.
35. Barnette, *Introduction to Communism*, 92. Barnette wrote another work on communism, where he claimed communists would court African-Americans to join their cause (*Communism: Who? What? Why?*, 47; 57–58). See also T. B. Maston, "Christianity and Communism."

support put themselves at risk in the era of McCarthyism, as the US government was increasingly suspect of foreign influences, particularly from the Soviet Union. In short, anyone who challenged the cultural status quo was viewed as subversive, including Black journalists, civil rights and labor organizations, and Martin Luther King Jr., himself, even though very few Blacks actually joined Communist movements.[36] Whites who appeared sympathetic to the Civil Rights Movement or who were accused of communist ties could suffer socially and economically, whether the charges were factual or not.[37] This threat led many to remain silent even though they despised the racial and political demagoguery of Southern politicians.

Southern whites attempted to regain the world they once knew through various means—ranging from propaganda, litigation, and violence—even if it meant losing their collective souls. They feared a slippery slope of integration leading to intermarriage, and thus, tainting the white race through diminished rationality and increased susceptibility to disease, and, consequently causing the nation's demise. Ultimately, a weakened society could be defeated by communists, either by frontal attacks, or by losing Americans to the ideological war. The illogical leaps create the now-common claim that government intervention equaled communism (or interchangeably socialism depending upon the speaker).

The *Brown* decision made desegregation "the symbol of a disappointed hope," ending the fantasies of a great southern revival.[38] The South's abiding differences with the rest of the nation, symbolized not just by *Brown*, provides a window into the southern mind. The South's outright rejection of what much of the nation might call "progress" continues today. Large swaths of the South have historically challenged or rejected government initiatives they deem to be overreaching, including: regulations of many varieties, environmental issues, the Equal Rights Amendment, abortion, gay marriage, unions and wages, workplace safety rules, and of course, healthcare.[39] The southern neuroses of losing everything and the doubling-down

---

36. A 1953 private FBI report on "The Communist Party and the Negro" came to similar conclusions as the 1949 House Committee on Un-American Activities hearings: Communism failed to attract even a small portion of the Negro population (Woods, *Black Struggle, Red Scare*, 87).

37. For example, see Clifford and Virginia Durr, Montgomery activists who had no Communist ties but were subpoenaed by Senator James Eastland to testify (Chappell, *Inside Agitators*, 53–61).

38. Manis, *Southern Civil Religions in Conflict*, 79.

39. Woodard, *American Nations*, 281–301. Jonathan Metzl details Tennessee's

on our most unsavory beliefs is a clear sign of a gone country. But, for a place that traffics in fatalism, things can always get worse. If you are always looking for enemies, then you will certainly find or create them.

---

rejection of the Affordable Care Act, both by the legislature and many white conservatives, linking racial animus toward President Barack Obama to the notion of all government programs being a slippery slope toward Communism (*Dying of Whiteness*, 121–88).

8

THE MORAL ARC OF THE UNIVERSE IS LONG, AND IT BENDS TOWARDS US

It was notoriously the women of the Fairchilds who since the Civil War, or—who knew?—since the Indian times, ran the household and had everything at their fingertips—not the men. The women it was who inherited the place—or their brothers, guiltily, handed it over. In the Delta the land belonged to the women—they only let the men have it, and sometimes they tried to take it back and give it to someone else.[1]

—Eudora Welty, *Delta Wedding*

Emmett Till was my George Floyd. He was my Rayshard Brooks, Sandra Bland and Breonna Taylor. He was 14 when he was killed, and I was only 15 years old at the time. I will never ever forget the moment when it became so clear that he could easily have been me. In those days, fear constrained us like an imaginary prison, and troubling thoughts of potential brutality committed for no understandable reason were the bars.[2]

—John Lewis

1. Welty, *Delta Wedding*, 190.
2. Lewis, "Together, You Can Redeem the Soul of Our Nation."

THE MORAL ARC OF THE UNIVERSE IS LONG, AND IT BENDS TOWARDS US

In the first section, I said whiteness provides a largely coherent world designed to work for us. I have set expectations for my universe, the first of which is that I am at the center of it. The American South, however, feels more like a bunch of multiverses that occasionally crossover with the others, each one containing their own routinized cultural norms and social expectations. For instance, I do not experience this place the same way my wife does. Another universe exists for my friends of color whose experiences are historically marked by the threat of violence. White supremacy has distorted relationships across races and genders, and yet the disruptions and brokenness for others have created the kind of peace benefitting white Southerners like myself.

Eudora Welty's novel *Delta Wedding* captures these multiverses' parallel existence to one another, with only rare intersections and always privileging the perceived main story. Seventeen-year old Dabney Fairchild's wedding nears, and the extended Fairchild family travels from all corners to help with the preparations at the family plantation, Shellmound. The Fairchild clan flits here and there, obsessing over the kind of things that are only important to the bride's family during a wedding. Welty's description of 1923 Mississippi reads like a year's subscription of *Southern Living* crammed into one book—every room, every place setting, every inheritance—punctuated by lowkey, largely manufactured, drama. The Fairchild women are the central characters in their own grand story.

Despite Welty's focus on the women, a cadre of named, but largely irrelevant, men populate the story, their function rarely exceeding the utility of wallpaper. Welty set her story between the two world wars, because she needed a time period where the men would be present and that "nothing very terrible had happened in the Delta by way of floods or fires or wars."[3] This facade of serenity is key for the mood *Delta Wedding* establishes, as if nothing harmful could invade the safe confines of the home. Order is not simply ornamental, like a properly set table; it is key to the entire family's understanding of the universe. Wars and rumors of war will come and go, but the Shellmound grounds will know peace, so long as everyone knows their station within it.

Similar to the place of men in the story, the only hint of the South's invisible labor appears in the background cooking, serving, cleaning, or keeping up the plantation house. Every single movement of theirs bends toward the service of Dabney Fairchild's special day. For Welty, Black

---

3. Donaldson, "Gender and History in Eudora Welty's *Delta Wedding*," 3.

characters exist to prepare the stage for the prima donna, but at times, the stagehands miss their mark; they step into scene when they should not. In one unexplained vignette, Dabney's groom-to-be, Troy, gets into a scrap with Root M'Hook, "a field Negro" who had assaulted another worker. Troy intervenes, shooting Root in the hand, and then orders the others to "Get the nigger out of here. I don't want to lay eyes on him."[4] Troy returns to his wedding day preparations.

And scene.

This abrupt episode is never referenced again or explained. The wedding happens; the party is held; Root presumably received some kind of medical attention. Who knows? The bizarre interruption illustrates the place of Black Southerners in the imagination of white Southerners in the early twentieth century: Silent, absent from white view, or the victims of sudden violence.

Delta Wedding exemplifies the South's creation of a supposed "organic society," one Joel Williamson sums up through "placeness," referring to societal station and the procedures one is expected to understand and master. "As young people grew up in this system," Williamson says, "they behaved as if they had been drilled in military fashion in the rituals of human interaction."[5] These rituals of human interaction nod toward the way in which southern sexual mores are intermingled with racial mores and foretell violence if they are crossed. Dabney Fairchild, the angelic expectant bride, exists under the protection of a family full of southern men. Protecting her day-to-day. Protecting her virtue, i.e., her virginity until she makes it to the most important day in a southern woman's life: her wedding.

School Lessons

In seventh-grade Tennessee history I caught my first hint of the South's intermingling of sex and violence with the mythology that accompanied Reelfoot Lake's formation: An indigenous chief named Kalopin, translated as "Reelfoot," ventured to speak with the neighboring Choctaw chief Copiah about marrying his daughter, Laughing Eyes. Chief Copiah forbid the match, insisting Laughing Eyes would only marry another Choctaw. Reelfoot, crestfallen but not defeated, consulted with the Great Spirit for his eternal advice, but the Great Spirit forbid Reelfoot from acting against

---

4. Welty, *Delta Wedding*, 257.
5. Williamson, *Crucible of Race*, 29–30.

Copiah's wishes, warning that his transgression would lead the Great Spirit to shake the earth and drown Reelfoot's people. Reelfoot defied the Great Spirit and charged southward, kidnapped Laughing Eyes and brought her back to his land where they were married. As the marriage celebration raged, the earth shook, the waters rose, and the Great Spirit exacted his price upon Reelfoot and his people, drowning them deep beneath the waters that still cover the upper northwest of Tennessee.[6] If you mess with a man's daughter there will be consequences and repercussions, if not from her family then from the Divine. Lesson learned.

Southern tradition, according to Lillian Smith, taught children three lessons that connected God, the body, and segregation: God loves *and* punishes children. We, in return, love and fear God. Parents possess a godlike quality, enforcing God's ways, and themselves are deserving of love and fear. The second lesson concerned God's gift of the body, which was to be kept clean and healthy. Be careful how you use this gift, for God's morality is "based on this mysterious matter of entrances and exits, and Sin hovering over all doors."[7] White skin was the most important feature of the body: This 'gift' gave whites status, dictated their control over space and movement, and children learned by watching their elders. The final lesson of southern tradition was that of segregation, an extension of the other two: You always obeyed authorities—"They Who Make the Rules"—and you valued and protected your white body. Even outside of the home "Custom and Church" would continue the education through words and actions.[8] The dance—the one that crippled the human spirit "step by step"—was "deep down into muscles" and every southern child learned "never to get out of step, for this was a precision dance which you must do with deadly accuracy."[9] Lessons shaped the Southerner's social imagination.

A direct line runs through southern history, preserving Smith's lessons through violence, a godlike presence that adjudicates between life and death. The line also stretches to the past to include what Jacquelyn Dowd Hall calls the "acceptable folk pornography in the Bible Belt." Lynchings told a story to the masses and imposed archetypal roles upon its perpetrators and victims. White men saw themselves to be "the protectors of

---

6. Reelfoot Tourism, "Legend of Reelfoot Lake."
7. Smith, *Killers of the Dream*, 88.
8. Smith, *Killers of the Dream*, 95.
9. Smith, *Killers of the Dream*, 96.

women, dispensers of justice, and guardians of communal values."[10] In the post-Reconstruction South, white men placed white women on pedestals vowing to protect them from the supposed threat posed by freed Blacks. White men's chivalric code protected southern women, so long as they continued to comport themselves as proper ladies. A woman's virginity was symbolically held to be "inaccessible sexual property . . . of white male supremacy," because her potentiality as matriarch for the Christian family meant their southern way of life would continue.[11]

Black men could exist in the white man's world, so long as they remained docile. The myth of the "black beast rapist" became the chimera upon which whites fixated, rather than on their own historical sexual offenses against Black women.[12] Black women, too, were vulnerable not only to the whims of white men, but also unwanted sexual contact by *all men*, because the law did not consider assault on a Black woman a crime. Contemporary poet Caroline Randall Williams frames the matter in stunning fashion, "I have rape-colored skin. My light-brown-blackness is a living testament to the rules, the practices of the Old South."[13] Conversely, white women could not consent to sex with Black men in the eyes of the law, and accordingly, any sexual contact was considered to be rape.[14]

A 2020 Equal Justice Initiative (EJI) report reveals nearly 6,500 lynchings in twelve southern states between 1865 and 1950, many premised on false allegations of rape or attempted rape against white women.[15] Any

---

10. Hall, *Revolt Against Chivalry*, 150–51. See also Ladelle McWhorter, *Racism and Sexual Oppression in Anglo-America*.

11. Hall, *Revolt Against Chivalry*, 155.

12. Bederman, *Manliness and Civilization*, 46; Hall, *Revolt Against Chivalry*, 146.

13. Williams, "You Want a Confederate Monument?"

14. This was due to the assumption that slave women, or those of African descent, constantly craved sexual intercourse (Morris, *Southern Slavery and the Law*, 305–6; Cf. Jordan, *White Over Black*, 151). There were consensual interracial relationships at the time, but forces like the Klan policed any hint of those relationships by beating the offenders, including white women. White women were also conscripted into policing other white women from these unthinkable liaisons (Feldman, "Home and Hearth," 57–99).

15. Equal Justice Initiative, "Reconstruction in America: Racial Violence after the Civil War." The NAACP reported of the 3224 lynching victims 2522 (78.2 percent) were Negroes (7). Over 28 percent of the 2522 Negro lynching victims were accused of rape or "attack upon white women," compared to 35.8 percent accused of murder (NAACP, *Thirty Years of Lynching in the United States, 1889–1918*, 10). Another study reveals that 16.7 percent were accused of rape, and 6.7 percent accused of attempted rape (Raper, *Tragedy of Lynching*, 36).

whisper of interracial dalliances would initiate a "ritual of transgression," where the alleged Black rapist would pay for his violation of the white virgin, punished in graphic fashion, involving medieval tortures. The ritual's performative structure included chasing down the accused, having the white woman identify him as her assailant, and announcing the public lynching site, like a save-the-date to a demonic carnival open to all white men, women, and children. The lynching ritual united white people of all classes, as they witnessed an emasculation of the "beast"—neutralizing his sexual threat—until he confessed. The event concluded with the burning, hanging, or shooting, of the victim and spectators gathering pieces of the victim's body as souvenirs.[16] Lynchers posed for photos like hunters with their trophies that were sold to the masses.[17] The lie of Black male violence justified the increased governmental presence in the form of law enforcement and prisons.[18] The plantation values just moved into established power. Although lynching steadily decreased from the late nineteenth century through World War II, it increased again with return of Black military veterans.[19]

Emmett

The South's story cannot be told without Emmett Till, whose "sin" was making himself visible on August 28, 1955. The Chicago-born teen was spending the summer with his Mississippi cousins, and his fateful trip to Bryant's Grocery and Meat Market was recounted by the only perspective that mattered according to the law: Carolyn Bryant. Bryant testified in court on September 22 that Till grabbed her by the hand when he was receiving his candy from her, asked her for a date, blocked her exit at the other end of the counter, where he grabbed her around the waist. Till said to her, Bryant testified, "You needn't be afraid of me. [I've], well, ——with white women before."[20]

Bryant's testimony was a lie.

---

16. Hale, *Making Whiteness*, 231; 203–4.
17. Wood, *Lynching and* Spectacle, 94–103. Cf. Hale, *Making Whiteness*, 229.
18. Potter, "History of Policing in the United States."
19. Between 1930 and 1967, 455 men were executed legally on the basis of rape convictions, and 405 of those executed were black (Davis, "Rape, Racism and the Myth of the Black Rapist," 156).
20. Tyson, *Blood of Emmett Till*, 4.

Roy Bryant, Carolyn's husband, drove with his brother, J. W. Milam, in the middle of the night to the house of Till's uncle, Moses Wright. They demanded that Wright produce the boy "the one that done the talking."[21] No mention of an assault. Just talk. From here, the facts are partially known with only the results being undisputed: Till was tortured and shot in the head; his body was weighted down with razor wire and tied to an iron fan, and thrown into the Tallahatchie River. Emmett Till's body was found on August 31 three days later.

Carolyn Bryant's word put him there. A word made Death.

Roy Bryant was arrested on August 29 and charged with kidnapping; Milam would submit to arrest the next day, and both men were indicted for murder. On September 2, Bryant told her attorney in private that Till grabbed her hand and asked for a date, saying "what's the matter, baby, can't you take it?"[22] No mention of an assault, as she would testify later in court—a testimony that satisfied the jury to acquit Roy Bryant and Milam. Their defense attorneys argued that Till simply had it coming. Fifty years later Carolyn revealed her testimony was not true. "Even though she didn't remember what *was* true," Timothy Tyson reported that Carolyn said, "nothing Emmett Till did could ever justify what happened to him."[23] In the summer of 2018, the FBI reopened the Till case, which was expected to conclude in 2020.

When the world refused to look itself in the mirror, Mamie Till opened her baby's casket to the world, bearing witness to a terror that deserved to be named and damned. That bravery impacted thousands like Rosa Parks, who just months after Till's funeral refused to move from her seat on a Montgomery bus. She said that Emmett Till was on her mind.

Too often, life in the South has demanded women of color to be heroic, to endure unimaginable loss—a sacrifice that in the end will be for some alleged greater good that delivers forgiveness to whites but little consolation to anyone else. University of North Carolina sociologist Tressie McMillan Cottom says of Black women, "we have remained firmly lodged in the cultural imagination as 'superwomen.'" But being viewed as extraordinarily strong has not translated into being welcomed into the dignity-affirming sphere of *competence*, where each of us is valued for our know-how. McMillan Cottom says,

21. Tyson, *Blood of Emmett Till*, 9. Emphasis added.
22. Tyson, *Blood of Emmett Till*, 52–53.
23. Tyson, *Blood of Emmett Till*, 7, 164–65.

> Black women are superheroes when we conform to others' expectations of us. When we are sassy but not smart; successful but not happy; competitive but not actualized—then, we have some inherent wisdom. That wisdom's value is only validated by our culture when it serves someone or something else . . . When we perform some existential service to men, to capital, to political power, to white women, and even to other "people of color" who are marginally closer to white than they are to black, then we are superwomen."[24]

A high-level Black administrator once confided to me how her advice was routinely doubted, even dismissed, by white students, who would go looking for second opinions like she had prescribed Tommy John surgery for elbow tendinitis. Her expertise was not sufficient to render her competent in a white space. The power of whiteness is that mediocrity is passable for sustained American success, as long as you're part of the good ol' boy network. Competence isn't a hurdle we white men have to clear. (And, before you get angry, think about how many no-account sons you know that have jobs because of their fathers.)

**

What we place at the center of our universe—assuming some notion of agency in the matter—necessarily moves other people to the margins. It's crucial to understand how white supremacy alters our relationships just by words. White supremacy is sticky like a high humidity, late-July day, where the shade doesn't shield but only offers the illusion of a reprieve; it will find you. White supremacy counters our stated virtue of hospitality with a protectionism against outsiders. White supremacy maims and memes people: Before there were internet Karens—waving guns around, threatening to call the police, displaying distorted notions of safety, security, and convenience—*we* created Uncle Toms, Sambos, Mammies, Jezebels, mass-marketed them, and sang "Zip-a-dee-doo-dah" to the bank.[25]

As Black and white worlds intersected, the South adapted its "law and order" to fit the needs of the white powerbrokers. For a time, our ancestors

---

24. Cottom, *THICK*, 93.

25. See Gates, *Stony the Road*. Gates includes dozens of mass-produced images of Black Americans by whites who were attempting to shape the white imagination of Blacks as a dangerous or frivolous people during the Reconstruction-Redemption eras. For a closer examination of the topic see Gilman, "Black Bodies, White Bodies," 204–42.

said the quiet part aloud: They didn't want integration, because it would mean interracial couples, interracial children, and eventually, a changed society. They didn't want "uppity" colleagues in their boardrooms, barracks, or classrooms. A couple of decades later, such overt racism could not be squared with southern civility, and whites coded their desires with "law and order" as a perfect catch-all term.[26] The problem was that "law and order" was just a repackaging of the same old racist ideas leading to Nixon's southern strategy, a reinstatement of the death penalty, Reagan's never-ending drug war, and George H. W. Bush and Clinton's expansion of mass incarceration.[27]

When I began working for Tennesseans for Alternatives to the Death Penalty, several things were colliding in criminal justice reform at once: Michelle Alexander pointed out in *The New Jim Crow* (2010) that "more African American adults are under correctional control today—in prison or jail, on probation or parole—than were enslaved in 1850."[28] Bryan Stevenson's *Just Mercy* (2014), the story of EJI's work to free Walter McMillian, wrongfully convicted of killing a white woman in Alabama, was everywhere—even being sold in Starbucks.[29] The *Serial* podcast, released in October 2014, was downloaded 40 million times by the end of the year.[30] An endless string of popular streaming series, documentaries, and podcasts followed, as America was waking up to injustices of our carceral system.

As I traveled across Tennessee, meeting with Christians, the mythic power of the death penalty became clear. Even though death sentences have been plummeting for years, the death penalty has the closest connection to

---

26. Political operative Lee Atwater's infamous quote from a 1981 interview sums up this coding: "You start out in 1954 saying, 'Nigger, nigger, nigger.' By 1968 you can't say 'nigger'—that hurts you, backfires. So you say stuff like, uh, forced busing, states' rights, and all that stuff, and you're getting so abstract" (Tisby, *Color of Compromise*, 152; Cf. 153, 157–58). See also Lassiter, *Silent Majority*, 251–75; Gilliard, *Rethinking Incarceration*, 46–54.

27. For a good description of the southern shift from the Democratic party to the Republicans, see Mark Newman's "Civil Rights in a Conservative Era" in *The Civil Rights Movement*, 134–61. Furthermore, Kristin Kobes Du Mez describes white evangelical engagement this way: "White evangelicals didn't just participate in this realignment, they helped instigate it. Billy Graham aided and abetted the southern strategy, advising Republicans on how to make inroads with southern evangelicals who, like him, were birthright Democrats" (*Jesus and John Wayne*, 107).

28. Alexander, *New Jim Crow*, 180.

29. Stevenson, *Just Mercy*.

30. Bootle, "S is for Serial."

lynching, particularly in the way the death penalty system protects white lives. Capital punishment has increasingly become a southern institution: By 2020, nearly two-thirds of states had abolished the death penalty, instituted moratoriums, or had not executed anyone in a decade.[31] The South routinely has the highest national homicide rate despite utilizing capital punishment more than any other region.[32] Multiple studies show that offenders who murder white people are more likely to receive death sentences than those with Black victims, a nod to which lives matter.[33] Perhaps the most haunting aspect of capital punishment is how it remains a death authored through words. As David Garland puts it, "A legislative act is announced, an indictment read, a sentence declared, a verdict upheld." Death moves from the public square to behind walls, delivered by a word to the media. Words end life with no evidence the act makes anyone safer, just mere belief.[34] A word made Death. Part of the white southern imaginary is to control spaces and people by the threat of incarceration or death—a system that recedes into the backdrop, becoming one more ornament in a perfectly decorated scene.

I've learned that the South has fearsome gods, none divine, yet they await our petitions to deliver justice. I learned something recently about that Reelfoot Lake school lesson; it appears that even the mythology might be—odd as this sounds—a myth:

> Early maps of Tennessee (circa 1795) show the area around modern-day Reelfoot Lake as the "Red Foot River." Modern mapmakers surmise that the name change was probably a mistake, thanks to sloppy penmanship, wherein the "d" was separated into an "e" and an "l."[35]

We have allowed certain narratives to shape our institutions, even knowing their fraudulent origins. It's not easy to admit how perfectly my universe

---

31. Death Penalty Information Center, "DPIC 2019 Year End Report."

32. Death Penalty Information Center, "Murder Rates by State by Region."

33. Medwed, "Black Deaths Matter."

34. Garland, *Peculiar Institution*, 312. See also Garland's five metaphors for why the death penalty persists in America, four of which are easily countered by statistical evidence; yet the fifth metaphor—an act of the people's will—cannot be countered intellectually. In other words, the death penalty is the will of the people until it isn't any longer. It must be defeated through elected officials abolishing the death penalty as an act of the people. Until then, the death penalty remains intact because elected officials believe their constituents want it. They believe it makes for a safer society (61–68).

35. Walker, "Fascinating Story Behind Reelfoot Lake."

protects me, blesses me, names me a good and welcomed presence. The South needs to challenge the narratives it has accepted as true and the repercussions of bending the universe toward ourselves.

SOUTHERN OUTRO

Will We Rise Again?

South Postpones Rising Again For Yet Another Year[1]
—*The Onion*

While I was doing doctoral work in southern California the ungodly hours of reading and writing were alleviated primarily by SEC football. My Saturday mornings consisted of downing coffee, while strolling through beautiful downtown Pasadena toward Barney's Beanery for breakfast and a personalized TV tuned to the Tennessee Volunteers for a 9 a.m. kickoff Pacific Coast Time.

The Vols rewarded my faithfulness on September 1, 2008, when they journeyed west to take on the UCLA Bruins. The Tennessee faithful always travel in force, and for a bit, the historic Rose Bowl felt a little bit like home. As kickoff neared, the Vol fans were worked into a booze-fueled delirium. The UCLA fans, on other hand, were enjoying a pleasant, sunny Labor Day. I passed the interminable wait by talking through the keys to the game with my friend Josh, an alumnus of UT's Pride of the Southland Band. He regaled me with stories of visiting hostile stadiums and being pelted with adult beverages after an upset win over LSU. At that moment, Josh had seen more hostile environments in a Kirkland's fine gifts store than the current home crowd at the bucolic Rose Bowl. Baton Rouge, this was not.

The kickoff team lined up, Vol Nation rose as one, the energy swelled, and then I felt a tug at the back of my shirt. I turned to see a perturbed

---

1. *The Onion*, "South Postpones Rising Again For Yet Another Year."

woman staring at me. Our seats were on the final row of the visitor's section before the ascending rows returned to the familiar blue and gold of disinterested Bruins.

"Will you please sit down?" she asked.

Sit down at a football game? I politely pointed to the crowd before us.

"Ma'am, there are three thousand people standing in front of me. You still won't be able to see even if we sit."

That did not go over well.

"Well, if you ask the people in front of you to sit and then they ask them to sit, then maybe . . . "

I scanned the fans in front of me, catching the back of a professional wrestler-sized gentleman who had an orange "Power-T" shaved into the back of his head, complimented by orange and white checkerboard overalls. She did not know my people.

"Ma'am, I can tell you it's not going to happen."

"Why not?" she asked in utter disbelief.

"We stand for kickoff at Tennessee."

She scoffed before letting me know that the police would be coming soon. I nodded to communicate that I understood her position, even though it was clear she did not comprehend mine. Her disdain for myself and the thousands of other guests to her lovely state exhibited quite the breach of intercultural competency, as her tolerance for regional distinctives was clearly limited. She and her husband left the stadium without incident by the second quarter. I stood victorious . . . at least until the game began.

Disembodiment + Division = Disorientation

My regional formation has largely reinforced my racial identity. The South is a majority white space that fought a war to maintain its racial hierarchy, and a place whose theories about people of color have become embedded through legal and cultural enforcement. In other words, if whiteness is a blessing, then the American South is truly God's country.

Disembodiment

Aside from lacking any broad agreement on what constitutes "the South"— boundaries being paramount to stating whether one is "in" or "out"—this place suffers from a disembodiment unique to its history. The South cannot simply be judged as the birthplace of the Confederacy, as many Southerners care very little about remembering Dixie. Yet the Confederacy looms because it persists as an idea even more so than a place of boundaries, a specter of odious ideals extending outside of the South. The flag still flies in curious places.[2] Our place remains one of unimaginable bounty held by the land, but only a limited portion of the population has ever really worked it in any consistent way, increasing our disconnect from it. Wendell Berry articulates this reality well:

> The white race in America has marketed and destroyed more of the fertility of the earth in less time than any other race that ever lived. In my part of the country, at least, this is largely to be accounted for by the racial division of the *experience* of the landscape. The white man, preoccupied with the abstractions of the economic exploitation and ownership of the land, necessarily has lived on the country as a destructive force, an ecological catastrophe, because he assigned the hand labor, and in that the possibility of intimate knowledge of the land, to a people he considered racially inferior; in thus debasing labor, he destroyed the possibility of a meaningful contact with the earth.[3]

Disconnection from the land is a kind of disembodiment from the ground that sustains us and to which we all eventually return. Healing this disconnect is not simply understanding which fruits and vegetables are in season and what it takes for my food to reach my plate. The true understanding comes, first, by walking outside my door and recognizing the true cost in human capital that it took to build these empires that provide for and protect us.

But, perhaps the greatest disembodiment of the Southerner are the stories told by those who no longer reside here. The Jim Crow South, with its limited economic opportunities and violence toward the ancestors of slaves, sparked "The Great Migration," when many Blacks moved North and West at staggering rates only exceeded by the immediate post-Emancipation migration.[4] By 1920, the North had gained 700,000 black migrants

---

2. Numerous Confederate flags were seen in Michigan during the 2020 COVID-19 protests at the state capitol. Additionally, Michigan State Senator Dale Zorn wore a Confederate flag mask on the Senate floor (Kornfield and Knowles, "Michigan Lawmaker Denies Wearing Confederate Flag Mask, Calls It History, Then Apologizes."). See also Richardson, *How the South Won the Civil War*.

3. Berry, *Hidden Wound*, 105.

4. Black migration in the US is believed to have peaked between 1870 and 1880, even

and nearly a quarter of a million headed West.[5] For this reason, the Great Migration was an act of self-assertion that would affect US race relations "as much as the Civil War or the Civil Rights Movement."[6] Whereas the South once held over 90 percent of the nation's total Black population at the beginning of the twentieth century, by 1960, only 59 percent of the Black population remained in the South. That number had fallen slightly to 55 percent by 2010.[7] Speaking of "the South" is to name an incomplete place. We as a people are missing part of the body. A starting point for the white Southerner to right these wrongs is, as Berry says, the "receiving into itself half of its own experience, vital and indispensable to it, which it has so far denied at great cost."[8]

Division

Something deep in the southern psyche remains after all this multi-generational conflict, a right to self-determination specifically concerning our standing versus the rest of the nation. More specifically, our racial divisions—codified, instituted, and normalized—remain a deep wound, one from which we are still in the process of healing. The process of awakening to injustices for white Southerners is painful, because it reveals just how deeply enmeshed we are within our region. Lillian Smith struggled to process how her elders divorced ideals from acts, creating a kind of schizophrenia:

> They did a thorough job of splitting the soul in two. They separated ideals from acts, beliefs from knowledge, and turned their children sometimes into exploiters but more often into moral weaklings who daydream about democracy and human dignity and freedom and integrity, yet cannot find the real desire to bring

---

though data for this period did not become readily available until the 1870 census. The largest sustained period of migration of blacks to the North is between 1915 and 1970 (Hall and Ruggles, "Restless in the Midst of Their Prosperity," 836).

5. Johnson and Campbell, *Black Migration in America*, 75. The actual figures are 695,000 migrants to the North and 245, 000 migrants to the West.

6. Tuck, *We Ain't What We Ought to Be*, 145.

7. Berlin, *Making of African America*, 153–55. Cf. Johnson and Campbell, *Black Migration in America*, 154; United States Census Bureau, "2010 Census Shows Black Population has Highest Concentration in the South."

8. Berry, *Hidden Wound*, 107.

these dreams into reality; always they keep dreaming and hoping, and fearing, that the next generation will do it.[9]

Smith names our bifurcated existence, one where the childhood lessons of compassion for and love of neighbor are not carried out in public. Her words harken back to the words of James, who says, "For if any are hearers of the word and not doers, they are like those who look at themselves in a mirror; for they look at themselves and, on going away, immediately forget what they were like" (1:23–24). If you don't practice what you preach then you create division even within yourself.

Disorientation

A bifurcated soul creates disorientation: Separating ideals from acts, like Smith says, leads to a people who cannot distinguish good news from fake news. When fear replaces faithfulness is it any wonder that allegedly good people—people we know and love—wear two faces and speak in forked tongues? Many of us know the feeling of hearing someone we love spit some racist venom, suddenly sounding like Voldemort after one too many soul-splitting's, whose horcruxes are locked away in retirement funds and inherited lands.

We cannot possibly know where we stand on this shifting new terrain, because we have only ever lied about the ground beneath our feet, about whose blood it holds. One thing is certain, though: We must face the past that still shapes us. Timothy Tyson says of the southern future, "The bloody and unjust arc of our history will not bend upward if we merely pretend that history did not happen here. We cannot transcend our past without confronting it."[10] The South leaned fully into an identity that would defend slavery, obstruct Reconstruction efforts, and enforce Jim Crow segregation, a system that became exemplary for evil regimes.[11] So, how will we remem-

---

9. Smith, *Killers of the Dream*, 153.
10. Tyson, *Blood of Emmett Till*, 203.
11. See George Fredrickson, who writes: "From the time they came to power in 1933, the Nazis harassed and abused Germany's half-million Jews. But it was with the passage of the Nuremberg Laws in 1935 that Germany became a full-fledged racist regime, comparable to those already established in the American South . . . One of the laws limited German citizenship to those who were of German or related ancestry, which excluded all Jews. (Blacks in the American South were nominally citizens, but the rights associated with citizenship had been effectively nullified.) . . . Another law prohibited marriage and sexual relations between Jews and German citizens. American laws against

ber these offenses? Germany posted Holocaust memorials, so that their atrocities could not be easily forgotten. No German citizen has the excuse of claiming that "things weren't really that bad," because the government has seen fit to provide reminders in public spaces and pay reparations to Holocaust victims.[12] In a similar spirit, organizations like EJI have erected public monuments to lynching so that generations will know our sins and hopefully not repeat them.

Quite early in the Nathan Bedford Forrest bust controversy, Republican Caucus chair of the Tennessee state legislature Jeremy Faison expressed a desire to remove the bust precisely due to concern expressed by his Black colleagues. Representative Faison, whose ancestor was a Confederate colonel, changed his mind about the bust when, Memphis lawmaker G. A. Hardaway asked Faison to study Forrest's ideology and legacy. Faison said, "Hitler has earned his place in history, but they don't put monuments of him in Germany anymore. There's plenty of people who are notable characters. That doesn't mean they deserve to be in a place of honor."[13]

Institutionalizing losers and traitors allows us to remain stuck in our victimhood until we supposedly rise again. Lacking an accurate public memory, we fall for the same old ploys that divide and defeat us. In short, we lie to ourselves, which makes for an utterly disorienting existence. But, Martin Luther King Jr.'s words provide some comfort in the midst of the disorientation: "When you can finally convert a white Southerner, you have one of the most genuine, committed human beings that you'll ever find."[14]

God, I hope so, because if true, it means not a one of us is fully locked into an unalterable state of being, fated by the sins of our past generations. But, often, conversion is a long, slow rising.

---

marriage between whites and people of color, then on the books in a majority of states, were the main foreign precedents for such legislation" (*Racism: A Short History*, 123–24). Similarly, see Colin Woodard, who says, "The Nazis had praised the Deep South's caste system, which they used as a model for their own race laws. Nazi publications approved lynching as a natural response to the threat of racial mixing" (*American Nations*, 289).

12. Tisby, *Color of Compromise*, 199.
13. Allison, "It's Time to Move the Nathan Bedford Forrest Bust."
14. Baldwin, *There is a Balm in Gilead*, 78.

Part III

AIN'T NO BODY
My Introduction to Evangelical Christianity

> It really does go back to being a southerner. It's something we intuitively do—it's not something we consciously do, I think. It's just in our genes, our bones ... It's a disease. To be southern and Christian.[15]
>
> —Will D. Campbell, on why Christianity captured him

Adolescence is a confounding time of life, and my church's response to our smelly collective of gangly limbs and out-of-whack hormones did not ease the anxiety. I don't recall many sermons from my youth, but the most memorable hook confirmed my suspicions that evangelicals had a body image problem. My pastor pointed to our large cross hanging high above our expansive modern sanctuary, yelling, *"He ain't on that cross! Ain't no body on that cross."*

While his positive point was the reality of the Resurrection, I took this comment to be an overt trolling of our brothers and sisters across town at the Immaculate Conception Catholic Church. We were Baptists, after all, and I learned that the body of Jesus was not all that important unless he was being crucified for us, which we heard about weekly in graphic detail. Christmas Eve sermons whizzed past the mystery of the Incarnation for the sake of the crucifixion: *"This child was born to die for us."* It's no surprise that

---
15. Ketchin, *Christ-Haunted Landscape*, 217.

I developed a thin theology of the body. Add to this the low Christology of the Lord's Supper (He ain't in that bread), and an underdeveloped ecclesiology (beliefs about the church) and pneumatology (beliefs about the Holy Spirit), Jesus—and Christianity, for that matter—began to feel a lot like my tiny communion cracker: light, airy, nearly absent, and very white.

Where there is no flesh to see, no wounds to touch, no scars to be healed, then of course, there can be no grace. I had a body but no idea what it was for exactly. Evangelicalism left me with far more questions than answers about how to live as an embodied creature. Was Christianity really just getting saved and then learning how to suppress all questions in the name of "having faith" or "trusting in God's will"? I suspect that for those of us who have stuck it out with the faith, despite lacking the freedom to consider anything outside the norms of evangelicalism, David Dark's explanation rings true: "Any God who is nervous, defensive, or angry in the face of questions is a false god."[16] The faith is, after all, a lifetime pursuit—of asking questions, resting assured that the absence of satisfactory answers does not lead to an unsatisfying God. A little mystery, it would seem, does the Body and the soul a lot of good.

Who is an Evangelical?

Evangelicals are a puzzle to many outside of the community, but our distinctive, communal marks are fairly straight-forward, famously organized by theologian David Bebbington: *Conversionism*—a "born-again" experience, proclaiming your belief in Jesus Christ; *Activism*—a missional component where one shares her faith, i.e., evangelism; *Biblicism*—the inspiration, authority, and trustworthiness of the Bible; *Crucicentrism*—salvation comes by the cross of Christ, and his sacrifice atones for humanity's sins.[17] Scholars debate who should be considered an evangelical, but the central evangelical beliefs remain intact for the rank-and-file members.[18]

---

16. Dark, *Sacredness of Questioning Everything*, 18.

17. Bebbington, "Nature of Evangelical Religion," 37–55.

18. Thomas Kidd includes Pentecostals due to many shared beliefs with evangelicalism and their emphasis on the Holy Spirit (*Who Is an Evangelical?*, 5). Even though prosperity gospel figures are sometimes dubbed "evangelicals," their deviations from orthodox Christianity places them in an entirely different category. See also Bowler, *Blessed*. Beliefs are not the sole demarcation for evangelicalism. Being counted an evangelical can be simply responding "yes" to a pollster's question, "Do you consider yourself an evangelical or born-again Christian?" (Kurtzleben, "Are you an Evangelical?")

Evangelicalism describes the historic divide from its fundamentalist heritage, while maintaining fundamentalism's "complete confidence in the Bible" and salvation through Christ alone.[19] Fundamentalism, while massively popular at the close of the nineteenth century, received a substantial cultural challenge from Protestant liberalism (e.g., the Social Gospel movement), due to their challenge of the Bible's authorship, the divinity of Jesus, and the diminishment of salvation in favor of social activism.[20] Fundamentalism meant separation from "the world" and even separatism within its own ranks, e.g., "neo-evangelicals" and eventually just "evangelicals." Evangelicals engaged society, while not forsaking their fundamentalist theological heritage.[21] The National Association of Evangelicals (NAE) formed in 1942 around essential evangelical doctrines, leaving secondary issues up to one's individual conscience.[22] Inaugural NAE President Harold John Ockenga expressed the sentiments of the new body: "I confess to you that I am disgusted with this division and strife. I have no interest whatsoever in being involved constantly in these internal quarrels with the brethren."[23] The NAE's academic star, Carl F. H. Henry, future founding dean at Fuller Theological Seminary and editor of *Christianity Today*, deplored the degeneration of the Gospel from a "world-changing message" to the fundamentalist's "world-resisting message."[24]

The South did not experience as much of the theological shift during the early twentieth century, because, first, the Social Gospel was a Northern, urban movement, and second, there was relative cultural homogeneity in the South. The South did, however, produce the most transformational figure on the road from fundamentalist withdrawal to evangelical

---

19. Fundamentalism is not a monolithic sect, but as Marsden puts it, a "religious movement" from within various denominations (*Fundamentalism and American Culture*, 3; 118–23). See also Sandeen, *Roots of Fundamentalism*, 188–207.

20. See Carpenter, *Revive Us Again*, 33–56.

21. "New evangelical" signifies the ecumenical approach of the organization, as well as the fact that no hard, fast division was yet complete with fundamentalists, as the words "evangelical" and "fundamentalist" were in Marsden's words, "interchangeable" (Marsden, *Reforming Fundamentalism*, 3, 48).

22. The NAE statement of faith included seven points: (1) The Bible as the inspired, authoritative, and infallible Word of God; (2) The Triune God of Father, Son, and Holy Spirit; (3) Christ's deity; (4) His virgin birth, His sinless life, and atonement for sin; (5) His bodily resurrection and ascension; (6) Christ's return in power and glory; (7) The necessity of the new birth (Wright, "Historical Statement of Events," 15).

23. Ockenga, "Unvoiced Multitudes," 32.

24. Henry, *Uneasy Conscience*, 19.

engagement in Southern Baptist evangelist Billy Graham, whose crusades reached millions in person or by radio and television.[25] Graham, more so than any other person, changed the face and tone of American evangelicalism, so much so that George Marsden wrote, "During the 1950s and 1960s the simplest, though very loose, definition of an evangelical in the broad sense was 'anyone who likes Billy Graham.'"[26]

By the 1980s, "evangelical" was nearly synonymous with "Republican." The majority of white evangelicals have supported every Republican presidential nominee since Eisenhower. Even though an organized Evangelical Left existed by then and still persists today, it has never matched the political power of conservative groups like Focus on the Family, the Moral Majority, and the Family Research Council, just to name a few. Support for or opposition to Donald Trump's presidency represents the latest fault-line for evangelicals. Thomas Kidd says, "White evangelicals' uncritical fealty to the GOP is real, and that fealty has done so much damage to the movement that it is uncertain whether the term *evangelical* can be rescued from its political and racial connotations."[27]

"Evangelical" may already be a bankrupt term that no one wants to be tagged with or claim for themselves; it is certainly not a desirable label for most Black Christians. Race remains at the center of evangelicalism's meaning. For example, Frances FitzGerald purposely omits Black, born-again Christians from her Pulitzer Prize-winning book *The Evangelicals* on white evangelical movements, saying,

> theirs is a different story, mainly one of resistance to slavery and segregation, but also of the creation of centers for self-help and community in a hostile world. Some African American denominations identify as evangelical, but because of their history, their religious traditions are not the same as those of white evangelicals.[28]

---

25. Evangelicals and Southern Baptists were not considered to be one-in-the-same during the period. They had different organizational apparatuses, with Southern Baptists generally preferring to work within their own denomination. Over time, historians have sometimes conflated the terms, since all Southern Baptists would be considered evangelicals, although not all evangelicals would be Southern Baptists. See Spain, *At Ease in Zion*, ix. See also Garrett et al., *Are Southern Baptists "Evangelicals?"*; Dockery, *Southern Baptists and American Evangelicals*; Hankins, *Uneasy in Babylon*, 14–40.

26. Marsden, *Understanding Fundamentalism and Evangelicalism*, 6.

27. Kidd, *Who Is an Evangelical?*, 154.

28. FitzGerald, *Evangelicals*, 3.

Jemar Tisby offers a helpful clarification for why FitzGerald's omission is appropriate, adding that while many Black Christians share theological beliefs with white evangelicals, many are reticent to refer to themselves as evangelicals.[29] Tisby poses crucial questions concerning why "white evangelicalism" swallows up other varieties of the faith:

> "What limits do white evangelicals place on black Christians?" or "When do black Christians distance themselves from white evangelicalism based on race and justice concerns?" In other words, can black Christians bring both their race and their religion with them into white evangelical spaces?[30]

This problem endemic to white evangelicalism—a disembodied faith concerned with matters of the soul—neglects or refuses to hear day-to-day experiences of people of color. Hence, a person of color raising matters of racial justice in white evangelical circles runs the risk of being dismissed as being "political" or a "social justice warrior."[31]

What is Our Problem?

White evangelicalism has been defined more by what it is against rather than the "good news" of Jesus. Dividing continually from ourselves contributes to our utter disorientation, and I cannot help but wonder whether or not a people who constantly divide become inured to being unreconciled? The church is a worshiping community under the shared claim that Jesus Christ has died; Christ has risen; Christ will come again. The church, more particularly, orients me within the world shaping my imagination of my place in God's kingdom and my calling to love my neighbor. Would the outside world categorize us this way now? Would we be known by our love? Uh, no.

The greatest problem for white evangelicals is that we are not who we claim to be. LifeWay, a Southern Baptist media outlet, released research in late 2017 showing that less than 45 percent of self-identified evangelicals

---

29. Tisby, "Are Black Christians Evangelicals?" 266. Tisby cites polling data from the Pew Religious Landscape in 2014, revealing only 6 percent of Black Protestants identify themselves as evangelicals (271).

30. Tisby, "Are Black Christians Evangelicals?" 272.

31. For an example, see Stewart, "As a Black Person, I'm Done Helping White Christians Feel Better About Race."

"strongly agree with core evangelical beliefs."[32] While theology alone is not enough to describe the current constitution of American evangelicalism, examining evangelical beliefs allows us to weigh serious charges against our failed praxis. Philosopher Tad Delay levies one of the strongest charges, calling white evangelicalism little more than a "reactionary, theological improvisation around whiteness" and "a faith organized around fantasies curating the enjoyment of—not the flight from—turmoil and anxiety."[33] At its worst, white evangelicals' self-understanding of religious "chosenness" merges into favored statuses of racial and national identities. The danger of "chosenness," in Delay's words, "means never second-guessing your narcissism or cruelty."[34] By the early 2000s, even some Southern Baptists were acknowledging the public's perception of the denomination as "mean and negative."[35]

In the proceeding essays, I want to show how white, southern evangelical beliefs and practices have cohered to protect the racial world we created for ourselves. Chicago pastor David Swanson frames the crisis well by drawing on James K. A. Smith's work, saying, "White Christianity is not making disciples who reflect and announce the division-healing kingdom of God," because they have "been blind to the powerful racial discipleship that has formed the imaginations of white Christians." Racial discipleship means our imaginations have been oriented away from God's kingdom toward the divisions our engulfing cultures have produced, and, as I've described, we've been a party to creating. Swanson puts it starkly, saying "Because White Christianity has largely ignored this deforming cultural discipleship, we have been unable to resist it."[36] So, let's resist it by first naming our malformation, particularly how evangelicalism's marks (re-ordered here) have been distorted on the issue of race: *Conversionism*—a born again experience where one believes her actions are now righteous, irrespective of the societal repercussions those beliefs produce; *Crucicentrism*—a reduction of Jesus Christ to his cross, diminishing his life, leaving few theological resources to comprehend complex societal problems; *Biblicism*—a way of

---

32. Smietana, "Many Who Call Themselves Evangelical Don't Actually Hold Evangelical Beliefs." See also LifeWay and Ligoner Ministries research summarized in Jeremy Weber, "Christian, What Do You Believe? Probably a Heresy about Jesus, Says Survey."

33. Delay, *Against*, 5, 8.

34. Delay, *Against*, 9.

35. FitzGerald quotes Jimmy Draper Jr., who was the head of Southern Baptist publishing (*Evangelicals*, 559).

36. Swanson, *Rediscipling the White Church*, 20, 24.

PART III: AIN'T NO BODY

honoring and interpreting Scripture that makes little room for individual experience, meaning he (and it's always he) who holds interpretive power is the sole authority; lastly, an *Activism* that promotes assimilationism to white, Western norms, essentially baptizes white supremacy.

In addition to the racial demographic shift coming in the United States during the next quarter century, "the Nones"—those who claim no religious affiliation—are rising, now a quarter of all Americans.[37] Regardless of their prior traditions, or *why* they claim no faith, the Nones' absence from the Body is a kind of disembodiment. As *Baptist News* writer Allan Bean says, "Aging white evangelicals are fighting like there's no tomorrow because . . . there isn't."[38] This apocalyptic fear becomes a metaphorical death-grip on the faithful, who in turn interpret Christianity to be one more arena in which to seize and keep power. Soong-Chan Rah claims, "American evangelical inability to move beyond Christian triumphalism arises from the inability to hear voices outside the dominant white male narrative."[39] Assuming the future will include white folk, Southerners, and evangelicals—even in some amalgamation of those colliding communities—we need to chart a way forward for the generations who will follow us.

So, what do we do? Baptist theologian James McClendon's words hearten me: "The best way to understand theology is to see it."[40] We go forward, following Jesus, and modeling him for others (1 Cor 11:1). Discipleship is not a set of intellectual exercises or a mental checklist of beliefs. Faith requires practice. Gushee and Stassen's term "incarnational discipleship" means "practicing the way of life that was embodied and practiced by Jesus, as recorded in Scriptures," an ethic contrasted by ones "more abstract than concrete, more disembodied than embodied."[41] Gushee and Stassen's definition contrasts with the version of white evangelicalism many of us know: One so focused on the absent body upon the cross or at the Table that one could begin to feel invisible personally. Total depravity is a fine doctrine, but when its preached *ad nauseum*, swallowing up every other thought the Church has ever produced, then your "somebody-ness" gets

---

37. Cooper et al.,"Exodus." Pew Study years later matched this finding with the atheists, agnostics, or "nothing in particular reaching 26 percent ("In U.S., Decline of Christianity Continues at Rapid Pace").
38. Bean, "Last Call for Aging White Evangelicals."
39. Rah, *Prophetic Lament*, 60.
40. McClendon, *Biography as Theology*, 20.
41. Gushee and Stassen, *Kingdom Ethics*, 2nd ed., 461.

lost, and you come to feel like you just ain't nobody. You decrease, not so much in the humble way John the Baptist acknowledged giving way to the Messiah's ministry (John 3:30), but instead, your diminishment becomes pathological, spilling out to appease an angry God, which is not grace. It's hell.

My good life is directly connected to your good life, never a possession of my own; life is only ever a gift. I want my relationships—personal and public, intimate and neighborly—to take on a grace that is beyond my comprehension. I want others to see me the way in which I want to be seen, and there is no way to do so apart from embodied existence. We understand theology by seeing it and doing it in community. McClendon reminds us that "presence" is the practice of "being there for and with the other . . . It is refusing the temptation to withdraw mentally and emotionally; but it is also on occasion putting our own body's weight and shape alongside the neighbor, the friend, the lover in need."[42] God's design for creation is clear through the revelatory vision of the Kingdom fulfilled in all its diverse glory:

> After this I looked, and there was a great multitude that no one could count, from every nation, from all tribes and peoples and languages, standing before the throne and before the Lamb, robed in white, with palm branches in their hands. They cried out in a loud voice, saying, "Salvation belongs to our God who is seated on the throne, and to the Lamb!" (Rev 7:9–10)

Discipleship is incomplete if we attempt to isolate ourselves into tribes. If we deny that we were made for intimate fellowship—one that emerges from our gathering together, in all our great diversity—then we will not live life as God intended. We might remain a white, southern evangelical, but I'm not so certain we'll feel very human.

---

42. McClendon, *Systematic Theology: Ethics*, 106.

9

GIVE ME THE BLOOD

American Messiah for the Possessed and Dispossessed

> In Texas, it was unclear whether the Southern Baptist pastors started looking like Texas politicians, or Texas politicians started looking like Southern Baptist preachers.[1]
>
> —Stanley Hauerwas

My first ministry position out of divinity school took me back to a West Tennessee congregation, just in time for the invasion of those dubbed "the neighborhood kids," meaning the poor, Black children from the neighborhood adjacent to the church. Jesus would have simply called them "neighbors."

One Wednesday night the kids began showing up to play basketball and stare at the white people having a nice dinner in the fellowship hall. Soon thereafter, the children joined us for mealtime, but not without some grumbling within the congregation. Our neighbors' presence sparked congregational meetings replete with sound theological reasoning for the "least of these," as well as calculations of how the neighborhood kids would end our church. The latter musings were typically proffered as cold pragmatism by "business guy," who prefaced nearly every statement with the deeply

---

1. Oppenheimer, "For God, Not Country."

undescriptive phrase, *"You see, in the business world...,"* followed by some inane conclusion about our path forward.

But "business guy" was superseded by "Business Man," and Business Man's net worth had two commas, so he was fully aware of the power his bank account held in our community, which he eventually wielded via a letter to the church's board:

> Will combining our Wednesday family night programs . . . with the mission project of healing the neighborhood kids hurt our Church? I think the mission project of trying to help teach our neighborhood kids about Jesus is great and I commend the people that are putting the effort to teach these kids. But let us face the unfortunate truth. How many of the neighborhood kids would come any night if we said that the gym was not available and if we did not serve a free meal[?]

Business Man warned that "several of our younger couples" were uncomfortable with the neighborhood kids, which was a clear warning shot to the board and clergy. Business Man's generous solution was to pay for a program for the kids, including Bible study, recreation, and a healthy meal . . . just not on Wednesday night.

You know, separate but equal.

He concluded with a hopeful tone projecting a thriving church with more young couples (who tithed) *and* a neighborhood influenced by Christ's love. The mission never began, and eventually our neighbors stopped showing up after we put in place a web of bureaucratic tape that no ten-year-old could possibly navigate. Any naiveté I had about money's power in the church evaporated when the last neighborhood kid crossed the church threshold for the last time. Business Man has also chewed up and spit out many a minister, and it never works the other way around.

Business Man thrives in American churches, because wealth and rugged individualism are adopted Christian virtues. Evangelical individualism is the syncretism of Christian theology with American ideals: God endows us with freedom, and limited government allows individuals the right to self-determination. But, to be "born again"—conversionism—means we turn from one way of living in exchange for the way of Jesus, which *should* direct our attention to loving our neighbors. Too often, the way of Jesus is confused with our way of life; self-interest, it would seem, is a poor substitute for the work of the Holy Spirit.

Business Man was operating out of what had been the southern norm for over fifty years (at that time). As one of the last bastions of Christendom, southern society has had little-to-no separation between its church-goers and those who ran city halls. Historians have debated whether southern evangelicals were "captive" to their culture in the mid-twentieth century, or that southern culture was so shaped by a version of Christianity that it made little sense to speak of them as two competing forces.[2] Robert Linder says the post-World War II years were an "era when evangelicals were most coopted by the forces of the status quo."[3] Kenneth Bailey says as southern Christians were confronted with the possibility of losing their newly-won members, they succumbed to filling their houses of prayer with "contrived appeals, of catch phrases, of canvasses, quotas, and pledges" and other strategies of the marketplace.[4] Likewise, Edward Queen says, "like anyone selling a product Baptists were unwilling to antagonize potential customers," and dealt with the issue of race with extreme caution.[5]

Following World War II, evangelical Southerners enjoyed massive growth and increasing cultural influence. The Southern Baptists, for example, saw rapid membership growth, doubling to nearly 10 million members from 1941 to 1961, leading to huge financial gains, and increasingly serving more urban and suburban areas than rural areas.[6] "The South is a Baptist empire," T. B. Maston said, meaning they were also responsible "for the solution of the pressing problems of the South, one of the greatest of which is the race problem."[7]

Southern Baptists responded to Jim Crow in three ways, according to Mark Newman: First, "militant segregationists" defended segregation using the Bible just as they had for slavery, an argument that was falling out of fashion.[8] Second, "moderate segregationists" employed social and cultural arguments to support segregation, avoiding making the issue a "moral"

---

2. Eighmy, *Churches in Cultural Captivity* and Hill, *Southern Churches in Crisis Revisited*.

3. Linder, "Resurgence of Evangelical Social Concern (1925–75)," 200.

4. Bailey, *Southern White Protestantism in the Twentieth Century*, 132.

5. Queen, *Baptists are the Center of Gravity*, 82.

6. By 1961 rural membership comprised less than 33 percent of SBC churches (Ammerman, *Baptist Battles*, 52).

7. Maston, *Of One*, 31.

8. Newman, *Getting Right with God*, ix.

PART III: AIN'T NO BODY

one, which would certainly require their ministerial response.[9] Third, the minority "progressives" challenged segregation and sought to improve racial relations long before the start of the formal civil rights movement.[10] The high walls of the white, southern evangelical empire protected its wealth and way of life, which was but whiteness, baptized and militarized. Churches were a safe place for booming families to worship the risen Lord, and for their rising tithes to lift everyone, including their neighbors, so long as they remained separated.

There Will Be Blood

Paul Thomas Anderson's haunting film, *There Will Be Blood* (2007), follows the life of ruthless oilman Daniel Plainview, who has an admitted unquenchable competition for annihilating his rivals. Plainview receives a tip about oil fields underneath the unfertile land of the Sunday family ranch, and he gains support for the sale within the family from Eli Sunday, the ambitious, charismatic preacher. Plainview buys the land, launches his drilling enterprise, and promises the townspeople flourishing schools, wells, infrastructure, and a church. It's salvation for this barren land.

Eli and his parishioners overstep their welcome, though, singing at the oil derrick and inviting workers to church, drawing Plainview's ire. Later, Plainview comes to Sunday's ramshackle church to be baptized, only because it was a negotiated condition by one of Sunday's congregants for Plainview to build a pipeline through his land. As Plainview kneels before the congregation, uncomfortably awaiting his baptism, Eli drags a public confession from him about his many sins. "Beg for the blood!" Eli bellows

---

9. State denominational papers like *The Baptist Standard* (Texas) plotted a middle ground, rejecting segregationist rhetoric, but also avoided making socially progressive statements. Editor Ewing S. James stated in 1955: "Personally, I think it would be good to keep the races segregated, but I cannot prove by the Bible that this is His plan; and I do not think that any other can do so . . . . If this were a moral question then Christians should initiate a referendum, but since the race problem is a social matter I believe God expects his people to do the best they can with whatever circumstances [they] may obtain" (Killingsworth, "Here I Am, Stuck in the Middle with You," 88).

10. Newman, *Getting Right with God*, 65–86. Newman shows that even progressive Baptists in the South had stages of adjustment to the developing realities of increased Black agency or even desegregation and integration.

to Plainview, who protests under his breath, saying, "Just give me the blood, Eli. Let me get out of here. Give me the blood, Lord, and let me get away."[11]

The young pastor strikes Plainview over and over—beating the devil out of him—until the oilman accepts Jesus as his Lord and Savior. As the baptismal waters trickle down his face, Plainview smiles slightly and speaks one last and audible word before exiting the church: Pipeline. It is the vessel through which the earth's "blood" will be freed from its earthly tombs. The choreographed devil's dance of unfettered capitalism and religious fundamentalism is complete, and tragedy awaits the preacher who believes he can play the game just as well as the oilman. In the final scene, a once-wealthy, now-chastened Eli slinks into Plainview's extravagant mansion, begging for financial help. Daniel laps it up and promises to help his old friend if Eli will just renounce his faith and declare himself to be a fraud. Eli relents, giving Plainview the satisfaction before he bludgeons the pastor to death, shouting, "I'm finished." Unlike the Christ, who defeated the last enemy of Death by taking violence upon himself, Plainview is a kind of antichrist, defeating his final competitor insuring he alone remains the victor: The finality of seeking and gaining it all—being possessed by winning. So much winning.

The fictionalized Plainview story is a recognizably American story of the cozy relationship between the wealthy and the religious. Kevin Kruse details in his book *One Nation Under God: How Corporate America Invented Christian America* how conservatives of all stripes sought to shape the nation for much of the last century. Beginning in the late 1930s, concerns grew among business titans and conservative Christian clergy about the long-term effects of FDR's New Deal, believing it would transform the country into one dependent upon government welfare. They linked their concerns to Christianity in this way: If following Jesus is a *personal* decision, which paralleled American individualism, "big government" handouts were not just anathema to that ideal, but a road to Communism.

Thus, a religious movement was underway, including campaigns and events, to make Americans more religious with the ancillary benefits of countering the Communist threat. The "Freedom Under God" celebration, for example, was organized in 1951 for the 175th anniversary of the signing of the Declaration of Independence, which included a who's who of mid-century giants: Former president Herbert Hoover, General Douglas MacArthur, Bing Crosby, Cecil B. DeMille, Walt Disney, Ronald Reagan, J. Howard Pew, Conrad Hilton, James L. Kraft, Harvey Firestone, E. F.

---

11. Anderson, *There Will Be Blood*.

Hutton, Fred Maytag, Henry Luce, J. C. Penny, Norman Vincent Peale, and many other conservative luminaries.[12] Through a highly-coordinated effort in virtually every available medium, Americans received messages from some of their most trusted celebrities and companies about the goodness of America and the proper, faithful posture a nation should maintain if it was to defeat Communism.

God-and-country messages found willing recipients among the American people, who were already steeped in apocalyptic visions of their world's end, and evangelists like a young Billy Graham implored his growing audience to turn back to God for the last days might be upon them. Historian Matthew Sutton summarizes that Graham "never doubted that faith and American nationalism walked hand in hand and he believed that God had selected the United States to help prepare the world for coming judgment."[13]

President Dwight D. Eisenhower's administration (1953–1961) oversaw the institutionalization of America's civil religion: "One nation under God" was inserted into the Pledge of Allegiance (1954) and "In God We Trust" became a permanent fixture on all currency and postal stamps (1955). Considering how evangelical influence extended across the nation—due to media savvy, growing institutions, and new parachurch organizations—it becomes easier to understand how the 1950s became revered as a golden age for white Christians. The nation became in Kruse's words, "fervent believers in a very vague religion,"[14] where piety and patriotism merged, creating an "interpretation of America's fundamental nature [that] would have a seemingly permanent place in the national imagination."[15]

Court Evangelicals

Proximity to power is an intoxicant, one evangelicals have been all-too-happy to imbibe regardless of their pietistic traditions. Billy Graham found open arms by the Eisenhower and Nixon administrations, until the latter's resignation over Watergate chastened the evangelist from further overt political engagement. Jimmy Carter's evangelical *bona fides* were undeniable, but he was defeated by Ronald Reagan, the great communicator who knew

12. Kruse, *One Nation Under God*, 27–34.
13. Sutton, *American Apocalypse*, 327.
14. Kruse, *One Nation Under God*, 68.
15. Kruse, *One Nation Under God*, 124.

how to talk the talk evangelicals wanted to hear. Reagan was the beneficiary of those Thomas Kidd calls "Republican insider evangelicals" for as long as he needed them; however, Reagan paid little mind to their agenda after his reelection in 1984.[16] George W. Bush enjoyed a resurgent evangelical movement during the 2000 presidential campaign and beyond, promoting "compassionate conservatism" and creating the White House Office of Faith-Based and Community Initiatives; yet he, too, never satisfied the white evangelical agenda to the satisfaction of the base.

Enter Donald Trump.

Four months prior to Trump's presidential victory, Robert Jones gave a premature eulogy for white Christian's political influence, stating, "After a long life spanning nearly two hundred and forty years, White Christian America—a prominent cultural force in the nation's history—has died."[17] But it was not yet so. Jones deemed Trump's evangelical supporters to be nostalgia voters rather than the "values voters" as they were once known to be.[18] Robert Jeffress, the pastor of First Baptist Church Dallas, summed up his rationale for supporting Trump: "I want the meanest, toughest, son-of-a-you-know-what I can find in that role, and I think that's where many evangelicals are."[19]

When values are thrown out the window in the name of cultural preservation, pastors sound like politicians. Calvin University historian Kristin Kobes DuMez says in *Jesus and John Wayne* that evangelicalism has been "inextricably linked to a staunch to patriarchal authority, gender difference, and Christian nationalism, and all of these intertwined with white racial identity."[20] White evangelicals' draw to strongmen, no matter how odious a figure might be, is too often a feature of the faith, not a bug. In other words, we're not captives to our culture; this is the culture we have created. DuMez writes:

> Despite evangelicals' frequent claims that the Bible is the source of their social and political commitments, evangelicalism must be seen as a cultural and political movement rather than as a community is defined chiefly by its theology. Evangelical views on any

---

16. Kidd, *Who Is an Evangelical?*, 94.
17. Jones, *End of White Christian America*, 1.
18. Sarah Pulliam Bailey, "How Nostalgia for White Christian America Drove So Many Americans to Vote for Trump."
19. DuMez, "Donald Trump and Militant Evangelical Masculinity."
20. DuMez, *Jesus and John Wayne*, 7

given issue are facets of this larger cultural identity, and no number of Bible verses will dislodge the greater truths at the heart of it.[21]

Which is why "Make America Great Again" was not so much a campaign promise, as a messianic mission.

Donald Trump wanted to save us: "Nobody knows the system better than me, which is why I alone can fix it."[22] White evangelicals needed a savior to shape the courts that could forestall what they understood to be nothing short of a cultural apocalypse of unchecked abortion and increasing LGBTQ rights. White, southern evangelicals knew better than most how federal judges could end or preserve a way of life. Trump's allies have bestowed upon him appellations such as the "King of Israel," "the second coming of God,"[23] "the most pro-Christian president that we've had,"[24] or simply the "chosen one."[25] Trump's promise to recapture the halcyon days of America also traded upon a pact steeped in bigotry. Trump's populist wave was an angry religious revival of America's worst elements, a message bereft of unity, justice, or compassion. Only the Donald would so brazenly abandon these virtues of civil religion. When you're an American messiah they let you do whatever you want.

Trump's flaws were excused or justified by those who Messiah College historian John Fea names "court evangelicals," including a coalition of the prosperity gospel personalities and a faction of the charismatic movement. Fea's category of the "New Old Religious Right" includes recognizable names like Franklin Graham, Jerry Falwell Jr. (now-former president of Liberty University), Dr. James Dobson, and those with sizable platforms like Rev. Jeffress and Tony Perkins.[26] What unites these figures is their performances of slobbering deference to build up Trump's fragile ego, likening him to biblical characters, most frequently to the Persian king, Cyrus, who freed ancient Israel from exile and ushered the return to the homeland.[27] With every bizarre pronouncement, with every alibi for unethical behavior, with every grift, "evangelical" comes to mean little more than a decaying

21. DuMez, *Jesus and John Wayne*, 298.
22. Jackson, "Donald Trump Accepts GOP Nomination, Says 'I Alone Can Fix' System."
23. Marcotte, "Evangelicals told Trump he was 'Chosen' by God."
24. Watts, "'Imaginary God' of Rev. Robert Jeffress."
25. Folley, "Rick Perry Says Trump is the 'Chosen One.'"
26. Fea, *Believe Me*, 115–52.
27. Howe, *Immoral Majority*, 48–68.

body housing a legion of demonic spirits. As Marva Dawn says, "We must let his Word describe our world rather than vice versa. To let ideologies control our theological work is to be subverted by powers other than God."[28] Writer and radio show host Eric Metaxas offers the clearest counterpoint for Trump supporters: "Trump makes us reexamine our theology."[29]

At the 2020 National Prayer Breakfast (another innovation of the Eisenhower era) Arthur Brooks called upon the nation to follow the commands of Jesus to "love your enemies and pray for those who persecute you" (Matt 5:44) in his keynote address. Trump responded saying, "Arthur, I don't know if I agree with you." Trump continued, "As everybody knows, my family, our great country, and your president, have been put through a terrible ordeal by some very dishonest and corrupt people." Trump aired his grievances concerning Senator Mitt Romney and Speaker Nancy Pelosi, both of whom said their faith informed their respective decisions against the president during the impeachment proceedings. Trump added, "I don't like people who use their faith as justification for doing what they know is wrong."[30] Weeks later, peaceful protesters were tear-gassed so Trump could stage a photo-op holding a Bible in front of St. John's Episcopal Church in downtown DC.

Fea says white evangelicals' political playbook has been "defined by the politics of fear, the pursuit of worldly power, and a nostalgic longing for a national past that never existed in the first place."[31] However, nostalgia comes with an unacknowledged price for many Americans who never found the 1950s to be so great.[32] Following the 2016 election, polling by the Public Religion Research Institute (PRRI) showed that while 74 percent of white evangelicals believed American culture had worsened since the fifties, 62 percent of African Americans and 57 percent of Hispanic Americans thought the culture had changed for the better.[33] In the runup to the 2020 election, the Pew Forum found that 77 percent of white Christians agreed that President Trump "fights for what I believe in," while no

---

28. Dawn, *Powers, Weakness, and the Tabernacling of God*, 84.
29. Fea, "Trump is the New King Cyrus."
30. Brooks, "Trump and I Disagreed at the National Prayer Breakfast."
31. Fea, *Believe Me*, 6–7.
32. See Coontz, *Way We Never Were*.
33. Bailey, "How Nostalgia for White Christian America Drove So Many Americans to Vote for Trump."

other demographic exceeded 39 percent in agreement with the statement.[34] Numbers never tell the entire story, but they reveal the rift between white evangelicals and people of color in the Trump era.

Nostalgia holds a kind of resurrecting power, breathing new life into communities and individuals. Nostalgia is, as Tad Delay says, a self-centered and "fictionalized" rendering of the past that "grabs those who see their declining status and prefer to blame a race or gender rather than a capitalist."[35] Evangelicals will never blame a capitalist, because too much of their funding might just be tied to how deeply they bend the knee at the altar of Trump. Gregory Thornbury, former president of King's College (2013–2017), a Christian liberal arts college in Manhattan, names the financial pressure Christian leaders face in this current political climate: "Who is an evangelical college president going to talk to, to raise $10 million a year? Right-wing crazy people." He adds, "All of the money that is behind these evangelical institutions is being given by Trump supporters."[36]

Trump's evangelicals must consider the long-term effect that ignoring his inflammatory rhetoric and racist policies will have on their ministries and institutions. White evangelicals who simultaneously want to reclaim their country, but also want some form of racial reconciliation, have backed themselves into a corner, the full repercussions of which are not yet known. Southern Seminary president Albert Mohler, for example, who called out Trump-supporting evangelicals in 2016, saying, "Sadly, many evangelicals overlooked his racial signaling and his crude nationalism," decided to support Trump in 2020.[37] Thornbury claims, "The white nationalism of fundamentalism was sleeping there like a latent gene, and it just came

---

34. Pew Research Center, "White Evangelicals See Trump as Fighting for their Beliefs, Though Many Have Mixed Feelings about his Personal Conduct."

35. Delay, *Against*, 139.

36. Morris, "False Idol—Why the Christian Right Worships Donald Trump."

37. Mohler, "Donald Trump Has Created an Excruciating Moment for Evangelicals"; Bailey, "Prominent Southern Baptist Albert Mohler"; See also Graham, "What It's Like to Be Black at Liberty University" who details Liberty employees who resigned due to a number of President Falwell's actions and inactions; Joel Anderson covers how Liberty's Black athletes have responded to Falwell's relationship to Trump and the university's political relationships ("Liberty University Poured Millions Into Sports").

roaring back with a vengeance."[38] Religious leaders who supported President Trump will have to answer to Black leaders within their ranks.[39]

Possessed or Dispossessed?

By November 2019, in the middle of the House impeachment hearings, Franklin Graham joined Metaxas's show and surmised that opposition to Trump was "almost a demonic power that is trying . . . " Metaxas interrupted, saying, "I would disagree. It's not *almost* demonic. You know and I know, at the heart, it's a spiritual battle."[40] Graham and Metaxas may be correct, just not in the way they think.

The Gerasene Demoniac (Mark 5)—a man never known by name, only by affliction—beckons us to understand our own possession.[41] The man was left alone with the dead, cutting himself night and day (Mark 5:5). His humanity had diminished to the point that his community could not suffer his presence, binding him with shackles and chains. They cast him out to live in the tombs, imposing impurity on him (vv. 3–4). The possessed man noticed Jesus coming "from a distance" (v. 6). The Gospel writer, Mark, signals Roman occupation to be a plague on this geography evidenced by the demon's name "Legion"—a conflation of the Roman empire's military occupation of the people and the demon's possession of the man. But Jesus had come, a king reclaiming his territory, saying: "Come out of the man, you unclean spirit!" (v. 8). In this exorcism, Obery Hendricks says Jesus is prophetically calling out "the Roman military presence in Israel exactly

---

38. Morris, "False Idol—Why the Christian Right Worships Donald Trump." Conservative evangelicals who joined the "Never Trump" movement denied their embrace of white nationalism, although others have supported Thornbury's claim. Rod Dreher challenges Thornbury's claims ("Religious Liberty and 'White Nationalism'"). Ben Howe says of the alt-right that it is "A movement . . . composed in no small part of self-identified Christians" (*Immoral Majority*, 136). Additionally, Anderson University theology professor Luke Stamps Tweeted (April 25, 2020), "I want to ignore them, but it is deeply discouraging to know that there are young alt-right ideologues coming out of our seminaries. I thought this mindset would die out." https://twitter.com/lukestamps/status/1254159118618820608.

39. See Blair, "SBC Leader Albert Mohler Indicates Support for Donald Trump"; Onwuchekwa, "4 Reasons We Left the SBC"; Burke, "'Why Black Christians are Bracing for a 'Whitelash.'"

40. Brown, "'Demonic Power': Franklin Graham Claims."

41. A version of this section appeared in *The Other Journal* (Phillips, "Jesus and the Dispossessed"). See also Phillips, "Lord, When Did We See You?" 275–79.

what it has proven to be to his people: a destructive, demonic, unclean presence."[42] Fittingly, Jesus drove the demon into the swine, another clear signal of the occupiers' uncleanliness. The demon's cry "not to send them out of the country" (5:10) reveals that the Legion is attached to the province and feels its kingdom slipping from its possession. The Legion has made itself a home, and it likes it there. As William Stringfellow says, there is but one ideal that "governs all demonic powers so long as they exist—survival."[43]

Earlier in Mark's Gospel, Jesus is confronted by another possessed man in the synagogue, and performs an exorcism (1:23). Jesus says that he is binding the strong man in order to plunder his house (3:27), proclaiming himself to be stronger than the powers that bind humanity.[44] Willie Jennings reminds us that, "The demonic moves in and through human interactions, social processes, and ways of thinking and acting so deeply inculcated in us that we could rightly call them ways of being possessed." And to punctuate the point, Jennings says, "These demons make us money."[45]

Consider the plight of the demoniac detailed in Mark's third act of the story, following the swine-dive:

> The herdsmen fled and told it in the city and in the country. And people came to see what it was that had happened. And they came to Jesus and saw the demon-possessed man, the one who had had the legion, sitting there, clothed and in his right mind, and they were afraid (5:14–15).

The freed demoniac, clothed and in his right mind, terrifies his people, so much so that they beg Jesus to leave them (v. 17). Though the healed man begs to come with Jesus, he says, "go home to your friends and tell them how much the Lord has done for you" (vv. 18–19). We do not know his story's ending, just that he had to return to the place he had terrorized.

I am possessed. I have enjoyed the benefits of empire. I have enjoyed the privileges of my race and protections of my home's embrace of racial division, a clear affliction by our regional demon. There is a Legion inside of us. As we have bound others, we ourselves have become bound, enslaved to the status quo that will always choose capital over communion. Brian Bantum explains:

---

42. Hendricks, *Politics of Jesus*, 147.

43. William Stringfellow quoted in Dawn's *Powers, Weakness, and the Tabernacling of God*, 75.

44. Myers, *Binding the Strong Man*, 191, 194.

45. Jennings, "Is America Wiling to be Freed from its Demons?"

> Race is a story. It is a story written onto our bodies and the patterns of our society. The story takes time to form, beginning with questions. "Who are those people? Why are they so different than us? How do we begin to make sense of those differences?" Like earth slowly compressed over time, the various stories that come from these questions harden, becoming stones from which walls and towers are built, the structure of a city and a people.[46]

Maybe as the possessed, we are called to rage in our tomb for a time, awaiting the Christ. Maybe this entombment provides time for our vision to be restored, so that when the cracks of light illuminate the darkness, the Christ can be seen for who he truly is, rather than one who conveniently blesses all of our endeavors. The great healer and prophet, the king, might even tell us to return home, a not-so-joyful occasion. After all, telling white evangelicals that they, too, are possessed—by racism, whiteness, mammonism—means one might be cast out. When the powers hear that the strong man has been bound by Jesus and their house is set to be plundered (3:27), it will not be received as good news.

---

46. Bantum, *Death of Race*, 158–59.

10

THE GAME IS RIGGED

Ignorance allows people to disregard the consequences of their actions. And sometimes it leads to consequences even they did not intend.[1]

—Michael Lewis, *The Fifth Risk*

Allow me to put on my tinfoil hat for a minute, when I tell you that the game is rigged. Playing Mouse Trap as a child taught me this.

My one-sided beef with the popular board game was renewed last Christmas, when my nephews asked me to play the updated Mouse Trap with them. In my day Mouse Trap never delivered on its advertised promise: When it worked, this well-oiled machine of ludicrously interconnected contraptions culminated in the incarceration of a plastic mouse. Alas, the beautifully orchestrated chain-reaction rarely worked, which turned out to be perfect training for the adult world, where reality seldom matches the advertisement, whether for a toy or grasping the American Dream. I didn't tell my nephews this before or during the game; they didn't need that kind of burden at the age of six.

I was mentally rehearsing my statement of solidarity with what I knew would be their imminent disappointment, until I noticed the new, sleeker apparatuses of the game. To my (I mean *our*) delight, the various elements worked as they were designed! The foot on a stick kicked the bucket with

---

1. Lewis, *Fifth Risk*, 115.

the cannonball, which rolled down the maze, launching the diver skyward to perform a perfect gainer into the pool, sending the trap rattling down atop the unsuspecting rodent. It was a Christmas miracle. After decades of working out the kinks, of refining the engineering, everything worked as intended. I joyfully played the game with them, feeling a bit less like I was trapped in a Smashing Pumpkins rage-fest during what was supposed to be play-time, no longer living like a rat in a cage of cynicism.

Evangelical Blind Spots

It defies our sense of American individualism to admit that we feel powerless in the face of circumstances outside of our own choosing—that we are caught in systems we do not understand. Furthermore, we (white people) expect those systems to work for us, and in general, they do, making "systemic racism" a difficult concept for us to comprehend. Our methods for investigating and diagnosing social ills, and thus understanding systemic problems, have been suspect. Saying, *"We live in a sinful world"* with a shrug is not a serious analysis of our problem. Yes, evangelical theology affirms that Jesus dies by crucifixion as penalty for the sins of humanity. The Bible also points to the role "powers and principalities" (powers, henceforth) play in our world, as well as how Jesus frees us from their rule. Systems play a role in our lives as much as our individual choices, and exploring this highly-complex subject can inform our work for racial equality.

Sociologists Michael Emerson and Christian Smith say white evangelicals have a limited "toolkit" to deal with racial matters. First, evangelicals interpret racism through the lens of "accountable free will individualism," meaning racism is *caused* by individual decisions and *resolved* by neighborly love. For this reason, "relationalism," the second tool, is key for evangelicals: We extend Christ's love to all people, because healthy relationships influence individuals to make good choices, like "iron sharpens iron" (Prov 27:17) as we are fond of referencing. These tools limit our vision to see individuals, rather than the world's complex structures, a blindness Emerson and Smith term "antistructuralism," the final tool. Evangelicals are taught that *individual* sins, require a *personal* confession of sins. Thus, when sin is blamed on an unseen system, to evangelicals, it sounds like avoiding accountability. Denying the system's existence, though, actually reproduces racial problems.[2]

2. Emerson and Smith, *Divided by Faith*, 76–79, 90. For an example outside of

PART III: AIN'T NO BODY

Even though we Americans value our individualism, we've also routinely received the "no 'I' in team" talk since youth sports. Additionally, our faith tradition is far less individualistic than we might believe. God addresses collectives in Israel and the church throughout the Scriptures, particularly how those communities are called to worship and do justice to each other and their outside neighbors.[3] Theologian Reinhold Niebuhr diagnoses incisively how sin functions: Self-preservation motivates individuals and groups. They assess threats to their life, loved ones, and/or possessions, all of which produce anxiety to protect them, sparking the temptation to sin. Individuals and groups are not identical, ethically speaking. An individual can change her mind through appeals to reason or empathy; she is capable of love.[4] Groups, however, do not respond to love. Niebuhr says, "The larger the group the more certainly will it express itself selfishly in the total human community. It will be more powerful and therefore more able to defy any social restraints which might be devised. It will also be less subject to internal moral restraints."[5]

Christians and their institutions are not immune from these behaviors. For example, I was in a fraternity at a Christian university, and at times, we had hilariously tame skirmishes with other frats. Because young men are, in general—and this is the correct theological term—*idiots*, the slightest misunderstanding could turn even the meekest of ministry students into a wannabe John Wick if among his group. Would they act this way on their own? Unlikely. But, individuals will do things under the cover of the group that they never would if they alone felt the repercussions.

Consider the nation-state, what Niebuhr calls, "the most absolute of all human associations."[6] The nation-state maintains its power by force and rationalizes *any* decisions in the name of its self-preservation. In the context of race, this has meant that the white majority protected its power at all costs. Niebuhr believed only coercion could alter a group's power: "However large the number of individual white men who do and who will identify themselves completely with the Negro cause, the white race in

---

theology that comes to the same conclusions in ethnic studies see Lipsitz, "Possessive Investment in Whiteness," 381.

3. See Stassen, *Thicker Jesus*. Stassen gives a robust analysis of Niebuhr and Dietrich Bonhoeffer on collective sin and repentance. Cf. Bonhoeffer, *Sanctorum Communio*.

4. Niebuhr, *Moral Man and Immoral Society*, 57.

5. Niebuhr, *Moral Man and Immoral Society*, 48.

6. Niebuhr, *Moral Man and Immoral Society*, 83.

America will not admit the Negro to equal rights if it is not forced to do so."[7] Contrary to the evangelical notion that social change comes simply by changing hearts and minds, our nation (a collective) has not responded to appeals to love.

Groups often resist just reforms, because their power is at stake, and they are particularly resistant to acknowledging any responsibility. No one likes to be blamed for something they did not perpetrate individually. And yet, as I've tried to describe throughout this book, we all have loyalties to "teams," few of which admit guilt or make amends without some arm-twisting. Two examples involving Martin Luther King Jr. illustrate Niebuhr's diagnosis of how collectives protect themselves: First, King's "Letter from Birmingham Jail" responded to eight white clergy who penned a letter against King's Easter weekend (1963) civil rights demonstrations. They varied in age, religious traditions, and even how to address racial tensions. Each one sacrificed their individuality when they co-signed the letter. The clergy called out "hatred and violence" by whites, but also affixed equal blame to demonstrators, stating, "We also point out that such actions as incite hatred and violence, however technically peaceful those actions may be, have not contributed to the resolution of our local problems."[8] Weeks later, peaceful marchers were met with police dogs and fire hoses that stripped the bark off of trees. By joining a coalition that did not represent the nuance of their individual positions, the progressive ministers let their convictions be tempered by the conservatives and gradualists. King's letter angered the ministers, as Rabbi Milton Grafman said, "Were we Klans people? Were we liberals? Were we moderates? He knew nothing about us."[9] Grafman's response proves Niebuhr's point about the impersonal nature of groups: Individuality fades into the background for the good of the team. In a brilliant maneuver, King honored their collective voice and responded to them *as one*, naming them "moderates," who he deemed "the arch-supporter[s] of the status quo."[10]

Second, King's assassination (April 4, 1968) did not lead to mass repentance by white Christians.[11] Some Southern Baptists attempted to do just that with the resolution, "A Statement Concerning the Crisis in

7. Niebuhr, *Moral Man and Immoral Society*, 253.
8. Bass, *Blessed Are the Peacemakers*, 236.
9. Bass, *Blessed Are the Peacemakers*, 6.
10. King, "Letter from Birmingham City Jail," 300.
11. Manis, "Silence or Shockwaves," 21–22.

our Nation," that read, "As a nation, we have allowed cultural patterns to persist that have deprived millions of black Americans, and other racial groups as well, of equality of recognition and opportunity in the areas of education, employment, citizenship, housing, and worship." The statement acknowledged "our share of responsibility for creating in our land conditions in which justice, order, and righteousness can prevail." The statement concluded with a final plea, asking God to "create in us a right spirit of repentance and to make us instruments of his redemption, his righteousness, his peace, and his love toward all men."[12]

Hudson Baggett, editor of the *Alabama Baptist*, rejected the statement, saying the convention "cannot confess the guilt or sins of all other Southern Baptists. Every person must confess his own sins, if they are confessed." He added, "many people resist the idea of collective guilt, especially if it is connected with certain things in which people felt they have no part directly or indirectly."[13] Baggett's words perfectly summarize the perspective that persists today among many whites, Christians included: In the absence of perceived guilt there is no reason to seek forgiveness. Sin works by blinding us to the realities of our failings, individually or collectively.

Powers that Be

One scriptural area worth exploring to address this evangelical blind spot comes in Paul's references to the mysterious "powers." The powers' identity and function is not perfectly clear. Some theologians hold that powers refer to spiritual warfare among angels and demons; others conceive them to be merely human structures.[14] Hendrik Berkhof revived the powers in theological studies, offering a mediating position between these poles: "Creation has a visible foreground, which is bound together with and dependent on an invisible background. The latter comprise 'the Powers.'" These order everyday existence within human life and keep society from

---

12. "A Statement Concerning the Crisis in our Nation."
13. "Baptist Leader Resists 'Collective Guilt' Idea," 25.
14. Rom 8:38 and 1 Pet 3:22 do not equate spiritual beings with the powers. Marva Dawn cites Rudolf Bultmann's *Theology of the New Testament* as the leading example of the "demythologizers" (*Powers, Weakness, and the Tabernacling of God*, 10). Theologians differ on how one participates in these structures in light of Christ's victory over the Powers. See Mouw, *Politics and the Biblical Drama*; Yoder, *Politics of Jesus*; Wolterstorff, "Theological Foundations for Evangelical Political Philosophy," 140–62.

falling into chaos.[15] The powers are good, created structures that order human life (Col 1:16); the powers are fallen—not left untouched by the consequences of humanity's sin (Rom 8:19-22, 38); yet the powers are also subservient under the reign of Christ following his crucifixion (Col 2:13-15; Eph 1:20-23;1 Pet 3:22).[16]

The powers also divide and dehumanize people, as they work through "structural evils such as nationalism, militarism, racism, classism, consumerism, and individualism."[17] Berkhof witnessed the powers assume a quasi-divine authority during the 1930s in Nazi-controlled Berlin: "The Powers of *Volk*, race, and state took a new grip on men," where they seemed to be "in the air."[18] Religious, political, and economic powers also imposed their rule through silence. The power of *Volk*, of blood and soil, was so engrained in Nazi Germany that it imposed fear upon some, acquiescence upon others, moving the ethical line toward genocide.[19]

In everyday language we speak about impersonal, yet impactful, forces quite often: *"The government never gets anything done,"* or *"The media can't be trusted."* This is a curious way of speaking for those who rigidly hold to individual accountability; it reveals a frustration with these structures that threaten to dominate us: The online human resources job portal where applicants never hear from a human being; small business owners stuck in a bureaucratic maze of loan applications; anyone who has dealt with health insurers. These experiences can arouse our inner Joker, willing to take our chances with a world of chaos than the so-called orderly one. These systems—the powers—expose our smallness, and no amount of requests filed through the "Contact Us" page will fix the feeling of our utter powerlessness.

The good news, revealed by Paul's letter to the Colossians (2:15ff) is that Jesus Christ breaks the hold of the powers over humanity, accomplishing three things: First, Jesus "disarms" the powers by exposing their illusory influence upon human affairs. Second, the crucified Jesus makes a "public example of them," showing their hypocrisy. After all, Jesus was crucified in

---

15. Berkhof, *Christ and the Powers*, 28–29.

16. Dawn, *Powers, Weakness, and the Tabernacling of God*, 6–7. Walter Wink organizes his view of the Powers as created good, fallen, and redeemed (Wink, *Engaging the Powers*, 65–74).

17. Boyd, "Power and Principalities," 613.

18. Berkhof, *Christ and the Powers*, 21, 32.

19. Walter Wink posits that these powers are secured and maintained by violence, or what he terms the "Domination System," (*Engaging the Powers*, 60–63, 109–13).

the name of the law: "The Pharisees, personifying piety, crucified Him in the name of piety," Berkhof says. "Pilate, representing Roman justice and law, shows what these are worth when called upon to do justice to the Truth Himself."[20] Third, Jesus "triumphs" over the powers through his Resurrection, showing his eternal innocence and sovereignty over the powers.

The G.I. Bill

Michael Lewis details in *The Fifth Risk* how the United States government—"the most complicated organization on the face of the earth," including two million federal employees taking orders from four thousand political appointees—requires constant attention to mitigate against risks. In other words, if there is a "deep state" it is simply the millions of dedicated public servants who guard against problems as broad as, "How to stop a virus, how to take a census, how to determine if some foreign country is seeking to obtain a nuclear weapon or if North Korean missiles can reach Kansas City."[21] Good systems hold societies in place.

The Servicemen's Readjustment Act of 1944—the "G.I. Bill"—is an example of a system working and failing at the same time. American folklore says the "greatest generation" carved their own path despite difficult times. They also benefited from a massive legislative effort that vastly expanded federal programs. Eleanor Roosevelt quoted a letter from a young soldier, aptly expressing their hopes and fears of returning home:

> There is one great fear in the heart of any serviceman, and it is not that he will be killed or maimed but that when he is finally allowed to go home and piece together what he can of life, he will be made to feel he has been a sucker for the sacrifice he has made.[22]

The U.S. government did not disappoint them. Many, like my grandfather, returned from war to enjoy the first fruits of a conflict-free period, keenly aware of the costs of achieving peace.

The G.I. Bill changed post-war America for 7.8 million veterans through four main benefits: First, the United States Employment Service (USES) placed veterans into jobs. Second, unemployment benefits were available to veterans for up to a year. Third, the Veterans Administration

---

20. Berkhof, *Christ and the Powers*, 37–39.
21. Lewis, *Fifth Risk*, 37–38.
22. Goodwin, *No Ordinary Time*, 512.

(VA) provided over four million low-interest home loans and two-hundred thousand other loans facilitated by the Federal Housing Administration (FHA).[23] The FHA insured low down-payments on long-term mortgages in order to encourage a flagging housing industry. In 1940, national homeownership was under 44 percent, but due to these federal interventions it rose to 55 percent by 1950 and increased to nearly 62 percent a decade later.[24] Fourth, the government paid for veterans' education at a university or vocational school. Fewer than half of the soldiers who served in World War II had high school diplomas, and approximately a fourth of all Americans had a college degree.[25] In less than a decade after the G.I. Bill's passage, the nation's college graduates had doubled.[26]

The bill's full benefits were not available to Black veterans, however, as universities, trade schools, job centers, banks, etc., maintained local control over the benefits. Local control meant the G.I. Bill's "roots were planted in poison soil," tended by segregationists like Mississippi Congressman and bill co-sponsor John Rankin.[27] Rankin's virulent racism was spurred on by his fear that Blacks, might become "the peer of the white man, and place him on terms of social and political equality with the member of the Caucasian race."[28] Local control allowed systemic abuses to short-circuit each benefit: Jobs offered to Black veterans were often unskilled, low-wage, labor positions, since the local USES office determined what "suitable" work was for each applicant. For example, in 1946, veterans in Mississippi were awarded skilled versus unskilled jobs nearly along racial lines, with whites holding 86 percent of the professional positions, and Blacks held 92 percent of the unskilled jobs.[29] If a Black veteran refused to take the job offered by the typically white USES counselor, he would lose his unemployment benefit.

The deepest systemic abuses were felt through housing. The FHA showed a consistent bias in favor of all-white subdivisions and *against*

23. Mettler, *Soldiers to Citizens*, 6.

24. U.S. Census Bureau, "Historical Census of Housing Tables: Homeownership."

25. Humes, *Over Here*, 33.

26. Bennett, *When Dreams Came True*, 242. In 1942, over 200,000 people had earned degrees. By 1950 that number more than doubled to approximately 497,000.

27. Humes, *Over Here*, 221; 26–38; 222–29.

28. Egerton, *Speak Now Against the Day*, 477; Rankin "Will Soldiers Vote?"; Herbold, "Never a Level Playing Field," 104. Rankin's quote comes following World War I, yet his racist sentiments remain the same throughout his political career.

29. Onkst, "First a Negro . . . Incidentally a Veteran," 521.

PART III: AIN'T NO BODY

heterogeneous or all-black neighborhoods. The two most heavily weighted criteria of The FHA's *Underwriting Manual* were "relative economic stability" and "protection from adverse influences," which were veiled phrases for segregation.[30] This FHA created a government monopoly over the lending process, and the effects were devastating. *Ebony* magazine found that of the three thousand VA home loans issued to Mississippi veterans in 1947 only *two* loans went to Black veterans.[31] Abuses were not limited to the South, as less than 2 percent of new homes insured by the FHA from 1949–1959 were available to Blacks across the nation.[32] Adam Gordon's summary of FHA policies in essence testifies to the reach of the powers: "Whether *intentionally* discriminatory or not, these legislative barriers provide a major reason to believe that government policies were responsible for a greater share of post-World War II racial segregation and disinvestment in urban areas than previously thought."[33] The government admitted as much in 1973 when the U.S. Commission on Civil Rights concluded that the "Government and private industry came together to create a system of residential segregation."[34]

Similarly, few Black veterans could take advantage of the college benefit, as only 17 percent of Blacks began their military service with a high school diploma, compared to 41 percent of whites.[35] Many Blacks were admitted to college, but often only to the under-funded Historically Black Colleges and Universities (HBCUs) after being turned away from white universities. Black institutions could not keep up with the post-World War II demand for science and technology fields, due to ill-equipped classroom spaces.[36] Lastly, Black veterans were dishonorably discharged at a disproportionate rate from white veterans, often for protesting civil rights violations, thus making them ineligible for G.I. Bill benefits. From slavery through modern abuses, an estimated twenty-four trillion dollars

---

30. Jackson, *Crabgrass Frontier*, 207.

31. Humes, *Over Here*, 226–27.

32. Gordon, "Creating of Homeownership," 217. Of the 67,000 G.I. Bill mortgages in the New York and New Jersey suburbs, less than one hundred went to Black veterans. Katznelson, *When Affirmative Action was White*, 140. See also Kushner, *Levittown*; Sugrue, "Jim Crow's Last Stand."

33. Gordon, "Creating of Homeownership," 213. Emphasis added.

34. Rothstein, *Color of Law*, 75.

35. Mettler, "Only Good Thing Was the G.I. Bill," 31.

36. Olson, *G.I. Bill, the Veterans, and the Colleges*, 74; Turner and Bound, "Closing the Gap or Widening the Divide," 152. See also Humes, "How the G.I. Bill Shunted Blacks into Vocational Training," 92–104; Atkins, "Negro Educational Institutions," 141–53.

has been stolen from Black families through lost wages, inaccessible land, educational impoverishment, and housing inequalities.[37]

All of it was legal within our system, like a game of Monopoly played over hundreds of years, where not everyone collected their rightfully-owed $200 each time they passed "Go."[38] Black veterans faced systemic abuses head-on, and as Steve Estes says, "Having survived the traditional rite of passage into manhood in military service, black veterans felt differently about themselves even if many white Americans still did not."[39] That generation would pave the way for the greatest exercise of democratic expression seen since our nation's founding.

Social Change

Expecting social change to come solely through individual conversion results in what Peter Heltzel calls a "half-gospel" that can never "fully integrate ministries of social justice."[40] History shows individual conversion to be an incomplete approach to forming a more equitable society. For this reason, the civil right movement should never be sentimentally reduced to one that simply "touched the hearts of the American people," but seen rather as the theological and democratic protest against death-dealing politics.[41] Jim Crow ended through legal challenges and legislative interventions by the federal government.[42] Hearts changed after the fact. Gradualism was little more than a halfway house for guilt-ridden white Christians who couldn't fathom becoming violent segregationists, and yet their foot-dragging caused generational wreckage in the interregnum between the powers' hold and meaningful reform.

---

37. Anderson, *White Rage*, 99. See also, Vinik, "Economics of Reparations."

38. See Waren, "Using Monopoly to Introduce Concepts of Race and Ethnic Relations," 28–35. Waren uses the game in introductory sociology courses to teach concepts of systemic racism.

39. Estes, *I am a Man!*, 37.

40. Heltzel, *Jesus and Justice*, 87. See also Hollinger, *Individualism and Social Ethics*, 39–40. See also Joel Goza on John Locke's emphasis on personal salvation helped create a lacuna within Christian social thought (*America's Unholy Ghosts*, 97–98).

41. Burgess et al., "Mike Pence said he came to Memphis"

42. See Dupont, *Mississippi Praying*, 13, 198–200. Dupont's excellent historical work uses Mississippi as a prime example of how a thoroughly Christian population was unswayed by appeals to individual conscience. Cf. Acharya et al., *Deep Roots*, 185.

PART III: AIN'T NO BODY

There is little evidence the powers exist when the status quo works for our good. Constancy brings comfort; it denotes a proper ordering and place for all things. Disruption of the powers' *modus operandi* reveals its problems, regardless of the era. The powers reign where division persists. Nationalism, racism, and greed fester, and we submit to the powers' vision of the world. Whether a clause dropped into legislation or group-think drowning out a prophetic word, ideas become implanted deep into our individual and collective psyche that this is the way things must be. Our imaginations shrink. Our hopes diminish.

The Wire (2002–2008), the phenomenal HBO drama, addresses how systems hold the potential for human flourishing or dehumanization. *The Wire* shows the interconnected web of Baltimore's drug dealers, police, homeless, dock workers, politicians, school systems, and its media. Bad apples do exist regardless of the institution, and even reformers fall prey to a poor system's trappings, unintentionally replicating the problems they were attempting to fix. Sometimes they just get exhausted by the fight. *The Wire* names the powerlessness we feel regarding the systems and structures we've built. An early scene explaining "the game," a metaphor for the drug trade, dispels the mythology of full personal autonomy: As two young dealers, Wallace and Bodie, play checkers using chess pieces, D'Angelo, an older member of their crew, convinces them to learn chess and explains the function of each piece in the game. The "kingpin" (the king) sits on the top line. Each piece receives a corresponding function within the drug game, including the pawns—"the soldiers"—who exist to protect the king. The intrigued young men lean in, and Wallace asks, "How do you get to be the king?" D'Angelo answers, "It ain't like that. See the king stay the king."[43] Everyone in the game remains locked in place with very little chance of upward mobility. D'Angelo explains how pawns are the single pieces that can be transformed during the game. If a pawn makes it to the opposite end of the board it becomes a queen, the most powerful piece, but D'Angelo cautions that the pawns are usually the first casualties of the game. Years later, Bodie recounts his entire life within the game—how he's always done things according to its rules and been a good soldier, but now the walls are closing in on him. He concludes, "The game is rigged, man" and likens himself to an expendable pawn.[44]

---

43. Medak, *Wire*, season 1, episode 3, "The Buys."
44. Dickerson, *Wire*, season 4, episode 13, "Final Grades."

Adulthood can feel like one long game with a child who keeps changing the rules to benefit himself. Any of us who have agreed to what we thought would be a low-key game of Candy Land or Nerf hoops know how quickly those games can confirm the doctrine of original sin. And yet, because humanity's brokenness is complex, simply settling or dismissing any issue with a quick reference to Genesis 3 just won't do. The depths of human pain necessitate investigation into the ways people feel powerless to change that which steals their agency.

In the first section of the book, I named myself to be part of a problem people, describing the various ways generational failures persist today. We were taught to be colorblind, to literally *not* notice race. The South, though, enforced an odd mix of not only *noticing* race but of *structuring* our places upon it, all the while still claiming colorblindness. White Southerners born in the last fifty years didn't realize that our ancestors' end-goal was a separate society, because the dirty work had already been done for us. Then, on top of all that, our churches did us few favors by limiting the scope of sin to individual acts. So, while we are not the originators of this reality, now we know and knowing means assuming responsibility to change it. For this reason, Christ's good news is more than just the escape plan he's hatched for us one glad morning. Dismantling a system rigged in your favor for the sake of your neighbor is no less good news.

11

BROKEN AND PUT BACK TOGETHER, I DON'T KNOW HOW MANY TIMES

(Or, Who's Afraid of Black Jesus?)

> Since whites have been the most violent race on the planet, their theologians and preachers are not in a position to tell black people, or any other people for that matter, what they must to do be like Jesus.[1]
>
> —James Cone

My second-grade teacher Ms. Harper made every subject exciting, but I especially loved when it was story time. In my view, every wonderful book had been written just for her to read to us. Ms. Harper was my first Black teacher. She walked with braces, a remnant of her childhood polio that caused her to bend forward at the waist. She moved methodically around thirty sets of tiny limbs and our accidents that must have created landmines for the path she had to navigate daily. Eventually we didn't notice the bodily differences that were plainly evident to us on the first day of class. Until one day during lunch, Ms. Harper slipped and fell hard with a sickening sound of metal and bone on the cafeteria floor. We whipped around from our tables to see her being lifted gingerly by other teachers,

---

1. Cone, *God of the Oppressed*, xvi.

and although it was obvious she was in pain, she assured us that she would survive. It was a reminder of her body—a point of fascination, mystery, and now deep concern to us. I watched her closely for the rest of the year, bracing for the next time she might fall.

Whose Jesus?

The Bible has little to say about the appearance of Jesus, and in that absence we have filled in those blanks with remarkably inaccurate self-portraits. We know that Jesus was born a Jewish boy growing up in first-century Roman-occupied Palestine. As M. Shawn Copeland powerfully puts it: "In his flesh, in his body, Jesus knew refugee status, occupation and colonization, social regulation and control."[2] Early in the church's history, Jesus's body was contested terrain. J. Kameron Carter's brilliant work, *Race: A Theological Account*, details the way "ethnic reasoning" invaded the first centuries of the church, which diminished the importance of Jesus's Jewish flesh for understanding Christianity. The logic goes as follows: The birth of Jesus completes the Jewish role in salvation history, and the church replaces Israel as God's chosen people, rendering the details of Jesus's life to be irrelevant.[3] Eliminating Jesus's Jewish heritage paved the way for Jesus to become "white," or as Willie Jennings says, "a social cipher for any and every redemptive vision of a people."[4] Even if the theological points do not interest you one bit, the process by which a historical figure can be transformed into an ahistorical, near-disembodied being should.

Edward Blum and Paul Harvey explain how images of Jesus shaped American Christianity in *The Color of Christ*, noting that "white Jesus" did not immediately dominate American history, for race was not a pervasive category in the American colonies. By the early nineteenth century, however, white maleness "was becoming a marker for political status, power, and opportunity." Racial and religious fusion became more pronounced, immigration diversified the nation, and "whiteness was increasingly attached

---

2. Copeland, *Enfleshing Freedom*, 58.

3. Carter, *Race*, 11–36 Carter focuses on Irenaeus's confrontation with the gnostics who diminished the reality of Jesus Christ incarnate. Carter cites Denise Buell for using the term "ethnic reasoning" (12).

4. Jennings,*Christian Imagination*, 259. For examples of how Jesus has been interpreted throughout U.S. history, see Noll, *America's God*; Prothero, *American Jesus*; Fox, *Jesus in America*; Nichols, *Jesus: Made in America*.

to civility, citizenship, and Christianity."[5] For the fifty years that followed the Civil War—itself a period of a contested Christ—Jesus was utilized to forward white supremacy. Some prominent examples include: Klan propaganda like Thomas Dixon Jr.'s novels and D. W. Griffith's film *Birth of a Nation*, screened at the White House for President Woodrow Wilson; images and pamphlets of a white Jesus for Sunday school materials; and religious movies that portrayed a white Jesus.[6]

The importance of representation is becoming a commonplace discussion in the twenty-first century, and so too do images of Jesus matter. Millions of white Christians like myself, grew up with images of Jesus that made his whiteness a "psychological certainty."[7] Warner Sallman's *Head of Christ* (1941) painting, featuring a bearded white Jesus with flowing brown hair and blue eyes, had been printed 500 million times by the 1990s, and at least one of these prints hung in the First Baptist Church of Union City.[8] Still today, that image remains lodged in my psyche when I pray or think about Jesus of Nazareth. The white Jesus became a product—mass-produced, marketed, and sold to eager consumers of all races.

Black Jesus

Graduating to "latchkey kid"—a Gen-X rite of passage—gave my sister and me access to 20+ channels after we completed our homework. For me, WGN Chicago offered everything I could desire in Cubs home games and what became my favorite syndicated show, *Good Times*. *Good Times* followed the Evans, a black, working-class family living in Chicago public housing. The catchy theme song addressed each daily challenge of being hassled, hustled, and ripped-off, punctuated with the refrain of "good times," a sign of resilience no matter the hardship. Eventually, *Good Times* also posed a theological dilemma for me: J. J., the eldest son and artist, painted a Black Jesus, which sparked a family debate about which Jesus should adorn their wall. It was the first time I considered that Jesus was not white.

I didn't know it at the time, but I was being prepped for James Cone.

You may never have heard of James Cone (1938–2018), the long-time theology professor at Union Theological Seminary (New York), but it's a

---

5. Blum and Harvey, *Color of Christ*, 77, 106.
6. Blum and Harvey, *Color of Christ*, 183–88.
7. Blum and Harvey, *Color of Christ*, 15.
8. Blum and Harvey, *Color of Christ*, 211.

near-certainty your pastor has, likely in seminary... for about fifteen minutes (or less) before his work was summarily dismissed. Cone was one of the first academic voices that provided a window into Black life for me. He was an intellectual powerhouse, ferociously brilliant, willing to say the difficult thing that needed to be said, no matter how misunderstood he might be, because putting flesh to reality was a God-given commission. So it was, in 1970, that white people lost their minds when Cone wrote, "God is black."[9] For the next half-century many white Christians go apoplectic at the mention of his name, still to this day, whether they had read his work or not.[10]

Cone gave voice to the centuries of pain experienced by people of color through his systematic theology, heretofore the territory of white men. He claimed that context directly shapes every person's questions and answers about God: "What people think about God cannot be divorced from their place and time in a definite history and culture," Cone said.[11] Everyone who reads a holy text, meditates on it, and preaches or teaches it, brings their perspective and for Cone, southern life directly shaped his work:

> I remember blacks in Arkansas trying to cope with despair—bad crops, terrible winter, and troublesome white folks—yet they still believed they could make it through the "storm of life" and not be defeated in this "mean old world." "Hard times" were real and concrete, an everyday struggle to survive with dignity in a society that did not recognize their humanity. The dialectic of sorrow and joy, despair and hope was central in the black experience.[12]

Black experiences shaped the conclusion that troubled white people: Jesus is Black. "God in Christ comes to the weak and the helpless, and becomes one with them, taking their condition of oppression as his own and thus transforming their slave-existence into a liberated existence."[13] Cone drew close the experiences of first-century Jews and Black folk, saying,

> [Jesus] truly becomes One with the oppressed blacks, taking their suffering as his suffering and revealing that he is found in the

---

9. Cone, *Black Theology of Liberation*, 63.

10. On December 29, 2019, Southeastern Seminary President Danny Akin tweeted that James Cone was "a heretic." For responses to Akin see Foley, "On the Assault of James Cone and Black Liberation Theology" and Gehrz, "What is a Heretic?"

11. Cone, *God of the Oppressed*, 37.

12. Cone, *Cross and the Lynching Tree*, 13.

13. Cone, *God of the Oppressed*, 71.

history of our struggle, the story of our pain, and the rhythm of our bodies .... The least in America are literally and symbolically present in black people. To say that Christ is black means that black people are God's poor people whom Christ has come to liberate.[14]

Cone believed that white professors, pastors, and lay people, who diminished the significance of Jesus's Jewishness, would certainly overlook the reiterative experiences of Black folk that suffered in their midst. Cone refuted any Christianity that even tacitly supported white supremacy, specifically the way that white theologians had incorporated Western philosophies that denigrated physical matter. The net result of their thought yielded a disembodied, non-Jewish Jesus, who became solely an *ideal* for humanity, rather than a concrete, historical figure.[15] Kelly Brown Douglas explains well that a Black Christ "does not begin with abstract speculation of Jesus' metaphysical nature. Instead, it starts in history with Jesus' ministry as that is recorded in the Gospels. What Jesus did becomes the basis for what it means for him to be Christ."[16]

Nowhere was Christ's "blackness" more evident than on his cross, a symbolic link to the South's lynching tree—both instruments used to incite terror, suffering, and submission. "Like Jesus, blacks knew torture and abandonment, with no community or government capable or willing to protect them from crazed mobs."[17] Whites were aware of this terror. For example, Henlee Barnette, pastor of a rural North Carolina church (and

---

14. Cone, *God of the Oppressed*, 125. Kelly Brown Douglas clarifies Cone's mention of a "literal" blackness, saying, "James Cone offered a symbolic version of Christ's Blackness. In this version Blackness did not refer to Jesus' ethnic characteristics. It was a symbol of Jesus' existential commitments. In this regard, Blackness was not incidental to who Christ was, but was an essential aspect of Christ's nature" (Douglas, *Black Christ*, 58).

15. Cone, *God of the Oppressed*, 125, 163–69. M. Shawn Copeland charges white Christianity with "*somatophobia* or a fear of the flesh" stemming from "a conceptual axis that compounds *both* distortions of Neoplatonism, with its tendency to idealism, suspicion of ambiguity, and discomfort with matter; *and* Pauline and Augustinian warnings about the flesh and its pleasures" (*Enfleshing Freedom*, 24). Copeland cites Kelly Brown Douglas, who says this mode of thinking comes from "uncritical absorption of Platonic and Stoic ideals" which created "dualistic thinking and ascetic sentiments." This is a "heretical tradition" and "a version of this tradition was assimilated into Southern evangelical Protestantism" (*Enfleshing Freedom*, 123). See also Grant, *White Women's Christ and Black Women's Jesus*.

16. Douglas, *Black Christ*, 113. Douglas says her knowledge of the creeds came in the Episcopal Church, yet they do not account for the life and ministry of Jesus.

17. Cone, *Cross and the Lynching Tree*, 75.

future Southern Seminary ethics professor), saw in 1936 a lynching photo in the local newspaper; and one of his deacons stood next to the hanging body. The image shook Barnette and shaped his ministry for racial justice.[18] Cone's Black Jesus was born out of slavery, lynching, and segregation. In contrast, my people's Jesus materialized out of everyday normal whiteness, transforming the cross "into a harmless, nonoffensive ornament that Christians wear around their necks," rather than the state's instrument of terror.[19]

Cone details the importance of the Black church for him: "I was born in Arkansas, a lynching state," Cone said, "During my childhood, white supremacy ruled supreme. White people were virtually free to do anything to blacks with impunity." But at Macedonia A.M.E. Church, he experienced the "powerful, living reality of God's Spirit" transforming "them from nobodies in white society to somebodies in the black church."[20] "The Black Church" is a theological and sociological shorthand for Black Protestant denominations, sharing common features, but not a monolith. This tradition parallels, but does not mimic, the development of white traditions, as its origins were formed in the crucible of slavery.[21] Jesus was understood to be a Redeemer in the tradition of Moses, who led his people out of bondage. Christ's suffering harkened to a God who was intimately involved with his people during times of distress. The Lord created all persons in his image, sought justice for all, and would ultimately enter history to liberate them through the cross. As Copeland says, Jesus of Nazareth is the one who "does not forget poor, dark, and despised bodies."[22]

This notion of liberation troubles many white Christians, because they think it distracts from the centrality of Christ's soul-saving sacrifice. But as Rev. Vernon Johns, Martin Luther King's predecessor at Dexter Ave. Baptist Church (Montgomery), emphatically put the matter at an interracial gathering of pastors: "The thing that disappoints me about the Southern white church is that it spends all of its time dealing with the Jesus after the cross, instead of dealing with Jesus before the cross."[23] The white Jesus preached in white churches blessed all aspects of white life. He encouraged

18. Stagg, "Henlee Hulix Barnette: Activist," 34.
19. Cone, *Said I Wasn't Gonna Tell Nobody*, 135.
20. Cone, *Cross and the Lynching Tree*, xv.
21. Lincoln and Mamiya, *Black Church in the African American Experience*, 1–2.
22. Copeland, *Enfleshing Freedom*, 53.
23. Branch, *Parting the Waters*, 339.

Black servility, tolerated lynchings, and calmed the guilt-ridden parishioners. This Jesus had to be banished, and Black churches became sites of worship as protest against inhumane forces, an act that forged a "defiant spirituality."[24] "The more Black people struggled against white supremacy," Cone says, "the more they found in the cross the spiritual power to resist the violence they so often suffered."[25] Although white evangelicalism is a product and reflection of racial division, Black Christians reimagined the tradition and so transformed their socio-political identities, drawing strength from Christ's death and resurrection. Black Christians claimed their liberation from white evangelicalism through slave preachers and abolitionists, by forming separate denominations, and raising up intellectuals and artists into the twentieth century, all of whom gave birth to James Cone.[26]

Jesus and Justice

Does the Jesus you imagine affect the way you live your life? I must consider, again and again, how to answer the same question Jesus posed to his disciples: "But who do you say that I am?" (Mark 8:29). As a younger Christian, my answer, sad to say, was shaped by a racialized world and distorted imagination. Reggie Williams sums up my early church formation well:

> Christians who see the connection between Jesus and justice are different than Christians who do not. Christians who miss, or deny, the connection between Jesus and justice are vulnerable to misunderstanding Christianity as a pursuit of righteousness, understood as individual piety. They may even use theology to justify practices of cruelty, or their apathy, about the suffering of others.[27]

Williams draws on Gushee and Stassen's work, who call attention to hundreds of "justice" references in Bible. The Hebrew words—*tsedaqah* ("delivering justice and community-restoring justice") and *mishpat* ("judgment according to right or rights, and thus judgment that vindicates the right(s) especially of the poor and powerless")—highlight ancient Israel's communal and restorative aspects of justice. God intends for humanity to live

---

24. Franklin, "With Liberty and Justice for All," 53.
25. Cone, *Cross and the Lynching Tree*, 22.
26. Blum and Harvey, *Color of Christ*, 194–204.
27. Williams, "How the Construct of Race Deforms Our Understanding of Christ."

together, make restitution, forgive, and be forgiven.[28] Jesus entered the lives of the suffering, seeking their justice, and we must do likewise in our time. Gushee and Stassen expand this notion:

> Jesus died for our sins, including our injustice. His confronting the injustice of the powerful was a major reason why they wanted him crucified. When we see his concern for justice—for an end to unjust economic structures, unjust domination, unjust violence, and unjust exclusion from community—we cannot help but rethink our entire conception of what Jesus was about in his preaching and teaching.[29]

While not every contemporary reference to justice matches the way of Jesus, my impulse is to at least listen to, rather than dismiss, the cries of those who feel pain. If I choose not to hear, then my loyalties will keep me separated from God's beloved children; that is the nature of what the powers do. If Jesus only reinforces my preconceived notions about the world and others, then I remain entrenched in a never-ending loop of self-justification.

Whether white evangelicals embrace Cone's entire project or not is beside the point. Cone called white Christians to pay attention to the experiences of people of color for nearly a half-century, and for too long, whites said "Nah. We're good." White evangelicals are not the hosts of God's kingdom, graciously granting entry into it. We hold neither the velvet rope nor the deed to the property, because the site of our inclusion is the crucified and resurrected (non-white) flesh of a poor Jewish man, who probably couldn't pick himself out of a lineup from our depictions of him.

Any resistance to hearing and learning from Black experiences should be tempered by considering how often pastors and professors use personal experiences as teaching points, whether universally relatable or not. For example, sermons about parenting can still be revelatory of theological truth, even if not directly applicable to every congregant. Personal experience is foundational to evangelical theology. Yes, sin clouds our perspective and cannot become our sole source of authority. Still, when evangelicals hear and accept an individual's personal testimony to follow Jesus, they are ostensibly welcoming the individual *and* the experiences that inform the individual's faith, not just their conversion. Jemar Tisby's question persists, "Can black Christians bring both their race and their religion with them

---

28. Gushee and Stassen, *Kingdom Ethics,* 2nd ed., 126–27.

29. Gushee and Stassen, *Kingdom Ethics,* 147. They glean these categories of injustice from their reading of Isaiah's deliverance passages in ch. 1 of *Kingdom Ethics* (3–20).

into white evangelical spaces?"[30] If a Black Christian's experiences are dismissed as "identity politics" or individualistic, how can *any* of us speak vulnerably about what Jesus has done for us? We need not fear that relying on experience, even a little, is a pathway to moral relativism. James K. A. Smith explains each individual's limits to understand the truth:

> Saying "It depends" is *not* the equivalent of saying "It's not true" or "I don't know." Owning up to our finitude is *not* tantamount to giving up on truth, revelation, or scriptural authority. It is simply to recognize the conditions of our knowledge that are coincident with our status as finite, created, social beings. And those conditions are pronounced "very good" by the Creator (Gen. 1:31).[31]

Being human is acknowledging that we do not have it all figured out and that we benefit from a multiplicity—a community—of thoughts. White evangelicals who create hermetically-sealed spaces are the poorer for it.[32]

I'll restate Stassen's earlier claim about how prior loyalties can cloud our judgment: "We regularly decide based on emotions and passions, and then devise rational reasons to justify what our emotions guided us to do. These emotions are not simply about our own internal wishes and interests; they are deeply connected with loyalties to others."[33] Try as we may to dub ourselves objective, facts-over-feelings, universal, rational actors, we constantly interpret everything—a gesture, a look, an intonation—to say nothing of every book we read, holy or otherwise. Carolyn Dupont's history of Mississippi's white, southern evangelicals during the civil rights movement offers a warning to modern worshipers, whose racial and ideological homogeneity limits their capacity to discern a different way than the only one they know. Consider how Dupont's summary of fundamentalist Bible-reading practices of nearly a century ago still applies today:

> The fundamentalist approach to the Bible relied on a thick consensus about its meanings. The literalist hermeneutic did not actually

---

30. Tisby, "Are Black Christians Evangelicals?" 272.

31. Smith, *Who's Afraid of Relativism?* 30.

32. For examples of Black exclusion specifically, historian Charles H. Lippy says that Black religious experiences not being taken seriously is just an extension of the same old patterns of exclusion and domination inherited from slavery, where "the domination of white evangelical Protestantism required ignoring the dynamics of black religion or at least seeing it as inferior to and on the periphery of the mainstream Christianity" (*Bibliography of Religion in the South*, 81). See Yancy, "Ugly Truth about Being a Black Professor in America."

33. Stassen, *Thicker Jesus*, 116.

take the entire Bible literally, of course. It required a myriad of interpretive shifts—emphasizing some texts while downplaying others, relying on historical context in some instances while ignoring it in others, understanding certain biblical passages as spiritual, some as allegorical or figurative, and others as literary or didactic. *Yet preachers, teachers, and their hearers denied making any interpretive choices and claimed that they simply took the Bible at face value.* To preserve this consensus about the Bible's meanings, Mississippians studied the Bible corporately. They expounded the meaning of Scripture in worship services structured around the sermon, in large and well-attended Sunday schools, and through reading religious literature—practices that cut against their claim that each believer could ascertain the meaning for him- or herself in private.[34]

We are always interpreting, and at times, we create the apparatuses that buttress our interpretations. Too often, we justify our gut reaction, because it's what we wanted to do in the first place. It's also the exhausting, lonely way of constant war and division, where I am righteous gatekeeper or shepherd and you are a heretic.

So, who's afraid of a Black Jesus? Maybe I am, if it means altering the tidy way I live out my faith. The white Christ of my youth kept me from eternal damnation, a belief that puts my mind at ease. Calling Jesus of Nazareth my Lord, though, has taken me a minute, because that means he gets the say on my bank account, my body, and my politics. The poor, first-century Palestinian Jewish man—a Black Jesus—contests my individualism, the autonomy I've known since birth in this white body, making it a bit more difficult to download a projection of my needs into the raceless vessel I've become accustomed to worshiping.[35] But, when I close my eyes to pray I don't want to pray to Sallman's Jesus anymore; I want to look into the face of Ms. Harper at her desk, thirty-five years ago.

---

34. Dupont, *Mississippi Praying*, 25. Emphasis added. Cf. Kristin Kobes Du Mez offers a similar analysis of Dupont but on the matter of masculinity: "Conservatives, however, insisted on a "populist hermeneutic," a method privileging "the simplest, most direct interpretations of scripture." For conservatives, this wasn't just the right method, it was also the masculine one" (*Jesus and John Wayne*, 108).

35. I'm indebted to David Dark's term "white supremacist antichrist poltergeist," which he routinely uses to describe the kind of "downloading" of whiteness into the flesh of Jesus, ultimately distorting his origins and ministry. https://twitter.com/DavidDark/status/1267109530699288576.

PART III: AIN'T NO BODY

**

The Christmas party in Ms. Harper's room was one of the most joyous school memories I recall. A half-day of school filled with games, snacks, and presents. In the middle of the festivities, I wandered over to Ms. Harper's desk, checking out all of the colorful ornaments and decorations she had displayed. A ceramic owl caught my eye, and I picked it up, popping the head right off of it. I lost my breath immediately and focused all of my attention on surgically replacing the head back on its rightful owner to no avail. I sat on the transgression for the full Christmas break, saying nothing to anyone, with it eating me up inside. I was crushed by what I had done to my beloved teacher's possession. Finally, I told my parents, and my dad agreed to accompany me to school for the early morning confession on the first day back from the break. I tearfully told Ms. Harper—gasping and snotting after every word—that I had broken her figurine. She asked, "Which one?" I pointed to the little owl with the stitched-up neckline. She examined it carefully, and then looked at me with the kind of compassion that only elementary school teachers have, saying, "Oh, you didn't break that thing. It's been broken and put back together I don't know how many times." She gave me a hug and thanked me for being honest. I felt restored.

It is admittedly a childish story, but I remember her forgiveness more vividly than literally any other moment from elementary school. I have no idea if I remember the encounter simply because Ms. Harper was my favorite teacher. Perhaps Ms. Harper was memorable because of her race or disability, and I was already suffering from white guilt before I even knew that was a thing. I would have other Black teachers, coaches, and professors, none of whom would have the distinction of *first* imprinting upon me that Black people were worthy of my respect; that they could be an authority for me; and that their instruction could be fun and beneficial to me. All I knew at seven years old is that I loved Ms. Harper, and she loved me. My teacher reminded me of Jesus. The ones who've been broken and put back together typically do.

12

MUY RAPIDO

Getting Saved in Uruguay

> My grandmother always told me that she loved my prayers. She believed my prayers were more powerful, because I prayed in English. Everyone knows that Jesus, who's white, speaks English. The Bible is in English. Yes, the Bible was not *written* in English, but the Bible came to South Africa in English so to us it's in English. Which made my prayers the best prayers because English prayers get answered first. How do we know this? Look at white people. Clearly they're getting through to the right person.[1]
>
> —Trevor Noah, *Born a Crime*

> I looked upon this world as a wrecked vessel ... God has given me a lifeboat and said to me, "Moody, save all you can."[2]
>
> —D.L. Moody

---

1. Noah, *Born a Crime*, 40.
2. Marsden, *Fundamentalism and American Culture*, 38.

PART III: AIN'T NO BODY

There he was, slouched on the loveseat with his arm around a young lady. His posture was that of a cocksure gunslinger, right arm lying motionless on his leg like a threat and a promise. The teen on the couch was the team's star pitcher, and he generally dismissed our presence in his space. We were a nuisance on his way to certain glory. We were twelve college boys on a mission trip in Uruguay, staying in the missionary's (Steve) home, and we had been teaching local kids how to play baseball. Tomorrow though was supposed to be a game against somewhat experienced teenaged players, and before tomorrow's game there was the psychological warfare of the joint pregame meal. He planned to make his name off us with the entire town watching. Even his food didn't interest him as much as trash-talking. He pushed his plate to the side and placed his elbows on the table, never breaking his gaze from us. It was a maneuver that resembled pulling pistols from a gunbelt, shown at just the right moment to communicate you mean business in spite of the lunchtime niceties.

"I throw muy rapido," he said in English-Spanish combo, adding a cackle and a sideways glance at his boys who were gaining confidence from their captain. How could they not with that registered weapon affixed to his AC joint? For our part, we named him "Muy Rapido," and I don't think he would have had it any other way.

This trip was my first and only foreign mission experience, fulfilling my duty as an evangelical to share my faith with others. We hopped on a plane the day after my college graduation, to play baseball with my friends and favorite professor, David Gushee, who was a promising late-thirties southpaw reliever at the time. Straight from the Montevideo airport to a central park in one poor neighborhood, we met local kids, and told them through our translators that we would be playing a series of sandlot games for anyone interested. The parks had few discernable geographical boundaries marking out actual fields of play, so we improvised virtually everything. Massive ditches carved gashes in the outfield landscape. We pounded balls into the ground, so we did not launch dingers onto tin rooftops. We tried to "go oppo" to avoid permanently maiming the disinterested child manning third base, who was wearing his glove as a toboggan, or the two horses wandering about unattended. Most games over those ten days were against children who enjoyed the spectacle of a quintessential American sport. None of them, however, were remotely within the talent-range of the junior-national level competition we had expected. Muy Rapido awaited us, though.

The next afternoon, Muy Rapido peeled off his windbreaker and sauntered onto the mound staring at us the entire stroll, ready to call down the lightning from the heavens, if necessary, to strike us down, or out, whichever came first. But, it did not go the way the young man planned, as we destroyed Muy Rapido's world, one deposited fastball at a time. When he was mercifully replaced a couple of innings later many members of our team encouraged him and talked to him about pitching mechanics, but the damage was done. He'd been thoroughly humbled, and now he had to listen to white boys talk about Jesus. Those are the universal rules of the mission trip.

Diseased Imagination Revisited

As I quoted in the first section, "Christianity in the Western world lives and moves within a diseased social imagination."[3] Jennings's book is a complex, symphonic work, one theme building upon the next, and it cannot properly be explained here; however, to understand Jennings's claim one must take a look at the history of missions which is intertwined with the European takeover of already-occupied lands.

Medieval colonialism forwarded both racial supremacy and a particular way of teaching Christian theology. Papal authorities blessed the "discovery" of the New World in order to attain lands under the auspices of propagating the Gospel. Four decades prior to Christopher Columbus's westward journey, Pope Nicholas V proclaimed that new expeditions were divinely authorized, and that any lands could be taken from "infidels," who held no right to them in the eyes of God. In 1493, Pope Alexander VI, decreed that conquerors and missionaries would make a "donation in perpetuity to the Spanish Crown," in gold and souls.[4] Those conquered peoples could swear allegiance to Catholic monarchs and convert to the faith or, if they refused, face enslavement.

Europeans destroyed the lands of native peoples through wars, mining, unfamiliar agriculture practices, and grazing; they imposed a foreign mentality upon a foreign land, all in the name of Jesus. The plunder was sent back to prop up a fading papal authority, stressed by a creeping influence of Islam and a Catholic hope to fund a reclamation of the Holy Land. As Columbus said, "Gold is extraordinary; gold becomes a treasure, and

3. Jennings, *Christian Imagination*, 6.
4. Rivera, *Violent Evangelism*, 29.

PART III: AIN'T NO BODY

with it, whoever has it can do anything he wishes in the world, and even send souls to Paradise."[5] Drawing on Jennings's work, Native American thinker Mark Charles says, "The diseased theological imagination (such as Christendom, the Doctrine of Discovery, and the myth of Anglo-Saxon purity) contributed to a dysfunctional social imagination (white supremacy) that has perpetuated unjust leaders, systems, and structures."[6] The gospel was a convenient window-dressing for imperialist aims.

By the 1790s, Protestant missions entered the global field, and the United States' participation exploded in the twentieth century. By the 1950s the US supplied two-thirds of the 43,000 Protestant missionaries around the world.[7] The Southern Baptist Convention's unprecedented growth led to the expansion or creation of several subsidiaries, including the entity that would become the International Mission Board (IMB), the sponsor of my trip to Uruguay.

At our first debriefing, Steve regaled us with all of God's good works in Uruguay. A team the previous month had witnessed thirty people get saved, and Steve asked us our "goal" for our trip. We paused to pray over the matter and reconvened a half-hour later. Steve asked again, how many souls did we want to see the Lord save this week? A teammate spoke up, "The Lord laid a number on my heart. I don't know why, but sixty just came to mind."

Sixty!

Ever the skeptic, I thought, "The Lord is going to have to keep a pretty good pace for us to pull this off." Steve was unfazed and flashed a "that's what I'm talking about" grin. I was uncomfortable with the idea of sixty as our divinely-registered number, because I was neither the most enthusiastic evangelizer nor particularly skilled at coaxing out the necessary verbal profession from would-be converts. If evangelicals had a power-poll among our membership, I would be in the bottom one percent of witnesses. Now, I had a quota of roughly five converts, a point that stressed me out—not having anything to do with those unnamed individual's salvation, but by being the perceived weak link of the evangelistic team.

We played on, preached the gospel, and saw some lost souls get saved. I think. The Uruguayan people did not seem to be experiencing the same level of anxiety or fervor I was used to seeing from the newly-saved. Most

5. Rivera, *Violent Evangelism*, 259.
6. Charles and Rah, *Unsettling Truths*, 33.
7. Jenkins, *Next Christendom*, 35.

seemed indifferent, confused even. My first and only two gospel-hearers were tweens who politely listened to me share my faith, and I asked if they would like to know Jesus, too? The kids paused for what felt like an eternity, not unexpected, when eternity is, in fact, the consideration. Finally, they responded, communicating more of an "okay, sure," rather than the far-more enthusiastic "conversion" my translator conveyed to me. To this day, I'm convinced they accepted Jesus out of sheer sadness . . . for me, not for their sins.

Billy Graham, I was not.

In all honesty, my vision for the trip became quickly clouded by the poverty I witnessed there. (Keep in mind, Uruguay was, and is, comparatively stable to the rest of South and Central America.) I couldn't stop thinking about their plight: The kids playing without shoes in the cold. How nice our equipment was compared to their possessions. The utterly unwinnable war against global poverty that Bono had not yet started waging. The whiteness of my skin. Maybe even the folly of my westernized faith. Was Jesus really enough? Here?

Doubts aside, I persevered. I played more baseball. I prayed with locals of clear devout faith. I even volunteered to share my testimony to the kids after our games. I'd hit them with a little muscular Christianity, which was really the only version of Christianity I knew at the time. I was less than two years removed from my cancer remission, so I had a compelling story to tell young folk. I had an awesomely gnarly scar across my stomach that served as a nice prop, too. Surely a message about physical and spiritual discipline, perseverance, letting God heal us to fight another day, could be pulled together on-the-fly.[8] I was proving true what Traci West says: "Contextually rooted sociopolitical interests are always embedded in Christological teaching."[9] The Spirit was moving and I got to preaching. Muy Rapido was squatting on the front row, staring intently at me, seemingly hanging on my every word . . . until he abruptly and aggressively began making out with his girlfriend during my sermon.

Billy Sunday, I was not.

---

8. See Ladd and Mathisen, *Muscular Christianity*.
9. West, "When a White Man-God Is the Truth and the Way," 124.

PART III: AIN'T NO BODY

New Standards for a "New World"

The earliest conquests in the Americas can be summed up as a mission to tame lands and peoples. Once those with the guns and crosses secured the land, they turned to the godlike task of recreating its inhabitants. "Europeans established a new organizing reality for identities, *themselves*," Jennings says, as they encountered indigenous peoples and saw themselves to be a "co-creator with God."[10] "Discovered" peoples were given a new identity, categorized typologically by their perceived intellectual capacity to learn theology and receive the Gospel. Jesuit missionaries established the standards by which the native peoples could be considered rational beings and began to instruct them in the tenets of Christianity. The criteria organized the "barbarians" according to their perceived rationality, emotional control, ability to speak the Europeans' language correctly, or their outright hostility to the conqueror-missionaries.[11]

Forget what you know. Follow us now. We know the way. If we did not, then why do your lands belong to us now?

Those who did not easily accept the conquerors' gospel were categorized as unintelligent or even demonic. According to the European standard, the native peoples were captives to their idols, to their land, and exhibited a general disinterest in learning European customs of language

---

10. Jennings, *Christian Imagination*, 58, emphasis added; 62.

11. This taxonomy is a composite from two sources of the era: First, Spanish Jesuit Bartolome de Las Casas, whose writing *Apologetica historia sumaria* (*Historical Context for Apologetic History of the Indies*), published in 1542, presented a four-fold taxonomy of the word "barbarian" to show possible converts to the faith: (1) Those who through actions, attitudes are generally reasonable but sometimes allows himself to be possessed by "great flares of passion and wildness." (2) Those who do not "speak our language correctly." (3) Those "wild beings, beastly in conduct and customs, the only ones to whom the term can be applied without correctives." (4) The term barbarian is "applied to the infidels, and these can either be guilty and consider themselves enemies of Christianity . . . . The natives of the New World fall in the second category and in the second division of the fourth" (Rivera, *Violent Evangelism*, 146). Second, Spanish Jesuit José de Acosta, missionary to Peru, wrote *De Procuranda Indorum Salute* (or *The Procurement of Indian Salvation*) in 1588. Acosta also categorizes peoples into distinct classes of barbarians: The first possess the highest civilization; they value reason and are receptive to gospel. Examples include the Chinese, Japanese, and people of eastern India. The second group lack developed system of writing, philosophy, and civil wisdom, like Mexicans and Peruvians. Acosta concludes they should be able to grow in the gospel. The third class of barbarians were like "wild animals" having no governmental sensibility; they might be dominated in force; can be attracted by flattery and, if that fails, by force (Jennings, *Christian Imagination*, 102–4).

and education, a disinterest which the settlers attributed to the indigenous peoples' intellectual deficiencies.[12] But as Jennings notes, indigenous people who rejected Christianity did so because the Europeans destroyed their familiar framework. In other words, the hold of the land and culture—that which one possesses, inhabits, and is *possessed by*—was replaced with a foreign imagination, one based on European texts and their understanding of rationality, and logic.[13] Allowing the "savages" to remain in their current state would ultimately be an act of defiance against God and the Crown. They had to be saved.

Christian faith was distorted, yet again. When Jesus is stripped of his flesh, he can be whoever we want him to be. When lands and peoples are stripped of their particularity, so too, can they be remade in our image. Before there was a "scientific" or social concept of race, there was a theological one under which we still suffer: Who will hear God's word? Those who will can be saved. Those who will not will be damned. Luis Rivera says bluntly, "The conquest of the Americas is the starting point for the modern system of slavery," with African slaves soon to arrive.[14] West says the evangelists had a ready-made metaphor for the enslaved blacks: "The bright, white light of Christ's truth was juxtaposed with the black darkness of evil and barbarism."[15]

I didn't know what colonialism was twenty years ago as a recent college graduate, but I definitely embodied its principles in the way I understood Uruguay and its people. I was the central character in this little movie. Not them. Not Jesus. Sad to say, I didn't "have a heart for them," in the parlance

---

12. Jennings, *Christian Imagination*, 102–15. He states further that "pedagogical imperialism" during the Middle Ages exhibited "an intellectual process guided by consultation with ancient Christian *texts*, a practical *rationality* whereby judgments that reflect the inner *logic* of Christian identity and story are made, and a way of envisioning the world scripturally" (112. Emphasis added).

13. For more on "white" rationality becoming the standard for all people, see Joel Goza's chapter on Thomas Hobbes in *America's Unholy Ghosts*, 36–51.

14. Rivera, *Violent Evangelism*, 181.

15. West, "When a White Man-God," 118. An advertisement in *Christianity Today* for the Moody Institute of Science's evangelistic film series shows a sketch of a white man sits next to a dark-skinned man with a nose-bone from an undetermined region. The headline asks, "Which is the untouchable?" leading into the prose promoting domestic missions: "Before you can reach a savage with the Gospel of Christ, you have to learn his language. You have to be able to communicate with him in the words and symbols he understands." The contrast—saved/unsaved, civilized/savage, white/black—has been a common trope (*Christianity Today*, April 9, 1965, 41).

of our faith. I pitied them, because they were not us. On my one and only foreign mission trip, I was completely disoriented because my evangelical logic was to invite them into God's family, sharing as equal brothers and sisters. But many of them were Catholic, and irrespective of their activity within the Catholic Church, they were *already* my brothers and sisters in the faith. I was there to make them *white, American* Christians. I pitied them, because in my imagination they would never have my wealth, my education, or my ability to travel overseas. I didn't reflect on my selfishness or injustices of this economic system or that one. Without even understanding it, I thought—no, *I knew*—myself to be their standard. In my mind, me and my teammates possessed everything our hosts could want. We came to export the great American pastimes: baseball and Christianity. Our strength and superiority was on display at every moment of the trip. We could be the vessels that saved their souls. We could be the only Jesus they would ever know.

White Saviorism

Seeing ourselves as the standard for everyone else—humanity as it is intended to be—is problematic for everyone who is *not* us. Like comedian Trevor Noah puts it, if "English prayers get answered first," it seems that white people are "getting through to the right person."[16] This feeling of blessedness is exhibited by earnest, young, white Christians who want to "make a difference" in the world. Christian colleges teem with this impulse to follow the Great Commission (Matt 28) and love their neighbor (Mark 12:31). I remember fondly the college students who burst into my office the day after Hurricane Katrina, while New Orleans was still underwater, who were ready to drive south that night, even though the National Guard was barring any entry.

The worst illustrations of this sincere impulse to serve degenerates into the White Savior Complex: white, Western Christians, revivifying a colonial imaginary, do more harm than good by circumventing local efforts through their superior money, power, and influence. As Teju Cole says, the mindset is that "a nobody from America or Europe can go to Africa and become a godlike savior or, at the very least, have his or her emotional needs satisfied."[17] The world exists as a broken-down renovation project,

---

16. Noah, *Born a Crime*, 40.
17. Cole, "White-Savior Industrial Complex."

and the fresh-faced HGN team will swoop in and spruce that warzone right up in seventy-two hours, accentuated by selfies with children of color. If we will but faithfully fling ourselves into the doom of brown and black nations, then surely God will be honored by our sacrifice.

Millennials will remember well the messianism propagated by the Invisible Children-Kony 2012 campaign aimed at ending Joseph Kony's child soldiering exploits in Uganda, all without any expertise on Ugandan politics. On an even larger stage, Malala Yousafzai's harrowing journey inspired a worldwide awareness of education efforts for Afghani women, culminating in Malala's Nobel Peace Prize; however, the predictable rendering of her story fit the white savior complex to a tee: "The story of an innocent brown child that was shot by savages for demanding an education and along comes the knight in shining armour to save her." White westerners applauded her inspiring story while never questioning US policies that exacerbated global conditions in which she lived.[18]

One of the more infamous cases of white saviorism recently ended: Reneé Bach, an American Christian, was sued in 2019 in Ugandan civil court because she and others in her NGO, Serving His Children, were practicing medicine without a license. Bach's mission served malnourished children in underserved areas of Uganda, and tragically, more than a hundred babies died at the mission between 2010 and 2015, the causes of which remain murky. Bach, now living in the US, reflected on her calling, "This sounds like such a white-savior thing to say, but I wanted to try to meet a need that wasn't being met."[19] In August 2020, the case was settled when Bach and Saving the Children agreed to pay about $9500 to each mother who lost a child. Serving His Children shuttered with the possibility of more litigation remaining, a stark warning to ill-prepared do-gooders.[20]

We risk perpetuating "poverty porn," where Black and brown needs becomes the site of all white attention. When we do not critically reflect upon root causes of problems that white, Western supremacy exacerbates, no doubt a far less adventurous task than hopping on a plane, we are not "doing good."[21] That said, I'm not questioning the heart of those who want to and do serve outside of their own contexts. Far from it. Many dear friends

18. Baig, "Malala Yousafzai and the White Saviour Complex."
19. Levy, "Missionary on Trial."
20. Aizenman, "U.S. Missionary with no Medical Training Settles Suit Over Child Deaths at her Center."
21. Kuja, "6 Harmful Consequences of the White Savior Complex."

serve across the globe, undergoing extensive linguistic and cultural training precisely so they do not replicate the sins of the past. They preach, teach in seminaries, bind wounds, deliver babies, and make peace in the name of Jesus with their neighbors of different faiths. Even my Uruguay trip remains formative for me, particularly the time spent in prayer with and for one another. I have recited our trip verse many days since then, typically when I'm facing uncertainty: "What no eye has seen, nor ear heard, nor the human heart conceived, what God has prepared for those who love him" (1 Cor 2:9).

My point remains that one's posture toward a people is difficult to alter, precisely due to the social imagination we enact just by being white Americans. The White Savior Complex is the natural outgrowth of a colonial (i.e., *diseased*) imagination put in motion centuries earlier through a now-nascent superiority that bears rotten fruit through cultural impositions, believing our solutions to be universal ones, abstracted from their origins. It shares the same genetic makeup of a mentality bent toward remaking lands and peoples into our image.

**

As the Uruguay trip progressed and the adrenaline wore off, exhaustion set in from multiple games a day, long travel between remote cities, and late-night returns to our hostel. The weariness set in one particular night, and such ensuing slumbers have always invariably led to vivid dreams for me. That night was no exception, as I experienced one of the few moments I can categorize as spiritual warfare. I dreamt about my grandfather's dying days. Buck wasn't visible to me, but he was somewhere in the darkness, and faintly I could hear an unfriendly voice taunting him (or me): *"You're coming home soon. You'll be ours soon."*

I woke up utterly distraught, still exhausted, and now nearly sick to my stomach. We were about to get back on the van, a mere four or five hours after arriving the night before, because we had salvation numbers we had to hit, metrics guiding our travel decisions. I barely thought about the games, my friends, or the people we were there to serve the next couple of days. As I try to recollect the trip, the haze in my memory does not lift until we land back home at the Memphis airport. It's far above my paygrade to assess the psychological-spiritual brain-dump that occurred in a dream two decades ago. But given what I could reason at the time, it meant one thing only: I had to get home. As a good evangelical, I knew there was no time to waste. Muy rapido.

EVANGELICAL OUTRO

A Desert and a Sea

Theologian Howard Thurman read the Bible to his grandmother nightly with clear instructions. Thurman said, "I might read many of the more devotional Psalms, some of Isaiah, the Gospels again and again. But the Pauline epistles, never."[1] When Thurman questioned his grandmother's excising of the great apostle, she told him that during her days as a slave, the master's minister would use Pauline texts to command their obedience. To Thurman, Paul was a curious man, who showed concern for all people, free or slaves, and came to read him empathetically:

> Paul was a Jew, even as Jesus was a Jew. By blood, training, and religion he belonged to the Jewish minority.... But unlike them, for the most part, he was a free Jew; he was a citizen of Rome. A desert and a sea were placed between his status in the empire and that of his fellow Jews.[2]

Paul navigated multiple personal communities in his life and ministry, each of which, in N. T. Wright's words, "overlapped and interlocked in all sorts of ways . . . part of what makes the world confusing and Paul such a complex character."[3] Paul's Roman citizenship gave him privileges not enjoyed by his people. He surely felt the push-and-pull of multiple loyalties and submitting to Jesus did not make those kinship and national negotiations any neater. Paul was transformed from the one who watched over the coats of Stephen's murderers (Acts 7:58), and a persecutor of the church (8:3), to the greatest

---

1. Thurman, *Jesus and the Disinherited*, 30.
2. Thurman, *Jesus and the Disinherited*, 32.
3. Wright, *Paul and the Faithfulness of God*, 76.

missionary to the Gentiles (9:15). His encounter with the risen Christ left him temporarily blinded, but it was also the beginning of his healing.

White, southern evangelicals' blindness is threefold: White supremacy, codified into law on American soil; the South's social caste system; and our evangelical notion of chosenness. White, southern evangelicalism is a cocktail imbibed early and often, sipped from birth, intoxicating a culture trapped in a nostalgic stupor. Each component of the narrative reinforces the others, making social change nearly unthinkable due to the holistic annihilation it would bring to our world.

Our communities, entrenched in disembodiment and division, have insulated us from seeing racism clearly. The theories we affixed to particular bodies made people into problems to be solved. In this era of distraction, impatience, and fear-mongering, we must seek the truth, which is this: We're beset by individualism and blinded by powerful forces and systems, because it never benefitted us to notice them. We excluded people of color from our institutions for generations, and we interpreted every square inch of the earth and its peoples by a white Christian standard. The disruption of these long-held practices brings our present disorientation.

Disembodiment + Division = Disorientation

Disembodiment

Paul's legacy of wrestling with "the flesh" has led to an unfortunate interpretation where our bodies are considered little more than sinful vessels, a stance that can lead to denigrating God's created beauty intended for our joy, cultivation, and stewardship. Paul valued the body, evidenced by his first letter to the Corinthians, who misunderstood their freedom to be, in Richard Hays's words, "the roots of their community-destroying insistence upon autonomy."[4] Paul's question—"Do you not know that your bodies are members of Christ?" (v. 15)—is meant to remind them of our spiritual and physical connection to one another. Paul addresses embodiment again at the end of the letter concerning the Corinthians' denial of the resurrection of the dead (15:35–58). Hays says, "They denied—whether they meant to or not—that these flawed bodies of ours are loved by God and will be

---

4. Hays, *First Corinthians*, 101.

redeemed.... they denied that what we do with these bodies is of the ultimate significance in God's eyes."[5]

We have too often failed to notice that "our bodies are the locus of conflict in which God and the Powers struggle to become embodied," as Walter Wink says.[6] Our neighbors certainly recognize the struggle far better than we do. Claiming "colorblindness" as a cure-all for our racial ills strips people of their particularity, making whiteness the frame of reference for what is "normal," and puts us on the way to a white Jesus, who names us the elect and answers our prayers. When we are blind to our bodies and others' bodies how can we understand the whole person of Christ, his Body, or the good news to the poor, the prisoner, the blind, and oppressed (Luke 4:18)? To say God cares about justice is to say that God cares about bodies, histories, and right now.

Division

Paul opens his letter to the Corinthians expressing his hope "that all of you be in agreement and that there be no divisions among you, but that you be united in the same mind and the same purpose" (1:10). The Corinthians were divided over who led them to the faith (1 Cor. 3); sexual practices (chs. 5–6); lawsuits among believers (ch. 6); cultural practices/witness (consuming idol meat) (ch. 8); class divisions (abuses of the Lord's Supper) (ch. 11); and the already-mentioned resurrection controversy (ch. 15). Paul attempts to spark what Hays calls a "'conversion of the imagination.' He invites them to see the world in dramatically new ways, in light of values shaped by the Christian story."[7]

Our current divisions are no less serious, albeit sometimes subterranean. Christina Cleveland's assessment that "invisible forces are thwarting church leaders' best-intentioned efforts to build unity" is true due to our distorted imaginations.[8] Let's be plain about it: Many of our racial divisions exist because too many white Christians do not read, listen to, live with, or sit under the authority of people of color. Spencer Perkins, son of John Perkins, named the white evangelical "prolife credibility gap" thirty years ago, saying that for him to consider joining white anti-abortion movements

5. Hays, *First Corinthians*, 277–78.
6. Wink, *Engaging the Powers*, 62.
7. Hays, *First Corinthians*, 11.
8. Cleveland, *Disunity in Christ*, 27.

white evangelicals needed to understand "God's concern for justice everywhere." Perkins saw "the gap" this way: "If we blacks took a stand on an issue, conservative evangelical Christians would line up on the opposite side of the street, blocking our way."[9] We would do well to consider the instances and issues where divisions persists among Christians. We should also ask why is it that when our brothers and sisters call out a problem, we do not believe them?

Disorientation

Our disorientation comes because we are a people that cannot decide if we are homeless in this world (Heb 13:14), or if it is ours to control. We are beset by a "melancholy," over what J. Kameron Carter describes as "evangelicalism's future, woven together with an anxiety over the American project," because we see it failing.[10] Similarly, Mark Charles and Soong-Chan Rah say a "traumatized white Christian America" is sorting through its collective losses without corresponding practices to cope with those losses.[11] Too often, rather than lamentation and repentance, white, southern evangelicals have decided to fight, and much like the Lost Cause, when God doesn't answer your prayers you go looking for new saviors. Eternal goals become reducible to winning elections and writing laws.

Paul's life and teachings remind us to press into our disorientation. Aside from mediating local theological controversies, Paul was imprisoned, beaten, and shipwrecked, and frequently sleepless, cold, hungry and thirsty (2 Cor 11:23–27). Paul adds: "And, besides other things, I am under daily pressure because of my anxiety for all the churches" (v. 28). Paul boasts in his weakness, because he knows the One who gives him strength (12:6–10). A desert and a sea placed between us and our fellow citizens, neighbors, family, or even within our own hearts and minds—whether by political rancor, pandemic-related stresses, racial tensions—feels like an impassable

---

9. Perkins, "Prolife Credibility Gap," 268. Similarly, at Urbana 2015, an InterVarsity Christian Fellowship's missions conference, Michelle Higgins spoke on black justice movements, including her Faith for Justice. Higgins, a black woman, called out white evangelicals' concern for ending legal abortion, while noting that "We can wipe out the adoption crisis tomorrow" were the will present to do so (Tisby, *Color of Compromise*, 183).

10. Carter, "Behind Christianity Today's Editorial is a Deeper Crisis."

11. Charles and Rah, *Unsettling Truths*, 185, 188–89.

gulf. The world seems to be testing the global limits of how much suffering it can hold before it bursts.

And yet, honest reflection about our unholy inheritances must be the first step in coping with the supposed end of our world, one twisted into our own image. I know that many of you are reticent to ponder troubling things. I suspect it's because these issues make you sad or angry; however, some of you avoid the subject because you know that seriously wrestling with your community's histories will require you to change. As David Swanson says, following Jesus means that "white Christians must become accustomed to the very thing whiteness has insulated us from: uncomfortable truth."[12] When I'm confronted by an uncomfortable, yet necessary, change, I'm reminded of Frederick Buechner's words that, "The Gospel is bad news before it is good news. It is the news that man is a sinner, to use the old word, that he is evil in the imagination of his heart . . . That is the tragedy." The good news, however is that we can partake in repairing the damage done, as Buechner reminds me that I am not the sum-total of my communal inheritances: "But it is also the news that he is loved anyways, cherished, forgiven, bleeding to be sure, but also bled for."[13]

**

Twenty years ago, I began my theological education at Duke Divinity School, a place where robust conversations on racial reconciliation were happening, led by incredible scholars of color. These conversations and new friendships altered the trajectory of my life. Racial reconciliation was the key to everything in my mind, but as my studies deepened I became more aware of power dynamics, racial trauma, and the simple fact that not all Black Christians were interested in reconciliation. We had not proven ourselves to be trustworthy reconciliation-partners, because a version of reconciliation mimicked our distorted Christianity: *"Please just forgive me, so that I can get on to other things."*

I believe in racial reconciliation as God's doing. The Church is the newly imagined way of existing in the world, reconciled in Christ's body, and yet this reality—that there is neither "Jew nor Gentile" (Gal 3:28), that "the dividing wall of hostility" has been destroyed (Eph 2:14)—has to be *lived in the flesh*. But, we also need to do some in-house cleaning before

---

12. Swanson, *Rediscipling the White Church*, 53.
13. Buechner, *Telling the Truth*, 7.

jumping into broader conversations that frankly we're not prepared to have. (The teacher in me wants to apply my standard rule: If you haven't done the reading, then don't speak up in class.) Our brothers and sister of color were not responsible for erecting our death-dealing systems, neither should they be responsible for educating us. Charles and Rah call for "racial conciliation," because reconciliation "implies a preexisting harmony and unity," which never existed. They add, "Conciliation does not happen without truth telling. Conciliation without truth is trying to bring health without a comprehensive diagnosis."[14] We would do well to mind Jemar Tisby's warning that "minor repairs by the weekend-warrior racial reconcilers won't fix a flawed foundation," adding, "The church needs the Carpenter from Nazareth to deconstruct the house that racism built and remake it into a house for all nations."[15]

The way forward is a Spirit-led community to see clearly through the fog of the powers. When that community is filled with diverse perspectives it will be better equipped to guard against white groupthink and testify to the multiple ways injustice afflicts our world.[16] But as my dear friend, Rev. Lisa Yebuah, reminds us, "Racial diversity is only as powerful as its ability to inspire institutions to move toward cultivating an equitable culture. Let's remember that some would say that plantations were diverse! Proximity doesn't equal intimacy."[17]

We need to risk. We need to go to some uncomfortable, even if familiar, places, just like the healed Gerasene demoniac. We need to be prepared to be misunderstood, precisely because we are now in our "right mind" (Mark 5:15). When the fear rises up inside of us, we would do well to remember that God tabernacled with a wandering people once before (Exod 25:8–9), and if God uproots our tentpoles then we will still have a stronger and firmer foundation than the little kingdoms we've forced others to build for us.

Christians were never promised power or comfort in this lifetime. Those who follow Jesus are promised the possibility of a cross (Luke 9:23). We were also promised the presence of Jesus to never leave us (Matt 28:20). For this reason, we can risk having no place. But, resting in the promise that God will never leave us requires us to know who the "us" is. If you think "us"

---

14. Charles and Rah, *Unsettling Truths*, 11.
15. Tisby, *Color of Compromise*, 24.
16. Christina Cleveland addresses this well in *Disunity in Christ*, 39–43.
17. Yebuah, "Diversity is Good, Equity is Greater."

means white, southern evangelicals—not the multi-ethnic, multi-national, multi-lingual worshiping throng, united in the Jewish Body of Christ—you are on the path to profound disappointment.

So, I ask, dear reader: Where does it hurt? Do you think you're losing a spot at the table? You are not. What you imagine you're giving up is not nearly as good as the kingdom you'll inherit by letting go.

CONCLUSION

The plane from Uruguay landed in Memphis. Groggy and dirty, I diverged off my normal route home toward my grandparents' house for an unexpected visit. I drove up their driveway unannounced. Buck was out in the yard tending to some chore that he had probably already completed five times over that day. He slowly broke into a slight smile, when he recognized my car. My grandmother sat me down at the kitchen table, and a plate of food magically appeared in front of me, a key tenet of the universal grandmother training program. I regaled them with stories from the mission trip, rattling off facts about the country and the weather. My grandparent's house had a way of buttoning my lip, but today, I was nervously chattering through an encyclopedia's worth of facts, avoiding a talk about Jesus.

My grandparents were no doubt aware of Jesus, as all Southerners are, and I even knew that my grandmother occasionally went to church. Beyond that, in my twenty-two years of life at the time, we had never talked about Jesus, not even mentioned his name. The following ten minutes or so, I delivered the sincerest gospel presentation that I could, and one that I may have been capable of delivering only during my earnest twenties. All that I recall is that I wrapped up my sermon by telling them that I loved them more than they could know.

My grandma listened so patiently and kindly, waiting for me to finish every thought. She looked at me so seriously, and said matter-of-factly, "Well, we love you, too." Buck just stared, sometimes at me; sometimes through me; sometimes at anything else in the room. My grandma and I chatted for a bit longer, back to the non-Jesus topics of conversation. Buck was silent. Not angry or agitated. Just silent, same as he always was. Eventually, we said our usual goodbyes, with Grandma telling me she loved me, and Buck giving his customary "come see us again," as I headed home with few assurances of anything.

I've tried to figure out my grandpa for years. I always loved Buck, even if I didn't know how best to love him. Being born in and of another time can sometimes feel like you're encountering aliens with few methods at your disposal to adequately translate your thoughts. The only thing that comes closest to explaining Buck is this: My dad has told me that at Fort Sill, Oklahoma, where Buck was once stationed, a posted sign read, "Ours is not to reason why ours is but to do and die." My grandfather's artillery company had adopted and paraphrased Alfred Lord Tennyson's "The Charge of the Light Brigade" as their own slogan. Commitment to one's nation required a kind of unquestioning obedience. The sign helped my dad begin to comprehend just what kind of life Buck had volunteered for—one that existed in absolutes with little room for curiosity. It was the very kind of structure my grandfather needed as a young man. The Army gave him a bed, three squares a day, a career, and little-to-no room for error.

I only knew my grandfather after his retirement from the Army, and he conveyed a kind of homelessness out of uniform. Our nation had his full allegiance. The national anthem was his favorite song. America was his God. She had given him orders for a quarter-century, and she told him when it was time to rest. Upsetting this kind of regimented life must have been an adjustment of cataclysmic proportions, because he rarely spoke of his service, at least not with me. If Buck had ever shared his stories I would have listened all day. He chose not to for whatever reason, but I also never asked.

Buck oscillated from mild amusement to mild annoyance. He exceeded his fairly restrained "range" once, during his fiftieth anniversary party. A year prior to our kitchen-table talk, most of the family had gathered to celebrate him and my grandma. Twenty-five of us crammed into their den, his children and grandchildren, finally cracked the armor. Buck began to weep slow, gentle tears, letting the moment wash over him like a baptism. It was like he couldn't believe his good fortune to have all of us with him— on his side—along with my grandma. This poor boy from Henry County finally had the good life.

He spoke quietly and briefly through the only tears I'd ever seen him shed, saying, "I don't deserve all of you." A man who had seen the horrors of war and brought some of it back home with him, who learned how to exist outside of the military and eventually without the help of a bottle, looked upon not his family, but his life, and offered the only confession I'd ever heard him make: "I don't deserve all of you."

Maybe none of us do.

Years later, we laid Buck to rest in his dress blues. When my dad came through town a few months after the funeral, we talked about how we were handling Buck's death. There is always something unmooring when the patriarch passes, often because too much has been left unsaid. Like a good evangelical, I asked my dad about the state of Buck's soul, remembering my dreams in Uruguay and my kitchen-table conversation with him and that blank, silent stare back at me. A man of few words and unseen actions, each executed without fanfare, leaves a short record to assess the fruits of the Spirit.

"Was he scared," I strained out the question, "about what was next?" After all of my degrees, I was little more than a well-educated fundamentalist. My faith had trained me to seek absolute certainty. I want to believe that Buck and my people will be taken care of, that God keeps his promises, like the blessed assurances I sung about in church.

It was likely Buck had been baptized when as a teenager, an apparent expectation in my great-grandfather's house that you walked that aisle by a certain age, which would also explain Buck's tenuous relationship with the church's threshold for the rest of his life. Dad summed it up well enough for the night, "I believe he's done what needed to be done in his own way. God's grace is greater than the meager gestures we can manage." Sometimes it feels like this is all we get.

What I miss about my grandfather is not his latter-day angst or his occasional grumblings about who knows what. He muttered a lot, a passive aggressive maneuver I'm appreciating more as I age. I miss his limited TV rotation of John Wayne and M*A*S*H. I miss the ludicrously large aluminum tins of potato chips and the endless supply of butter pecan ice cream. I miss the sixty seconds I could get him to stay on a phone call before he handed me over to my grandma. Really I just miss being in a room with Buck, like when I first came out of surgery and his face was the first I saw, sitting motionless by my bed, like a soldier at his post.

More than anything, I miss the chance to ask him all of the questions I have now. I never asked what it was like for him to see the military integrated. How did you feel the first time you saluted a Black officer? I never asked him how the Dodgers came to be his favorite baseball team, or what his reaction was to Jackie Robinson breaking the color barrier. I didn't ask him one, single time if what I read in my large history tomes matched his experiences. I could guess what he might have said on a variety of topics, race especially, but I never gave the man a chance to surprise me. I thought silence was better. I was wrong. All I have now is the silence.

BIBLIOGRAPHY

Acharya, Avidit, et al. *Deep Roots: How Slavery Still Shapes Southern Politics.* Princeton: Princeton University Press, 2018.
Adams Family Papers. An Electronic Archive. Massachusetts Historical Society. https://www.masshist.org/digitaladams/archive/doc?id=L17800512jasecond.
"An Address by Dr. W.A. Criswell, Pastor, First Baptist Church, Dallas, Texas, To the Joint Assembly (Wednesday, February 22, 1956)." Duke University Library, Special Collections.
Adichie, Chimamanda Ngozi. "The Danger of a Single Story." TED Talk, October 7, 2009. https://www.youtube.com/watch?v=D9Ihs241zeg.
Ahlstrom, Sydney E. *A Religious History of the American People.* 2nd ed. Foreword and concluding chapter by David D. Hall. New Haven, CT: Yale University Press, 2004.
Aizenman, Nurith. "U.S. Missionary with no Medical Training Settles Suit Over Child Deaths at her Center." *NPR,* July 31, 2020. https://www.npr.org/sections/goatsandsoda/2020/07/31/897773274/u-s-missionary-with-no-medical-training-settles-suit-over-child-deaths-at-her-ce.
Aldredge-Canton, Jann. *Counseling People with Cancer.* Louisville: Westminster John Knox, 1998.
Alexander, Michelle. *The New Jim Crow: Mass Incarceration in the Age of Colorblindness.* New York: The New Press, 2011.
Al Jazeera. "New Zealand Mosque Attacks Suspect Praised Trump in Manifesto." *Al Jazeera,* March 16, 2019. https://www.aljazeera.com/news/2019/03/zealand-mosques-attack-suspect-praised-trump-manifesto-190315100143150.html.
Allison, Natalie. "Gov. Bill Lee Pictured in Auburn Yearbook Wearing Confederate Army Uniform." *The Tennessean,* February 21, 2019. https://www.tennessean.com/story/news/politics/2019/02/21/bill-lee-tennessee-governor-auburn-yearbook-confederate-yearbook/2939636002/.
———. "It's Time to Move the Nathan Bedford Forrest Bust from Tennessee's Capitol, GOP Leader Says." *The Tennessean,* December 10, 2019. https://www.tennessean.com/story/news/politics/2019/12/10/nathan-bedford-forrest-monument-tennessee-rep-calls-removal/4380485002/.
———. "Tennessee Gov. Signs Nathan Bedford Forrest Day Proclamation. Bedford Was Early KKK Leader." *The Tennessean,* July 15, 2019. https://www.tennessean.com/story/news/2019/07/15/kkk-tennessee-nathan-bedford-forrest-day-gov-bill-lee-signs-proclamation-confederate-general/1733261001/.

———. "Tennessee Legislature Cracks Down On Protesters, Making It a Felony Camp Overnight Outside the Capitol." *The Tennessean*, August 12, 2020. https://www.tennessean.com/story/news/politics/2020/08/12/tennessee-passes-law-targeting-protesters-makes-capitol-camping-felony/3354879001/.

Alund, Natalie Neysa. "Report Finds 103 Incidents of White Supremacist Propaganda in Tennessee Since 2018." *The Tennessean*, February 13, 2020). https://www.tennessean.com/story/news/local/2020/02/13/report-white-supremacist-propaganda-tennessee/4747354002/.

Ammerman, Nancy Tatom. *Baptist Battles: Social Change and Religious Conflict in the Southern Baptist Convention*. New Brunswick/London: Rutgers University Press, 1990.

Anderson, Carol. *White Rage: The Unspoken Truth of Our Racial Divide*. New York: Bloomsbury, 2016.

Anderson, Elijah. "The White Space." *Sociology of Race and Ethnicity* 1 (2015) 10–21.

Anderson, Joel. "Liberty University Poured Millions Into Sports: Now Its Black Athletes are Leaving." *Slate*, August 2, 2020. https://slate.com/culture/2020/08/liberty-university-falwell-black-athletes-football-sports.html.

Anderson, Paul Thomas, dir. *There Will Be Blood*. Paramount Vantage and Miramax Films, 2007.

"Andrews Bald." http://hikinginthesmokys.com/andrewsbald.htm.

Applebaum, Yoni. "How America Ends." *The Atlantic*, December 2019. https://www.theatlantic.com/magazine/archive/2019/12/how-america-ends/600757/.

Arrested Development. "Tennessee." Track 14 on *3 Years 5 Months and 2 Days in the Life of—*, Capitol Records, 1992.

Atkins, James A. "Negro Educational Institutions and the Veterans' Educational Facilities Program." *The Journal of Negro Education* 17 (1948) 141–53.

Baig, Assed. "Malala Yousafzai and the White Saviour Complex." *Huff Post*, July 15, 2013. https://www.huffingtonpost.co.uk/assed-baig/malala-yousafzai-white-saviour_b_3592165.html.

Bailey, Kenneth K. *Southern White Protestantism in the Twentieth Century*. New York: Harper & Row, 1964.

Bailey, Sarah Pulliam. "How Nostalgia for White Christian America Drove So Many Americans to Vote for Trump." *The Washington Post*, January 5, 2017. https://www.washingtonpost.com/local/social-issues/how-nostalgia-for-white-christian-america-drove-so-many-americans-to-vote-for-trump/2017/01/04/4ef6d686-b033-11e6-be1c-8cec35b1ad25_story.html

———. "Prominent Southern Baptist Albert Mohler opposed Trump in 2016. Now, He Says He Will Vote for the President." *The Washington Post*, April 16, 2020. https://www.washingtonpost.com/religion/2020/04/16/souther-baptist-albert-mohler-to-vote-trump/.

Baldwin, James. "White Man's Guilt." In *Black on White: Black Writers on What it Means to be White*, edited by David R. Roediger, 320–25. New York: Schocken, 1998.

Baldwin, Lewis V. *There is a Balm in Gilead: The Cultural Roots of Martin Luther King, Jr.* Minneapolis: Fortress, 1991.

Bantum, Brian. *The Death of Race: Building a New Christianity in a Racial World*. Minneapolis: Fortress, 2016.

Baptist, Edward E. *The Half Has Never Been Told: Slavery and the Making of American Capitalism*. New York: Basic, 2014.

BIBLIOGRAPHY

"Baptist Leader Resists 'Collective Guilt' Idea." *Rome News-Tribune*, May 22, 1968.

Barnette, Henlee H. *An Introduction to Communism*. Grand Rapids: Baker Book House, 1964.

———. *Communism: Who? What? Why?* Nashville: Broadman, 1962.

Bartley, Numan V. *The Rise of Massive Resistance: Race and Politics in the South During the 1950's*. Baton Rouge: Louisiana State University Press, 1969.

Bass, S. Jonathan. *Blessed Are the Peacemakers: Martin Luther King Jr., Eight White Religious Leaders, and the "Letter from Birmingham Jail."* Baton Rouge: Louisiana State University Press, 2001.

Bean, Alan. "Last Call for Aging White Evangelicals: The Political Marriage to Trump Will Collapse. What Then?" *Baptist News*, December 31, 2019. https://baptistnews.com/article/last-call-for-aging-white-evangelicals-the-political-marriage-to-trump-will-collapse-what-then/#.Xx8e0S2ZPBI.

Bebbington, David W. "The Nature of Evangelical Religion." In *Evangelicals: Who They Have Been, Are Now, and Could Be*, edited by Mark A. Noll et al., 37–55. Grand Rapids: Eerdmans, 2019.

Bederman, Gail. *Manliness and Civilization: A Cultural History of Gender and Race in the United States, 1880–1917*. Chicago: University of Chicago Press, 1995.

Berlin, Ira. *The Making of African America: The Four Great Migrations*. New York: Viking, 2010.

Bennett, Michael J. *When Dreams Came True: The G.I. Bill and the Making of Modern America*. Washington/London: Brassey's, 1996.

Berends, Kurt O. "Confederate Sacrifice and the "Redemption" of the South." In *Religion in the American South: Protestants and Others in History and Culture*, edited by Beth Barton Schweiger and Donald G. Mathews, 99–124. Chapel Hill, NC: University of North Carolina Press, 2004.

Berkhof, Hendrik. *Christ and the Powers*. Translated by John Howard Yoder. Scottdale, PA: Herald, 1977.

Berry, Wendell. *Citizenship* Papers. Washington, DC: Shoemaker & Hoard, 2003.

———. *The Hidden Wound*. New York: North Point, 1989.

———. *Jayber Crow: A Novel*. Berkeley: Counterpoint, 2000.

———. "A Native Hill." In *The Art of the Commonplace: The Agrarian Essays of Wendell Berry*, edited and introduced by Norman Wirzba, 3–31. Berkeley: Counterpoint, 2002.

———. *Sex, Economy, Freedom, and Community*. New York/San Francisco: Pantheon, 1992.

Blair, Leonardo. "SBC Leader Albert Mohler Indicates Support for Donald Trump in Reversal of 2016 Position." *Christian Post*, April 17, 2020. https://www.christianpost.com/news/sbc-leader-albert-mohler-indicates-support-for-donald-trump-in-reversal-of-2016-position.html.

Blum, Edward J., and Paul Harvey. *The Color of Christ: The Son of God and the Saga of Race in America*. Chapel Hill, NC: University of North Carolina Press, 2012.

Bonhoeffer, Dietrich. *Sanctorum Communio: A Theological Study of the Sociology of the Church. Dietrich Bonhoeffer Works*. Edited by Clifford J. Green. English edition edited by Clifford J. Green. Translated by Reinhard Krauss and Nancy Lukens. Minneapolis: Augsburg Fortress, 1998.

Bolaffi, Guido, et al., eds. *Dictionary of Race, Ethnicity and Culture*. London: Sage, 2003.

Bonilla-Silva, Eduardo. *Racism without Racists: Color-Blind Racism and the Persistence of Racial Inequality in the United States*. 2nd ed. Oxford: Rowman & Littlefield, 2006.

Bootle, Emily. "S is for Serial: The Podcast that Left Us Permanently Plugged In." *New Statesman America*, December 23, 2019. https://www.newstatesman.com/culture/tv-radio/2019/12/s-serial-podcast-left-us-permanently-plugged.

Bowler, Kate. *Blessed: A History of the American Prosperity Gospel*. Oxford: Oxford University Press, 2013.

Boyd, Greg. "Power and Principalities." In *Dictionary of Scripture and Ethics*, edited by Joel B. Green, 611–13. Grand Rapids: BakerAcademic, 2011.

Branch, Taylor. *At Canaan's Edge: America in the King Years 1965–68*. New York: Simon & Schuster, 2006.

———. *Parting the Waters: America in the King Years, 1954–63*. New York: Simon & Schuster, 1988.

Brooks, Arthur. "Trump and I Disagreed at the National Prayer Breakfast. But We Listened To Each Other." *The Washington Post*, February 14, 2020. https://www.washingtonpost.com/opinions/trump-and-i-disagreed-at-the-national-prayer-breakfast-but-we-listened-to-each-other/2020/02/14/ae8d019c-4f40-11ea-9b5c-eac5b16dafaa_story.html.

Brown, Austin Channing. *I'm Still Here: Black Dignity in a World Made for Whiteness*. New York: Convergent, 2018.

Brown, Jon. "'Demonic Power': Franklin Graham Claims Supernatural Element Behind Attacks On Trump." *Washington Examiner*, November 12, 2019. https://www.washingtonexaminer.com/news/franklin-graham-claims-demonic-power-behind-attacks-on-trump.

Brundage, W. Fitzhugh. *The Southern Past: A Clash of Race and Memory*. Cambridge, MA: Belknap Press of Harvard Press, 2005.

Bryce, James D. C. L. *The Relations of the Advanced and the Backward Races of Mankind in Anti-Black Thought, 1863–1925: "The Negro Problem."* In *Volume Eight—Racial Determinism and the Fear of Miscegenation Post-1900: Race and "The Negro Problem" Part II*, edited by John David Smith, 7–46. New York & London: Garland, 1993.

Buechner, Frederick. *Telling the Truth: The Gospel as Tragedy, Comedy, and Fairy Tale*. New York: Harper & Row, 1977.

Burgess, Katharine et al. "Mike Pence Said He Came to Memphis 'to Pay a Debt of Honor and Respect to' Rev. Martin Luther King, Jr." *The Commercial Appeal*, January 19, 2020. https://www.commercialappeal.com/story/news/2020/01/19/mike-pence-memphis-visits-national-civil-rights-museum-cogic-church/4503674002/.

Burke, Daniel. "Why Black Christians are Bracing for a 'Whitelash.'" *CNN*, July 12, 2020. https://www.cnn.com/2020/07/10/us/white-black-christians-racism-burke/index.html?fbclid=IwAR3F061MXr9kcT8mSG8uI8_xZ-K4wiNundP25ySL2-cQhHIvw-QXoLpFSdk.

Campbell, Will D. *Brother to a Dragonfly, 25th Anniversary Edition*. New York: Seabury/New Continuum, 2009.

———. "Reverend Will Davis Campbell." Interview by Harmon Wray, *Civil Rights Oral History Project*. Nashville: Nashville Public Library, 2003.

Carpenter, Joel. *Revive Us Again: The Reawakening of American Fundamentalism*. New York/Oxford: Oxford University Press, 1997.

Carter, J. Kameron. "Behind Christianity Today's Editorial is a Deeper Crisis." *Religion News Service*, December 24, 2019. https://religionnews.com/2019/12/24/behind-christianity-todays-editorial-is-a-deeper-crisis-of-americas-religion-of-white ness/?fbclid=IwAR2X7sXycItvV-sHmFkUGSYlmcdXAt1mJ5Je6nwSgM4RN-eOjjR42FuOsxcU.

———. *Race: A Theological Account*. Oxford: Oxford University Press, 2008.

Cash, W. J. *The Mind of the South*. Repr. New York: Vintage, 1991.

Chadwin, Dean. *Those Damn Yankees*. New York: Verso, 1999.

Chappell, David L. *Inside Agitators: White Southerners in the Civil Rights Movement*. Baltimore: Johns Hopkins University Press, 1994.

———. *A Stone of Hope: Prophetic Religion and the Death of Jim Crow*. Chapel Hill, NC: University of North Carolina Press, 2004.

Charles, Mark, and Soong-Chan Rah. *Unsettling Truths: The Ongoing, Dehumanizing Legacy of the Doctrine of Discovery*. Downers Grove, IL: InterVarsity, 2019.

Charlton, Lauretta. "What is the Great Replacement?" *The New York Times*, August 6, 2019. https://www.nytimes.com/2019/08/06/us/politics/grand-replacement-explainer.html.

Charyn, Jerome. *Joe DiMaggio: The Long Vigil*. New Haven, CT: Yale University Press, 2011.

Cleveland, Christina. *Disunity in Christ: Uncovering the Hidden Forces that Keep Us Apart*. Downers Grove, IL: InterVarsity, 2013.

Coates, Ta-Nehisi. *Between the World and Me*. New York: Spiegel & Grau, 2015.

———. *We Were Eight Years in Power*. New York: One World, 2017.

Cobb, James C. *Away Down South: A History of Southern Identity*. Oxford: Oxford University Press, 2005.

Cole, Teju. "The White-Savior Industrial Complex." *The Atlantic*, March 21, 2012. https://www.theatlantic.com/international/archive/2012/03/the-white-savior-industrial-complex/254843/.

Cone, James H. *A Black Theology of Liberation*. Twentieth Anniversary Edition. New York: Orbis, 2001.

———. *The Cross and the Lynching Tree*. New York: Orbis, 2011.

———. *God of the Oppressed*. New York: Orbis, 1997.

———. *Said I Wasn't Gonna Tell Nobody*. Maryknoll, NY: Orbis, 2018.

Coontz, Stephanie. *The Way We Never Were: American Families and the Nostalgia Trap*. New York: Basic, 2000.

Cooper, Betsy et al. "Exodus: Why Americans are Leaving Religion—And Why They're Unlikely to Come Back." *PRRI*, September 22, 2016. https://www.prri.org/research/prri-rns-poll-nones-atheist-leaving-religion/.

Copeland, M. Shawn. *Enfleshing Freedom: Body, Race, and Being*. Minneapolis: Fortress, 2010.

Coppola, Francis Ford, dir. *The Godfather*. Paramount Pictures, 1972.

Cox, Daniel. "White Christians Side with Trump." *PRRI*, November 9, 2016. https://www.prri.org/spotlight/religion-vote-presidential-election-2004-2016/.

Cramer, Richard Ben. *Joe DiMaggio: The Hero's Life*. New York: Simon & Schuster, 2000.

Crist, Carolyn. "Police-Involved Deaths Vary by Race and Place." *Reuters*, July 31, 2018. https://www.reuters.com/article/us-health-race-police-deaths-police-involved-deaths-vary-by-race-and-place-idUSKBN1KL2M4.

Dailey, Jane. "Sex, Segregation, and the Sacred after Brown." *The Journal of American History* 91 (June 2004) 119–44.

Dark, David. *Life's Too Short to Pretend You're Not Religious.* Downer's Grove, IL: InterVarsity, 2016.

———. *The Sacredness of Questioning Everything.* Grand Rapids: Zondervan, 2009.

Davis, Angela Y. "Rape, Racism and the Myth of the Black Rapist." In *Public Women, Public Words: A Documentary History of American Feminism, Volume III: 1960 to the Present*, edited by Dawn Keetley and John Pettegrew, 155–58. Lanham: Rowman & Littlefield, 2002.

Dawn, Marva J. *Powers, Weakness, and the Tabernacling of God.* Grand Rapids: Eerdmans, 2001.

Death Penalty Information Center. "DPIC 2019 Year End Report." https://deathpenaltyinfo.org/facts-and-research/dpic-reports/dpic-year-end-reports/the-death-penalty-in-2019-year-end-report.

———. "Murder Rates by State by Region." https://deathpenaltyinfo.org/facts-and-research/murder-rates/murder-rates-by-state-by-region.

"Declaration of Constitutional Principles: The Southern Manifesto." http://americanradioworks.publicradio.org/features/marshall/manifesto.html.

Delay, Tad. *Against: What Does the White Evangelical Want?* Eugene, OR: Cascade, 2019.

Delgado, Richard, and Jean Sefancic. *Critical Race Theory: An Introduction.* New York: New York University Press, 2012.

DiAngelo, Robin. *White Fragility: Why It's So Hard for White People to Talk About Racism.* Boston: Beacon, 2018.

Dickerson, Ernest R., dir. *The Wire.* Season 4, episode 13, "Final Grades." Aired December 10, 2006, on HBO.

Dockery, David S., ed. *Southern Baptists and American Evangelicals: The Conversation Continues.* Nashville: Broadman & Holman, 1993.

Donaldson, Susan V. "Gender and History in Eudora Welty's "Delta Wedding." *South Central Review* 14 (1997) 3–14.

Douglas, Kelly Brown. *The Black Christ.* Maryknoll, NY: Orbis, 1994.

Douglass, Frederick. *Narrative of the Life of Frederick Douglass, an American Slave.* New York: Library of America, 2014.

Dreher, Rod. "Religious Liberty and 'White Nationalism.'" *The American Conservative*, December 3, 2019. https://www.theamericanconservative.com/dreher/religious-liberty-and-white-nationalism/.

Du Bois, W. E. B. *The Souls of Black Folk.* Oxford: Oxford University Press, 2008.

DuMez, Kristin. "Donald Trump and Militant Evangelical Masculinity," *Religion and Politics*, January 17, 2017. https://religionandpolitics.org/2017/01/17/donald-trump-and-militant-evangelical-masculinity/

———. *Jesus and John Wayne: How White Evangelicals Corrupted a Faith and Fractured a Nation.* New York: Liveright, 2020.

Dupont, Carolyn Renee. *Mississippi Praying: Southern White Evangelicals and the Civil Rights Movement, 1945–1975.* New York: New York University Press, 2013.

Ebert, Roger. "Review of *The Breakfast Club.*" RogerEbert.com, April 29, 1984. https://www.rogerebert.com/rogers-journal/john-hughes-when-youre-16-youre-more-serious-than-youll-ever-be-again.

Eddo-Lodge, Reni. *Why I'm No Longer Talking to White People About Race.* London: Bloomsbury, 2017.

Egerton, John. *Speak Now Against the Day: The Generation Before the Civil Rights Movement in the South.* Chapel Hill, NC: University of North Carolina Press, 1995.

BIBLIOGRAPHY

Eighmy, John Lee. *Churches in Cultural Captivity: A History of the Social Attitudes of Southern Baptists.* Knoxville: University of Tennessee Press, 1972.

Emerson, Michael O., and Christian Smith. *Divided By Faith: Evangelical Religion and the Problem of Race in America.* Oxford: Oxford University Press, 2000.

Engelberg, Morris, and Marv Schneider. *DiMaggio: Setting the Record Straight.* St. Paul, MN: MBI, 2003.

Equal Justice Initiative. "Reconstruction in America: Racial Violence after the Civil War." https://eji.org/reports/reconstruction-in-america-overview/.

ESPN News Services. "Adam Ottavino Says 'No Disrespect' Intended With Swipe of Babe Ruth." https://www.espn.com/mlb/story/_/id/25853053/adam-ottavino-says-no-disrespect-intended-swipe-babe-ruth.

Estes, Steve. *I am a Man! Race, Manhood, and the Civil Rights Movement.* Chapel Hill, NC: University of North Carolina Press, 2005.

Farmer, James O., Jr. *The Metaphysical Confederacy: James Henley Thornwell and the Synthesis of Southern Values.* Macon, GA: Mercer University Press, 1999.

Fea, John. *Believe Me: The Evangelical Road to Donald Trump.* Grand Rapids: Eerdmans, 2018.

———. "Trump is the New King Cyrus. No, He's Queen Esther. No, He's Daniel. No, He's David. No, He's ACTUALLY Samson." https://thewayofimprovement.com/2020/03/07/trump-is-the-new-king-cyrus-no-hes-queen-esther-no-hes-daniel-no-hes-david-no-hes-actually-sampson/.

Feldman, Glenn. "Introduction." In *Politics and Religion in the White South*, edited by Glenn Feldman, 1–10. Lexington: University of Kentucky Press, 2005.

———. "Home and Hearth: Women, the Klan, Conservative Religion, and Traditional Family Values." In *Politics and Religion in the White South*, edited by Glenn Feldman, 57–99. Lexington: University of Kentucky Press, 2005.

FitzGerald, Frances. *The Evangelicals: The Struggle to Shape America.* New York: Simon & Schuster, 2017.

Flynt, Wayne J. *Alabama Baptists: Southern Baptists in the Heart of Dixie.* Tuscaloosa: University of Alabama Press, 1998.

Foley, Malcom. "On the Assault of James Cone & Black Liberation Theology." *The Witness*, January 3, 2020. https://thewitnessbcc.com/on-the-assault-of-james-cone-black-liberation-theology/.

Folley, Arris. "Rick Perry Says Trump Is the 'Chosen One' Sent to Do Great Things." *The Hill*, November 25, 2019. https://thehill.com/homenews/administration/471868-rick-perry-says-trump-is-the-chosen-one.

Ford, Matt. "Donald Trump's New Lost Cause." *New Republic*, October 3, 2019. https://newrepublic.com/article/155245/donald-trumps-new-lost-cause.

Fox, Richard Wightman. *Jesus in America: Personal Savior, Cultural Hero, National Obsession.* San Francisco: HarperSanFrancisco, 2004.

Frady, Marshall. *Southerners: A Journalist's Odyssey.* New York: The New American Library, 1980.

Franklin, Robert M. "'With Liberty and Justice for All': The Public Mission of the Black Churches." In *Public Faith: Reflections on the Political Rule of American Churches.* St. Louis: CBP, 1990.

Frederickson, George. *Racism: A Short History.* Princeton: Princeton University Press, 2002.

Freeman, Curtis W. "'Never Had I Been So Blind': W. A. Criswell's 'Change' on Racial Segregation." *The Journal of Southern Religion* 10 (2007) 1–12.

Frey, William H. "The US Will Become 'Minority White' in 2045, Census Projects." The Brookings Institution, March 14, 2018. https://www.brookings.edu/blog/the-avenue/2018/03/14/the-us-will-become-minority-white-in-2045-census-projects/.

Frost, Michael. "Colin Kaepernick vs. Tim Tebow: A tale of two Christians on their knees." *The Washington Post*, September 24, 2017. https://www.washingtonpost.com/news/acts-of-faith/wp/2017/09/24/colin-kaepernick-vs-tim-tebow-a-tale-of-two-christianities-on-its-knees/?arc404=true.

Fukunaga, Cary Joji, dir. *True Detective*. Season 1, episode 10, "Who Goes There." Aired February 9, 2014 on HBO.

Garland, David. *Peculiar Institution: America's Death Penalty in an Age of Abolition.* Cambridge, MA: Belknap Press of Harvard University Press, 2010.

Garrett, James Leo, et al., eds. *Are Southern Baptists "Evangelicals?"* Macon, GA: Mercer University Press, 1983.

Gates, Henry Louis, Jr. "The 'Lost Cause' That Built Jim Crow." *The New York Times*, November 8, 2019. https://www.nytimes.com/2019/11/08/opinion/sunday/jim-crow-laws.html?searchResultPosition=2.

———. *Stony the Road: Reconstruction, White Supremacy, and The Rise of Jim Crow*. New York: Penguin, 2019.

Genovese, Eugene D. *A Consuming Fire: The Fall of the Confederacy in the Mind of the White Christian South*. Athens: University of Georgia Press, 1998.

Gehrz, Chris. "What is a Heretic?" *The Anxious Bench*, January 14, 2020. https://www.patheos.com/blogs/anxiousbench/2020/01/heretic-history-joey-cochran/?utm_source=Newsletter&utm_medium=email&utm_campaign=Best+of+Patheos&utm_content=57.

Gilliard, Dominique DuBois. *Rethinking Incarceration: Advocating for Justice that Restores.* Downers Grove, IL: Intervarsity, 2018.

Gilman, Sander L. "Black Bodies, White Bodies: Toward an Iconography of Female Sexuality in Late Nineteenth-Century Art, Medicine, and Literature." *Critical Inquiry* 12 (1985) 204–42.

Glenn, H. Stephen, and Joel W. Warner. *Developing Capable Young People*. Seattle: Humansphere, 1985.

Goodwin, Doris Kearns. *No Ordinary Time: Franklin and Eleanor Roosevelt: The Home Front in World War II*. New York: Simon & Schuster, 1994.

Gordon, Adam. "The Creating of Homeownership: How New Deal Changes in Banking Regulation Simultaneously Made Homeownership Accessible to Whites and Out of Reach for Blacks." *The Yale Law Journal* 115 (2005) 186–223.

Goza, Joel Edward. *America's Unholy Ghosts: The Racist Roots of Our Faith and Politics*. Eugene, OR: Cascade, 2018.

Graham, Ruth. "What It's Like to Be Black at Liberty University." *Slate*, June 16, 2020. https://slate.com/human-interest/2020/06/liberty-university-black-students-faculty.html.

Grant, Jacquelyn. *White Women's Christ and Black Women's Jesus: Feminist Christology and Womanist Response*. Atlanta: Scholars, 1989.

Greenwood, Max. "Trump on Removing Confederate Statues: 'They're Trying to Take Away Our Culture.'" *The Hill*, August 22, 2017. https://thehill.com/homenews/

administration/347589-trump-on-removing-confederate-statues-theyre-trying-to-take-away-our.
Gushee, David P. *Righteous Gentiles of the Holocaust: Genocide and Moral Obligation.* St. Paul: Paragon, 2003.
Gushee, David P., and Glen H. Stassen. *Kingdom Ethics: Following Jesus in Contemporary Context.* 2nd ed. Grand Rapids: Eerdmans, 2016.
Hackney, Sheldon. "Southern Violence." *The American Historical Review* 74 (1969) 924–25.
Hale, Grace Elizabeth. *Making Whiteness: The Culture of Segregation in the South, 1890–1940.* New York: Vintage, 1998.
Hall, Amy Laura. *Conceiving Parenthood: American Protestantism and the Spirit of Reproduction.* Grand Rapids: Eerdmans, 2008.
Hall, Jacquelyn Dowd. *Revolt Against Chivalry: Jessie Daniel Ames and the Women's Campaign Against Lynching.* New York: Columbia University Press, 1993.
Hall, Patricia Kelly, and Steven Ruggles. "Restless in the Midst of Their Prosperity: New Evidence on the Internal Migration of Americans, 1850–2000." *The Journal of American History* 91 (2004) 829–46.
Hankins, Barry. *Uneasy in Babylon: Southern Baptist Conservatives and American Culture.* Tuscaloosa: University of Alabama Press, 2002.
Harlow, Luke E. "Slavery, Race, and Political Ideology in the White Christian South Before and After the Civil War." In *Religion and American Politics: From the Colonial Period to the Present,* edited by Mark A. Noll and Luke E. Harlow, 203–24. Oxford: Oxford University Press, 2007.
Hartman, Saidiya. *Lose Your Mother: A Journey Along the Atlantic Slave Route.* New York: Farrar, Straus and Giroux, 2007.
Hartmann, Douglas, et al. "An Empirical Assessment of Whiteness Theory: Hidden from How Many?" *Social Problems* 56 (2009) 403–24.
Harvey, Paul. *Freedom's Coming: Religious Culture and the Shaping of the South from the Civil War through the Civil Rights Era.* Chapel Hill, NC: University of North Carolina, 2005.
———. "'Yankee Faith' and Southern Redemption: White Southern Baptist Ministers, 1850–1890." In *Religion and the American Civil War,* edited by Randall M. Miller et al., 167–86. Oxford: Oxford University Press, 1998.
Hauerwas, Stanley. *Hannah's Child: A Theologian's Memoir.* Grand Rapids: Eerdmans, 2010.
Hayden, Michael Edison. "Stephen Miller's Affinity for White Nationalism Revealed in Leaked Emails." The Southern Poverty Law Center, November 12, 2019. https://www.splcenter.org/hatewatch/2019/11/12/stephen-millers-affinity-white-nationalism-revealed-leaked-emails.
Hays, Richard B. *First Corinthians, Interpretation: A Bible Commentary for Teaching and Preaching.* Louisville: John Knox, 1997.
Helderman, Rosalind S., and Jon Cohen, "As Republican Convention Emphasizes Diversity, Racial Incidents Intrude." *The Washington Post,* August 29, 2012. https://www.washingtonpost.com/politics/2012/08/29/b9023a52-f1ec-11e1-892d-bc92fee603a7_story.html.
Heltzel, Peter Goodwin. *Jesus and Justice: Evangelicals, Race, and American Politics.* New Haven, CT: Yale University Press, 2009.
Hendricks, Jr, Obery M. *The Politics of Jesus.* New York: Doubleday, 2006.

BIBLIOGRAPHY

Henry, Carl F. H. *The Uneasy Conscience of Modern Fundamentalism*. Grand Rapids: Eerdmans, 1947.

Herbold, Hilary. "Never a Level Playing Field: Blacks and the GI Bill." *The Journal of Blacks in Higher Education* (1994/1995) 104–8.

Herman, Arthur. *The Cave and the Light: Plato Versus Aristotle and the Struggle for the Soul of Western Civilization*. New York: Random, 2014.

Herndon, Astead W. "'Nothing Less Than a Civil War': These White Voters on the Far Right See Doom Without Trump." *The New York Times*, December 28, 2019. https://www.nytimes.com/2019/12/28/us/politics/trump-2020-trumpstock.html.

Hill, Samuel S. *Southern Churches in Crisis Revisited*. Tuscaloosa: University of Alabama Press, 1999.

Hollinger, Dennis P. *Individualism and Social Ethics: An Evangelical Syncretism*. Lanham, MD: University Press of America, 1983.

hooks, bell. *Killing Rage: Ending Racism*. New York: Henry Holt and Company, 1995.

Howe, Ben. *The Immoral Majority: Why Evangelicals Chose Political Power over Christian Values*. New York: Broadside, 2019.

Horowitz, Juliana Menasce. "Most Americans Say the Legacy of Slavery Still Affects Black People In the U.S. Today." *Pew Research Center*, June 17, 2019. https://www.pewresearch.org/fact-tank/2019/06/17/most-americans-say-the-legacy-of-slavery-still-affects-black-people-in-the-u-s-today/.

Hudnut-Beumler, James. *Looking for God in the Suburbs: The Religion of the American Dream and Its Critics, 1945–1965*. New Brunswick, NJ: Rutgers University Press, 1994.

Hughes, John, dir. *The Breakfast Club*. Universal Pictures, 1985.

Humes, Edward. "How the G.I. Bill Shunted Blacks into Vocational Training." *The Journal of Blacks in Higher Education* 53 (2006) 92–104.

———. *Over Here: How the G.I. Bill Transformed the American Dream*. New York: Harcourt, 2006.

Huppke, Rex. "Trump Uses Textbook White Supremacist Language Day After Chicago Man Is Charged with a Hate Crime." *Chicago Tribune*, July 13, 2018. https://www.chicagotribune.com/columns/rex-huppke/ct-met-hate-crime-puerto-rico-shirt-video-huppke-20180713-story.html.

Isenberg, Nancy. *White Trash: The 400-Year Untold History of Class in America*. New York: Penguin, 2016.

Jackson, David. "Donald Trump Accepts GOP Nomination, Says 'I Alone Can Fix' System." *USA Today*, July 21, 2016. https://www.usatoday.com/story/news/politics/elections/2016/07/21/donald-trump-republican-convention-acceptance-speech/87385658/.

Jackson, Kenneth T. *Crabgrass Frontier: The Suburbanization of the United States*. Oxford: Oxford University Press, 1985.

Jacobson, Matthew Frye. *Whiteness of a Different Color: European Immigrants and the Alchemy of Race*. Cambridge, MA: Harvard University Press, 1998.

Jacoway, Elizabeth. *Turn Away Thy Son: Little Rock, The Crisis that Shocked the Nation*. New York: Free, 2007.

Jaffe, Alexandra, and Corky Siemaszko "Outrage as Trump Inspired Candidate wants to 'Make America White Again." *NBC News*, June 23, 2016. https://www.nbcnews.com/news/us-news/outrage-trump-inspired-congressional-candidate-wants-make-america-white-again-n597916.

BIBLIOGRAPHY

Jenkins, Philip. *The Next Christendom: The Coming of Global Christianity*. Oxford: Oxford University Press, 2002.

Jennings, Willie James. *The Christian Imagination: Theology and The Origins of Race*. New Haven, CT: Yale University Press, 2010.

———. "Is America Wiling to be Freed from its Demons?" *Religion Dispatches*, July 11, 2016. https://religiondispatches.org/is-america-willing-to-be-freed-from-its-demons/.

Johnson, Daniel M., and Rex R. Campbell. *Black Migration in America: A Social Demographic History*. Durham, NC: Duke University Press, 1981.

Johnson, Martenzie. "All the Quarterbacks Who Signed Since Colin Kaepernick Became a Free Agent." *The Undefeated*, November 15, 2019. https://theundefeated.com/features/33-quarterbacks-signed-before-colin-kaepernick-free-agent/.

Jones, Robert P. *The End of White Christian America*. New York: Simon & Schuster, 2016.

Jordan, Winthrop D. *The White Man's Burden: Historical Origins of Racism in the United States*. Oxford: Oxford University Press, 1974.

———. *White Over Black: American Attitudes Toward the Negro, 1550–1812*. Chapel Hill, NC: University of North Carolina Press, 1968.

Katznelson, Ira. *When Affirmative Action was White: The Untold History of Racial Inequality in Twentieth Century America*. New York: W. W. Norton, 2005.

Keel, Terence. *Divine Variations: How Christian Thought Became Racial Science*. Palo Alto: Stanford University Press, 2019.

Kelly, Caroline. "Virginia Governor Apologizes for 'Racist And Offensive' Costume In Photo Showing People In Blackface and Kkk Garb." *CNN*, February 7, 2019. https://www.cnn.com/2019/02/01/politics/northam-blackface-photo/index.html.

Kendi, Ibram X. *How to Be an Antiracist*. New York: One World, 2019.

———. *Stamped From the Beginning: The Definitive History of Racist Ideas in America*. New York: Nation, 2016.

Kennedy, Thomas D. "Will D. Campbell." In *Twentieth-Century Shapers of American Popular Religion*, edited by Charles H. Lippy, 65–72. Westport, CT: Greenwood, 1989.

Kidd, Thomas. *Who Is an Evangelical?* New Haven, CT: Yale University Press, 2019.

Killingsworth, Blake. "Here I am, Stuck in the Middle with You": The Baptist Standard, Texas Baptist Leadership, and School Desegregation, 1954 to 1956." *Baptist History and Heritage* 41 (2006) 78–92.

King, Martin Luther, Jr. "Letter from Birmingham City Jail." In *A Testament of Hope: The Essential Writings and Speeches of Martin Luther King, Jr.*, edited by James M. Washington, 289–302. San Francisco: HarperSanFrancisco, 1991.

Kirwan Institute for the Study of Race and Ethnicity at The Ohio State University. "Understanding Implicit Bias." http://kirwaninstitute.osu.edu/research/understanding-implicit-bias/.

Kluger, Richard. *Simple Justice: The History of Brown v. Board of Education and Black America's Struggle for Equality*. New York: Alfred A. Knopf, 2004.

Kolchin, Peter. *American Slavery, 1619–1877*. New York: Hill and Wang, 1993.

Kornfield, Meryl and Hannah Knowles. "Michigan Lawmaker Denies Wearing Confederate Flag Mask, Calls It History, Then Apologizes." *The Washington Post*, April 25, 2020. https://www.washingtonpost.com/nation/2020/04/25/dale-zorn-confederate-flag-mask/.

BIBLIOGRAPHY

Kruse, Kevin M. *One Nation Under God: How Corporate America Invented Christian America*. New York: Basic, 2015.

Kuja, Ryan. "6 Harmful Consequences of the White Savior Complex." *Sojourners*, July 24, 2019. https://sojo.net/articles/6-harmful-consequences-white-savior-complex?fbclid=IwAR2Zct4P5mccYGxc2LPPyOEojehyMhJatjoSx_wdg956wFyc14oRxMiNHQc.

Kurtzleben, Danielle. "Are you an Evangelical? Are you sure?" *NPR*, December 19, 2015. https://www.npr.org/2015/12/19/458058251/are-you-an-evangelical-are-you-sure.

Kushner, David. *Levittown: Two Families, One Tycoon, and the Fight for Civil Rights in America's Legendary Suburb*. New York: Walker & Company, 2009.

Ladd, Tony, and James A. Mathisen. *Muscular Christianity: Evangelical Protestants and the Development of American Sport*. Grand Rapids: Baker, 1999.

"Lariat Letters: Rope Failed In Attempting Parody of Religion Prof." *Baylor Lariat*, October 26, 2011. https://baylorlariat.com/2011/10/26/lariat-letters-rope-failed-in-attempting-parody-of-religion-prof/.

Lassiter, Matthew D. *The Silent Majority: Suburban Politics in the Sunbelt South*. Princeton: Princeton University Press, 2006.

"Legend of Reelfoot Lake." http://reelfoottourism.com/reelfootlake/history/219-2/.

Leonard, Bill J. "A Theology for Racism: Southern Fundamentalists and the Civil Rights Movement." *Baptist History and Heritage* 34 (1999) 49–68.

LeRoy, Mervyn, dir. *The House I Live In*. RKO Radio Pictures, 1945.

Letcher, Michael, and Ossie Davis. *God's Will*. DVD. Tuscaloosa, AL: University of Alabama Center for Public Television and Radio, 2000.

Lewis, David Levering. *W. E. B. Du Bois: Biography of a Race, 1868–1919*. New York: Henry Holt, 1993.

Lewis, John. "John Lewis: Together, You Can Redeem the Soul of Our Nation." *The New York Times*, July 30, 2020. https://www.nytimes.com/2020/07/30/opinion/letters/john-lewis-civil-rights.html.

Lewis, Michael. *The Fifth Risk*. New York: W. W. Norton, 2018.

Levy, Ariel. "A Missionary on Trial." *The New Yorker*, April 6, 2020. https://www.newyorker.com/magazine/2020/04/13/a-missionary-on-trial.

Lincoln, C. Eric, and Lawrence H. Mamiya. *The Black Church in the African American Experience*. Durham: Duke University Press, 1990.

Linder, Robert D. "The Resurgence of Evangelical Social Concern (1925–75)." In *The Evangelicals: What They Believe, Who They Are, Where They Are Changing*, edited by David F. Wells and John D. Woodridge. Nashville: Abingdon, 1975.

Lippy, Charles H. *Bibliography of Religion in the South*. Macon, GA: Mercer University Press, 1985.

Lipsitz, George. "The Possessive Investment in Whiteness: Racialized Social Democracy and the 'White' Problem in American Studies." *American Quarterly* 47 (1995) 369–87.

Logan, Rayford W., ed. *What the Negro Wants*. Chapel Hill, NC: University of North Carolina Press, 1944.

Lubin, Alex. *Romance and Rights: The Politics of Interracial Intimacy, 1945–1954*. Jackson: University of Mississippi Press, 2005.

Mangine, Genevieve. "Seeing Life Full Size: An interview with Wendell Berry." *The Other Side* 30 (1994).

Manis, Andrew Michael. "Silence or Shockwaves: Southern Baptist Responses to the Assassination of Martin Luther King, Jr. *Baptist History and Heritage* 15 (1980) 19–27, 35.

———. *Southern Civil Religions in Conflict: Black and White Baptists and Civil Rights, 1947–1957*. Athens: University of Georgia Press, 1987.

Marcotte, Amanda. "Evangelicals Told Trump He Was 'Chosen' By God. Now He Says It Himself." *Salon*, August 22, 2019. https://www.salon.com/2019/08/22/evangelicals-told-trump-he-was-chosen-by-god-now-he-says-it-himself/.

Marsden, George M. *Fundamentalism and American Culture: The Shaping of Twentieth-Century Evangelicalism, 1870–1925*. Oxford: Oxford University Press, 1980.

———. *Reforming Fundamentalism: Fuller Seminary and the New Evangelicalism*. Grand Rapids: Eerdmans, 1987.

———. *Understanding Fundamentalism and Evangelicalism*. Grand Rapids: Eerdmans, 1991.

Marsh, Charles. *The Beloved Community: How Faith Shapes Social Justice From the Civil Rights Movement to Today*. New York: Basic, 2005.

———. *God's Long Summer: Stories of Faith and Civil Rights*. Princeton: Princeton University Press, 1997.

Marshall, Christopher D. *Compassionate Justice: An Interdisciplinary Dialogue with Two Gospel Parables on Law, Crime, and Restorative Justice*. Eugene, OR: Cascade, 2012.

Mason, John Edwin. "History, Mine and Ours: Charlotteville's Blue Ribbon Commission and the Terror Attacks of August 2017." In *Charlottesville 2017: The Legacy of Race and Inequity*, edited by Louis P. Nelson and Claudrena N. Harold, 19–36. Charlottesville: University of Virginia Press, 2018.

Maston, T.B. "Christianity and Communism." *The Review and Expositor* 45 (1948) 271–80.

———. *Of One: A Study of Christian Principles and Race Relations*. Atlanta: Home Mission Board of the Southern Baptist Convention, 1946.

McCardle, Mairead. "FBI Director: White-Supremacist Violence Accounts for Majority of Domestic-Terrorism Arrests Since Last October." *The National Review*, July 23, 2019. https://www.nationalreview.com/news/fbi-director-white-supremacist-violence-accounts-for-majority-of-domestic-terrorism-arrests-since-last-october/.

McClendon, James William, Jr. *Biography as Theology: How Life Stories Can Remake Today's Theology*. Philadelphia: Trinity Press International, 1990.

———. *Ethics: Systematic Theology, Vol. 1*. Nashville: Abingdon, 1986.

McEvers, Kelly. "Ex-Green Beret and NFL Player on his Role in, Reaction to Anthem Protests." *NPR*, October 17, 2017. https://www.npr.org/2017/10/17/558390590/former-green-beret-and-nfl-player-talks-about-take-a-knee-protests.

McMillan Cottom, Tressie. *THICK: And Other Essays*. New York: The New Press, 2019.

McWhorter, Ladelle. *Racism and Sexual Oppression in Anglo-America: A Genealogy*. Bloomington; Indianapolis: Indiana University Press, 2009.

Medak, Peter, dir. *The Wire*. Season 1, episode 3, "The Buys." Aired June 16, 2002 on HBO.

Medwed, Daniel S. "Black Deaths Matter: The Race-of-Victim Effect and Capital Punishment." *Northeastern Public Law and Theory Faculty Research Paper Series* 367–2020 (January 28, 2020).

Mettler, Suzanne. "The Only Good Thing Was the G.I. Bill": Effects of the Education and Training Provisions on African-American Veterans' Political Participation." *Studies in American Political Development* 19 (2005) 31–52.

———. *Soldiers to Citizens: The G.I. Bill and the Making of the Greatest Generation.* Oxford: Oxford University Press, 2005.

Metzl, Jonathan. *Dying of Whiteness: How the Politics of Racial Resentment is killing America's Heartland.* New York: Basic, 2019.

Mohler, R. Albert, Jr. "Donald Trump Has Created an Excruciating Moment for Evangelicals." *The Washington Post*, October 9, 2016. https://www.washingtonpost.com/news/acts-of-faith/wp/2016/10/09/donald-trump-has-created-an-excruciating-moment-for-evangelicals/.

Moore, Russell. "The Cross and the Confederate Flag." https://www.russellmoore.com/2015/06/19/the-cross-and-the-confederate-flag/.

Morris, Alex. "False Idol—Why the Christian Right Worships Donald Trump." *Rolling Stone*, December 2, 2019. https://www.rollingstone.com/politics/politics-features/christian-right-worships-donald-trump-915381/.

Morris, Thomas D. *Southern Slavery and the Law, 1619–1860.* Chapel Hill, NC: University of North Carolina, 1996.

Morrison, Toni. *Playing in the Dark: Whiteness and the Literary Imagination.* Cambridge, MA: Harvard University Press, 1992.

Mouw, Richard J. *Politics and the Biblical Drama.* Grand Rapids: Baker, 1976.

Myers, Ched. *Binding the Strong Man: A Political Reading of Mark's Story of Jesus.* New York: Orbis, 2008.

Myrdal, Gunnar. *An American Dilemma: The Negro Problem and Modern Democracy.* New York/London: Harper & Brothers, 1944.

The National Association For the Advancement of Colored People. *Thirty Years of Lynching in the United States, 1889–1918.* New York: Negro Universities Press, 1919.

NBC Bay Area Sports Staff. "Trump to Anthem Protesters: 'Get That Son of a B—— Off the Field.'" *NBC Bay Area Sports*, September 22, 2017. https://www.nbcsports.com/bayarea/49ers/trump-anthem-protesters-get-son-b-field.

NBC News. "These 5 States Still Use Confederate Symbols in Their Flags." *MSNBC*, June 23, 2015. http://www.msnbc.com/msnbc/these-5-states-still-use-confederate-symbols-their-flags.

Newman, Mark. *The Civil Rights Movement.* Westport, CT: Praeger, 2004.

———. *Getting Right with God: Southern Baptists and Desegregation, 1945–1995.* Tuscaloosa: University of Alabama Press, 2001.

Newson, Ryan Andrew. "Epistemological Crises Made Stone: Confederate Monuments and the End of Memory." *Journal of the Society of Christian Ethics* 37 (2017) 135–51.

NewsOne Now. "Roland Martin Confronts White Nationalist Richard Spencer on NewsOne Now." https://newsone.com/3597206/roland-martin-confronts-white-nationalist-richard-spencer-on-newsone-now/.

NFL.com Staff. "Drew Brees Facing Intense Criticism for Comments On Flag Disrespect." NFL.com, June 3, 2020. https://www.nfl.com/news/drew-brees-facing-intense-criticism-for-comments-on-flag-disrespect.

Nichols, Stephen J. *Jesus: Made in America.* Downers Grove, IL: Intervarsity, 2008.

Niebuhr, Reinhold. *Moral Man and Immoral Society: A Study in Ethics and Politics/* New York/London: Charles Scribner's Sons, 1934.

Noah, Trevor. *Born a Crime: Stories From a South African Childhood.* New York: Spiegel & Grau, 2016.

Noll, Mark A. *America's God: From Jonathan Edwards to Abraham Lincoln.* Oxford: Oxford University Press, 2002.

BIBLIOGRAPHY

———. *God and Race in American Politics: A Short History.* Princeton: Princeton University Press, 2008.

Norrell, Robert J. *The House I Live In: Race in the American Century.* Oxford: Oxford University Press, 2005.

Ockenga, Harold John. "The Unvoiced Multitudes." Keynote conference address contained in *Evangelical Action! A Report of the Organization of the National Association of Evangelicals for United Action.* Compiled and Edited by the Executive Committee. Boston, Mass: United Action Press, 1942.

Olson, Keith W. *The G.I. Bill, the Veterans, and the Colleges.* Lexington: University of Kentucky Press, 1974.

Onkst, David H. "First a Negro. . .Incidentally a Veteran: Black World War Two Veterans and the G.I. Bill Of Rights In the Deep South, 1944–1948." *Journal of Social History* 31 (1998) 517–43.

The Onion "South Postpones Rising Again for Yet Another Year." https://www.theonion.com/south-postpones-rising-again-for-yet-another-year-1819565548.

Onwuchekwa, John. "4 Reasons We Left the SBC." *The Front Porch*, July 9, 2020. https://thefrontporch.org/2020/07/4-reasons-we-left-the-SBC/,.

Oppenheimer, Mark. "For God, Not Country: The un-American Theology of Stanley Hauerwas." *Lingua Franca* 11 (2001). http://linguafranca.mirror.theinfo.org/print/0109/feature.html.

Painter, Nell Irvin. *The History of White People.* New York: W. W. Norton, 2010.

Palmer, Parker J. *Healing the Heart of Democracy: The Courage to Create a Politics Worthy of the Human Spirit.* San Francisco: Jossey-Bass, 2011.

Patterson, James T. *Brown v. Board of Education: A Civil Rights Milestone and Its Troubled Legacy.* Oxford: Oxford University Press, 2001.

Perkins, Spencer. "The Prolife Credibility Gap." In *Readings in Christian Ethics*, edited by David K. Clark and Robert V. Rakestraw, 268–71. Grand Rapids: Baker Academic, 1996.

Pew Research Center. "In U.S., Decline of Christianity Continues at Rapid Pace." https://www.pewforum.org/2019/10/17/in-u-s-decline-of-christianity-continues-at-rapid-pace/.

———. "White Evangelicals See Trump as Fighting for their Beliefs, Though Many Have Mixed Feelings about his Personal Conduct." https://www.pewforum.org/2020/03/12/white-evangelicals-see-trump-as-fighting-for-their-beliefs-though-many-have-mixed-feelings-about-his-personal-conduct/.

Phillips, Clinton E., and Raymond J. Corsini, *Give In or Give Up.* Chicago: Burnham, 1982.

Phillips, Justin Randall. "How Cancer Made Me Less of a Bastard (and More Human)." *The Other Journal*, May 11, 2015. https://theotherjournal.com/2015/05/11/how-cancer-made-me-less-of-a-bastard-and-more-human/.

———. "Jesus and the Dispossessed." *The Other Journal*, October 31, 2016. https://theotherjournal.com/2016/10/31/jesus-and-the-dispossessed/.

———. "Lord, When Did We See You? The Ethical Vision of White Progressive Baptists in the South During the Civil Rights Movement." PhD diss., Fuller Theological Seminary, 2013.

Pinches, Charles R. "Stout, Hauerwas, and the Body of America." *Political Theology* 8 (2007) 9–31.

BIBLIOGRAPHY

Pittman, Ashton. "Lt. Gov. Tate Reeves' Fraternity Wore Black Face, Hurled the N-Word at Black Students." *Jackson Free Press*, February 8, 2019. https://www.jacksonfreepress.com/news/2019/feb/08/lt-gov-tate-reeves-fraternity-wore-black-face-hurl/.

Positano, Rock, and John Positano. *Dinner with DiMaggio: Memories of an American Hero.* New York: Simon & Schuster, 2017.

Potter, Gary. "The History of Policing in the United States." Eastern Kentucky University Police Studies Online, June 25, 2013. https://plsonline.eku.edu/insidelook/history-policing-united-states-part-1.

Prothero, Stephen. *American Jesus: How the Son of God Became a National Icon.* New York: Farrar, Straus and Giroux, 2003.

Quarles, Benjamin. *The Negro in the Making of America.* New York: Collier, 1987.

Queen, Edward L., II. *In the South the Baptists are the Center of Gravity: Southern Baptists and Social Change, 1930–1980.* Brooklyn: Carlson, 1991.

Raboteau, Albert J. *Slave Religion: The "Invisible Institution" in the Antebellum South.* Oxford: Oxford University Press, 2004.

Rah, Soong-Chan. *Prophetic Lament: A Call for Justice in Troubled Times.* Downers Grove, IL: InterVarsity, 2015.

Raper, Arthur F. *The Tragedy of Lynching.* New York: Dover, 1970.

Rauschenbusch, Walter. *Christianity and the Social Crisis in the 21st Century.* Edited by Paul Raushenbush. New York: HarperOne, 2007.

Richardson, Heather Cox. *How the South Won the Civil War: Oligarchy, Democracy, and the Continuing Fight for the Soul of America.* Oxford: Oxford University Press, 2020.

Ringwald, Molly. "What About 'The Breakfast Club?'" *The New Yorker*, April 6, 2018. https://www.newyorker.com/culture/personal-history/what-about-the-breakfast-club-molly-ringwald-metoo-john-hughes-pretty-in-pink.

Rivera, Luis N. *A Violent Evangelism: The Political and Religious Conquest of the Americas.* Louisville: Westminster John Knox, 1992.

Rock, Chris. "Bigger and Blacker." HBO Productions, July 10, 1999.

Roediger, David R. *Working Toward Whiteness: How America's Immigrants Became White—The Strange Journey from Ellis Island to the Suburbs.* New York: Basic, 2005.

Rothstein, Richard. *The Color of Law: A Forgotten History of How Our Government Segregated America.* New York/London: Liveright, 2017.

"Ruby Sales: Where Does it Hurt?" *On Being with Krista Tippett*, September 15, 2016. https://onbeing.org/programs/ruby-sales-where-does-it-hurt/.

Sandeen, Ernest. *The Roots of Fundamentalism: British and American Millenarianism, 1800–1930.* Chicago: University of Chicago Press, 1970.

Sides, John, et al. *Identity Politics: The 2016 Presidential Campaign and the Battle for the Meaning of America.* Princeton: Princeton University Press, 2018.

Smietana, Bob. "Many Who Call Themselves Evangelical Don't Actually Hold Evangelical Beliefs." *LifeWay Research*, December 6, 2017. https://lifewayresearch.com/2017/12/06/many-evangelicals-dont-hold-evangelical-beliefs/.

Simon & Garfunkel, "Mrs. Robinson." Sony Music Entertainment, B00270WH3Y, 1985.

Smith, H. Shelton. *In His Image, but. . .: Racism in Southern Religion, 1780–1910.* Durham: Duke University Press, 1972.

Smith, James K. A. *Desiring the Kingdom: Worship, Worldview, and Cultural Formation.* Cultural Liturgies 1. Grand Rapids: BakerAcademic, 2009.

———. *Who's Afraid of Relativism? Community, Contingency, and Creaturehood.* Grand Rapids: BakerAcademic, 2014.

BIBLIOGRAPHY

———. *You Are What You Love: The Spiritual Power of Habit*. Grand Rapids: Brazos, 2016.

Smith, Lillian. *Killers of the Dream*. New York: W. W. Norton, 1994.

Sokol, Jason. *There Goes My Everything: White Southerners in the Age of Civil Rights, 1945–1975*. New York: Alfred A. Knopf, 2006.

The Southern Poverty Law Center. "Whose Heritage? Public Symbols of the Confederacy." https://www.splcenter.org/sites/default/files/com_whose_heritage.pdf.

Spain, Rufus B. *At Ease in Zion: Social History of Southern Baptists, 1865–1900*. Nashville: Vanderbilt University Press, 1961.

Stagg, Frank. "Henlee Hulix Barnette: Activist." In *Perspectives in Religious Studies: Essays in Honor of Henlee Hulix Barnette*, edited by Rollin S. Armour, 34. Macon, GA: Mercer University Press, 1991.

Stassen, Glen H. *Thicker Jesus: Incarnational Discipleship in a Secular Age*. Louisville: Westminster/John Knox, 2012.

Stassen, Glen H., and David P. Gushee, *Kingdom Ethics: Following Jesus in Contemporary Context*. 1st ed. Downers Grove, IL: InterVarsity, 2003.

"A Statement Concerning the Crisis in our Nation." *Baptist Press* (May 20, 1968). http://media.sbhla.org.s3.amazonaws.com/2604,20-May-1968.pdf.

Stephens, Alexander H. "Cornerstone" Speech. https://teachingamericanhistory.org/library/document/cornerstone-speech/.

Stevenson, Bryan. *Just Mercy: A Story of Justice and Redemption*. New York: Spiegel & Grau, 2014.

Stewart, Dante. "As a Black Person, I'm Done Helping White Christians Feel Better About Race." *The Washington Post*, July 13, 2020. https://www.washingtonpost.com/outlook/2020/07/13/black-pastor-white-churches/?fbclid=IwAR120Qgsi3Nab4P_cydpg10F_ER-s2qxf_uXavvaKSsfuKrvastJTinTcFI.

Stout, Harry S. *Upon the Altar of the Nation: A Moral History of the Civil War*. New York: Penguin, 2006.

Sugrue, Thomas J. "Jim Crow's Last Stand: The Struggle to Integrate Levittown." In *Second Suburb: Levittown, Pennsylvania*, edited by Dianne Harris, 175–99. Pittsburgh: University of Pittsburgh Press, 2010.

Sutton, Matthew Avery. *American Apocalypse: A History of Modern Evangelicalism*. Cambridge, MA: Belknap Press of Harvard University Press, 2014.

Swanson, David W. *Rediscipling the White Church: From Cheap Diversity to True Solidarity*. Downers Grove, IL: InterVarsity, 2020.

Taylor, Charles. *A Secular Age*. Cambridge, MA: Belknap Press of Harvard University Press, 2007.

Taylor, Jessica. "Alabama Gov. Kay Ivey Apologizes For Wearing Blackface During College Skit." *NPR*, August 29, 2019. https://www.npr.org/2019/08/29/755649657/alabama-gov-kay-ivey-apologizes-for-wearing-blackface-during-college-skit.

Tennessee Office of the Governor. Transcript (June 10, 2020). https://www.tn.gov/governor/covid-19/governors-response/commitment-to-accessibility/covid-19-briefing-transcripts/june-10—2020.html.

———. Transcript (June 18, 2020). https://www.tn.gov/governor/covid-19/governors-response/commitment-to-accessibility/covid-19-briefing-transcripts/june-18—2020.html.

———. Transcript (July 8, 2020). https://www.tn.gov/governor/covid-19/governors-response/commitment-to-accessibility/covid-19-briefing-transcripts/july-8-2020.html.

Thomas, Angie. *The Hate U Give*. New York: Balzer + Bray, 2017.

Thompson, Tracy. *The New Mind of the South*. New York: Simon & Schuster, 2013.

Thurman, Howard. *Jesus and the Disinherited*. Boston: Beacon, 1996.

Tilson, Everett. *Segregation and the Bible*. New York/Nashville: Abingdon, 1963.

Tisby, Jemar. "Are Black Christians Evangelicals?" In *Evangelicals: Who They Have Been, Are Now, and Could Be*, edited Mark A. Noll et al., 262–72. Grand Rapids: Eerdmans, 2019.

———. *The Color of Compromise: The Truth about the American Church's Complicity in Racism*. Grand Rapids: Zondervan, 2019.

"Transcript of President Trump's Remarks at Trump Tower on Charlottesville." *Los Angeles Times*, August 15, 2017. https://www.latimes.com/politics/la-na-pol-trump-charlottesville-transcript-20170815-story.html.

Tuck, Stephen. *We Ain't What We Ought to Be: The Black Freedom Struggle from Emancipation to Obama*. Cambridge, MA: Belknap Press of Harvard University Press, 2010.

Turner, Sarah, and John Bound. "Closing the Gap or Widening the Divide: The Effects of the G.I. Bill and World War II on the Educational Outcomes of Black Americans." *The Journal of Economic History* 63 (2003) 145–77.

Tyson, Timothy B. *The Blood of Emmett Till*. New York: Simon & Schuster, 2017.

U.S. Census Bureau: Census of Housing. "Historical Census of Housing Tables: Homeownership." www.census.gov/hhes/www/housing/census/historic/owner.html

———. "2010 Census Shows Black Population has Highest Concentration in the South." https://www.census.gov/newsroom/releases/archives/2010_census/cb11-cn185.html.

Vinik, Danny. "The Economics of Reparations: Why Congress Should Meet Ta-Nehesi Coates's Modest Demands." *The New Republic*, May 21, 2014. https://newrepublic.com/article/117856/academic-evidence-reparations-costs-are-limited.

Walker, Emma. "The Fascinating Story Behind Reelfoot Lake." *Roots Rated*, December 12, 2016. https://rootsrated.com/stories/the-fascinating-story-behind-reelfoot-lake.

Walzer, Michael. *Interpretation and Social Criticism*. Cambridge, MA: Harvard University Press, 1987.

Waren, Warren. "Using Monopoly to Introduce Concepts of Race and Ethnic Relations." *The Journal of Effective Teaching* 11 (2011) 28–35.

Watts, Craig M. "The 'Imaginary God' of Rev. Robert Jeffress." *Red Letter Christians*, July 5, 2019. https://www.redletterchristians.org/the-imaginary-god-of-rev-robert-jeffress/.

Weber, Jeremy. "Christian, What Do You Believe? Probably a Heresy about Jesus, Says Survey." *Christianity Today*, October 16, 2018. https://www.christianitytoday.com/news/2018/october/what-do-christians-believe-ligonier-state-theology-heresy.html.

Welty, Eudora. *Delta Wedding*. Orlando: A Harvest Book, 1974.

West, Cornel. "A Genealogy of Modern Racism." In *Race Critical Theories*, edited by Philomena Essed and David Theo Goldberg, 90–112. Hoboken, NJ: Wiley-Blackwell, 2002.

BIBLIOGRAPHY

———. "Untitled Address." A speech presented the President's Forum at Hobart and William Smith Colleges, Geneva, New York (October 5, 2009). https://www.hws.edu/about/presidentsforum/west_speech.aspx.

West, Traci C. "When a White Man-God Is the Truth and the Way for Black Christians." In *Christology and Whiteness: What Would Jesus Do?* edited by George Yancy, 114–27. London: Routledge, 2012.

"Will Soldiers Vote?" *Time*, February 14, 1944. https://archive.org/stream/timecapsuleoonewy/timecapsuleoonewy_djvu.txt.

Williams, Caroline Randall. "You Want a Confederate Monument? My Body is a Confederate Monument." *The New York Times*, June 26, 2020. https://www.nytimes.com/2020/06/26/opinion/confederate-monuments-racism.html.

Williams, Hank, Jr. "A Country Boy Can Survive." Single, Curb Records, 1981.

Williams, Reggie L. "How the Construct of Race Deforms Our Understanding of Christ." *Sojourners*, June 16, 2016. https://sojo.net/articles/faith-action/how-construct-race-deforms-our-understanding-christ.

Williamson, Joel. *The Crucible of Race: Black-White Relations in the American South Since Emancipation.* Oxford: Oxford University Press, 1984.

Wilson, Charles Reagan. *Baptized in Blood: The Religion of the Lost Cause, 1865–1920.* Athens: University of Georgia, 2009.

———. *Judgment and Grace in Dixie: Southern Faiths from Faulkner to Elvis.* Athens: University of Georgia Press, 1995.

Wink, Walter. *Engaging the Powers: Discernment and Resistance in a World of Domination.* Minneapolis: Fortress, 1992.

Wolterstorff, Nicholas. "Theological Foundations for Evangelical Political Philosophy." In *Toward an Evangelical Public Policy: Political Strategies for the Health of the Nation*, edited by Ronald J. Sider and Diane Knippers, 140–62. Grand Rapids: Baker, 2005.

Wood, Amy Louise. *Lynching and Spectacle: Witnessing Racial Violence in America, 1890–1940.* Chapel Hill, NC: University of North Carolina Press, 2009.

Woodard, Colin. *American Character: A History of the Epic Struggle Between Individual Liberty and the Common Good.* New York: Viking, 2016.

———. *American Nations: A History of the Eleven Rival Regional Cultures of North America.* New York: Viking, 2011.

Woods, Jeff. *Black Struggle, Red Scare: Segregation and Anti-Communism in the South, 1948–1968.* Baton Rouge: Louisiana State University Press, 2004.

Wright, Lawrence. *Saints and Sinners.* New York: Alfred A. Knopf, 1993.

Wright, N. T. *Paul and the Faithfulness of God, Parts I and II.* Minneapolis: Fortress, 2013.

Yancy, George. "The Ugly Truth about Being a Black Professor in America." *The Chronicle of Higher Education*, April 29, 2018. https://www.chronicle.com/article/The-Ugly-Truth-of-Being-a/243234.

Yebuah, Lisa. "Diversity is Good, Equity is Greater." https://mailchi.mp/armstrongmcguire/diversity-is-good.

Yoder, John Howard. *The Politics of Jesus.* Grand Rapids: Eerdmans, 1972.

Young, Jabari. "Colin Kaepernick's Botched Nfl Workout Could Strengthen Case for Second Collusion Lawsuit, Sports Lawyer Says." *CNBC*, November 21, 2019. https://www.cnbc.com/2019/11/21/kaepernicks-botched-nfl-workout-strengthens-case-for-second-collusion-lawsuit.html.

Yu, Jessica, dir. *The West Wing.* Season 2, episode 16, "Somebody's Going to Emergency, Somebody's Going to Jail." Aired February 28, 2001, on NBC.

Made in the USA
Las Vegas, NV
29 September 2021